W9-BAZ-788

NATIONS OF THE MODERN WORLD

ARGENTINA — H. S. Ferns
Professor of Political Science, University of Birmingham

AUSTRALIA — O. H. K. Spate
Director, Research School of Pacific Studies, Australian National University, Canberra

AUSTRIA — Karl R. Stadler
Professor of Modern and Contemporary History, University of Linz

BELGIUM — Vernon Mallinson
Professor of Comparative Education, University of Reading

BURMA — F. S. V. Donnison
Formerly Chief Secretary to the Government of Burma Historian, Cabinet Office, Historical Section 1949–66

CYPRUS — H. D. Purcell
Professor of English, University of Libya, Benghazi

DENMARK — W. Glyn Jones
Reader in Danish, University College London

MODERN EGYPT — Tom Little
Former Managing Director and General Manager of Regional News Services (Middle East), Ltd, London

EL SALVADOR — Alastair White
Lecturer in Sociology, University of Stirling

ENGLAND A Portrait — John Bowle
Formerly Professor of Political Theory, Collège d'Europe, Bruges 1950–67

FINLAND — W. R. Mead
Professor of Geography, University College London

EAST GERMANY	David Childs *Lecturer in Politics, University of Nottingham*
WEST GERMANY	Michael Balfour *Professor of European History, University of East Anglia*
MODERN GREECE	John Campbell *Fellow of St Antony's College, Oxford*
	Philip Sherrard *Lecturer in the History of the Orthodox Church, King's College, London*
HUNGARY	Paul Ignotus *Formerly Hungarian Press Counsellor, London, 1947–49, and Member, Presidential Board, Hungarian Writers' Association*
MODERN INDIA	Sir Percival Griffiths, K.B.E., C.I.E., I.C.S. (RET.) *President India, Pakistan and Burma Association*
ITALY	Muriel Grindrod *Formerly Editor of* International Affairs *and* The World Today *Assistant Editor* The Annual Register
KENYA	A. Marshall MacPhee *Formerly Managing Editor with the* East African Standard *Group*
LIBYA	John Wright *Formerly of the* Sunday Ghibli, *Tripoli*
MALAYSIA	J. M. Gullick *Formerly of the Malayan Civil Service*
MEXICO	Peter Calvert *Senior Lecturer in Politics, University of Southampton*
NORWAY	Ronald G. Popperwell *Fellow of Clare Hall, and Lecturer in Norwegian, Cambridge*
PAKISTAN	Ian Stephens *Formerly Editor of* The Statesman, *Calcutta and Delhi, 1942–51* *Fellow, King's College, Cambridge, 1952–58*

PERU	Sir Robert Marett *H.M. Ambassador in Lima, 1963–67*
THE PHILIPPINES	Keith Lightfoot *Naval, Military, and Air Attaché, British Embassy, Manila, 1964–67*
POLAND	Václav L. Beneš *Professor of Political Science, Indiana University*
	Norman J. G. Pounds *Professor of History and Geography, Indiana University*
SOUTH AFRICA	John Cope *Formerly Editor-in-Chief of* The Forum *and South Africa Correspondent of* The Guardian
THE SOVIET UNION	Elisabeth Koutaissoff *Professor of Russian, Victoria University, Wellington*
SPAIN	George Hills *Formerly Correspondent and Spanish Programme Organizer, British Broadcasting Corporation*
SWEDEN	Irene Scobbie *Senior Lecturer in Swedish, University of Aberdeen*
SYRIA	Tabitha Petran
TURKEY	Geoffrey Lewis *Senior Lecturer in Islamic Studies, Oxford*
YUGOSLAVIA	Stevan K. Pavlowitch *Lecturer in Balkan History, University of Southampton*

NATIONS OF THE MODERN WORLD

THE PHILIPPINES

THE PHILIPPINES

By

KEITH LIGHTFOOT

PRAEGER PUBLISHERS
New York · Washington

BOOKS THAT MATTER

Published in the United States of America in 1973
by Praeger Publishers, Inc.
111 Fourth Avenue, New York, N.Y. 10003

Library of Congress Cataloging in Publication Data

Lightfoot, Keith.
The Philippines
(Nations of the modern world)
Bibliography: p.
1. Philippine Islands. I. Title. II. Series.
DS655.L5 1973 915.99'03 72-93294

Printed in Great Britain

Author's Note

ALTHOUGH SOME SPECIALIZED RESEARCH has been necessary to complement the original material which forms the base of this book, much of the kaleidoscopic detail was gathered over the three years which I spent in the Philippines, during which I was able to complement reading with conversation and discussion. These exchanges were not only possible within the more evolved sections of the population, but also, during my frequent travels in the islands, with persons of the rural-dwelling communities, many of whom lived and continue to live in fairly primitive and unrewarding circumstances. It is to all these people, with their spontaneous generosity and open comment, so characteristic of the Filipino, that I owe much for the balance of this book.

It was also during these three years that I learned to check and double-check the written word of others when mention was made of the islands. Factual information on the Philippines is sometimes clouded by a degree of wishful thinking and the future and present tenses are often confounded, both in official handouts and in press reporting. In addition, many of the printed works relating to the country are North American in origin and, here, approaches to problems can sometimes be tinged with an unobjectivity, born of sentimentalism, generally resulting from too close an identification of the author with the subject environment. In all humility, I would like to offer a warning to the reader who is tempted to go further with his researches on the Philippines: here, if ever, be sure of your material if you wish to indulge in logical conclusions or extensions.

I would like to thank Sir John Addis, K.C.M.G., at present British Ambassador in Peking, and the Honourable Jaime Zobel, the Philippines' Ambassador in London, for the interest and help which they have given me, although I feel that I must immediately dissociate them from any personal comments made in this book. Others, Colonel Pete Los Baños of the Philippine Air Force, for instance, have also assisted me with information during the final compilation of the book in Europe and to them I offer my warmest thanks. Nevertheless, it is to those Filipino, American, and European friends, both in Manila and outside, who made the garnering of detail so painless by their spontaneous and uninhibited discussion, often accompanied by a traditional hospitality, that I owe so much.

Paris
May 1973

K.J.L.

Reference to currencies in this work mentions the Philippine peso, the US dollar, and the pound sterling. Until 1963, the rate of the Philippine peso to the US dollar was 2 to 1: from 1963 until the monetary crisis in 1970, the rate was 3.90 to 1. From February 1970 onwards, the peso was floated against all currencies, reaching a rate of 6.40 pesos to US$1 in June of the same year. The pound sterling was valued at a little less than 11 pesos in the 1963–69 period and stood at 16.87 pesos on 30 April 1973.

Contents

PART THREE

THE REPUBLIC OF THE PHILIPPINES

List of Illustrations

(*All are inserted between pages* 144 *and* 145)

Maps

Acknowledgements

ACKNOWLEDGEMENT for kind permission to reproduce illustrations is made to the following, to whom the copyright of the illustrations belongs:

Dr Nicholas Bayne: 2, 22, 23, 24
Camera Press Limited: 3, 10, 19
Foreign Information Service, Manila: 12, 13, 14
Philippine Tourist and Travel Association, Manila: 4, 9, 16, 17, 18, 21, 25, 26
Paul Popper Limited: 7, 8, 11, 15, 20
U.S. Signal Corps, Photo No. III–SC–93272, National Archives, Washington, D.C.: 5

Introduction

To BOTH the great world powers which, in their turn, colonized the Philippines, this strung-out archipelago in the East Indies was at the ends of Earth. To the Spaniard, even when the eastabout route was finally used, it was a journey through the Mediterranean to the Indian Ocean and then onwards to the South China Sea. To the American of the United States it was at least the width of the Pacific away and for the east-coaster planning to bring in copra or sugar from the islands, or the administrator, based on Washington and posted to serve a term with the Insular government, the journey included a passage of the Panama Canal and many long days steaming across the Gulf of Mexico and along the West Atlantic seaboard. Even now, with direct air routes from many Western capitals to Manila, both the comparative remoteness of the republic and its past close association with the United States military and economic spheres of influence would still seem to provide a barrier between the European and any balanced appreciation of this Malay nation. The American, with his shared history and Filipinos living both in the Hawaiian Group and on the continent itself, maintains a sentimental attachment for the people of these islands, although time is slowly destroying the memories of the colonial and tutelage days, and even the relationships founded on the post-1940–45 War treaties and customs are now being broken down by changing economic patterns and a desire by successive Philippine governments to establish an Asian identity.

After the departure of the Spaniards at the turn of the century the Philippines ceased to be a normal European zone of activity, although, unbeknown to the masses back in their highly industrialized states, the British, the French, and the Germans have, over the years, had a large share in the liberalization and development of the country's economy. It is unfortunate that the latter's scope has been diminished by selective clauses in post-war treaties which give overwhelming prerogatives to United States citizens. This situation is also regretted in the islands, where the 1946 and 1950 agreements are considered to have been thrust upon the newly emerging country unfairly and at a time when Philippine say was limited.

The Philippines has been a sovereign state since 1946 and real independence is growing rapidly. Already Japan has become her major trading partner and she is less tied to the former neo-colonial economic régime which followed on from the assumption of sovereign control. Although United States anti-Communist policies and mutual defence measures have continued to find a sympathetic political audience in Manila, initiative in establishing solid relations with the Third World has been taken and latterly, diplomatic and trade relations with Communist countries have been established for the first time.

In 1972, the population of the Philippines numbered 39,500,000, an increase of 12,420,000 on the previous figure taken twelve years before in 1960. A predominantly Roman Catholic nation, her people are markedly Malay in ethnic origin. Of an earlier East Indian character, tempered by over three hundred years of Spanish colonial rule, then forty-eight years of United States tutelage, the population is at once strikingly mature in its political institutions and evolving rapidly in its practical approach to the world as a whole. The Philippines can be seen at present as a nation in search of her real place – both politically and characteristically – and encountering many fundamental difficulties in doing so.

In 1960 less than 2 per cent of the islands' population claimed to speak Spanish, yet the Filipino still professes pride in so many of the things which were brought in during the long colonial period and which have remained imbedded in his day-to-day life. The majority religion is one of these and with it goes much of the lowlander culture of the Christian parts of the country, with its Iberian type music and dancing, a formalized dress, and the powerful place of women in both the household and in public life. Against this, two divergent currents stand out sharply: the first is a new awareness of the lack of any precise knowledge of what the Philippines was really like before Spanish colonization and the second is the almost oppressive nature of United States residual influence, which remains strikingly evident, even after twenty-eight years of independence.

For many years now, vigorous attempts have been made to align the Filipino image with a pre-Hispanic ancestor, even with the peoples who came in to populate the island chains from Stone Age days onwards. In much the same way, similarities with neighbouring pre-colonial cultures within the area have been studied and their importance stressed. As a result, an unproven but reassuring doctrine of origin did emerge, supported by some apocryphal reference, even giving details of day-to-day life in this earlier society. With a return to reality, it can be said that, at the present state of our knowledge, not overmuch is known of pre-Hispanic life beyond a general impression of customs and social organization, enriched by some detail obtained from the chronicles of the earlier Spanish expeditions and from the excavation of burial grounds. To these have been added the fruits of studies amongst the least undisturbed elements of the population: the Moslem communities of Mindanao and the Sulu Archipelago and certain isolated pagan groups which stood outside major European penetration until the twentieth century. There is, however, a striking dearth of any pre-Hispanic historical narrative, although the great Indo-Malay empires of Sri-Vishaya and Madjahpahit rose and fell over nearly six centuries of our era in neighbouring Sumatra and Java, with currents running northwards to Kalimantan and the Sulu and Visayan Seas. What are probably the greatest obstacles to any attempt at defining an earlier Filipino-Malay civilization are the almost complete absence of any earlier architectural remains outside the burial grounds[1] and a quasi-total destruction of all indigenous literature which took place soon after the setting-up of colonial rule in the late sixteenth century.

As an extension, we can also say that no formal proof of the origins of the Filipino people at present exists, but that, again, circumstantial evidence leads us to believe that settlers did come from the North, probably from the north-west, and that the majority travelled across the short sea routes and over the East Indian arc, in common with the peoples of what are now Malaysia and Indonesia. Again some affinity with the latter can be discerned, for all were in some way influenced by the cultures of southern India and the Moslem countries of West Asia. But in the Philippines these currents have been felt on a markedly decreased scale and we shall see that, today, political association with the other countries of the East Indian community is more difficult than with those states outside this restricted area.

On 1 May 1898 the United States Asiatic Squadron attacked the Spanish fleet in Manila Bay. The subsequent American military occupation of the islands was confirmed by the Treaty of Paris (10 December 1898) when Spain ceded her Philippine territories for the sum of US $20 million. The ensuing tutelage period brought with it modern social and industrial techniques, liberal political institutions, and a wider, more varied pattern of economic activity. Today, the Philippines uses a broad spectrum of such political, technical, and socio-economic methods inherited from that time, generally with pride and acumen, as they now form part of the national heritage. Although Japan has recently replaced the United States as the priority trading partner, institutional and infrastructural ties with America are still strong and have in some cases produced impediments to a logical development of the country's resources. The veneer of American practice is immediately apparent and, for better or for worse, those formative years between 1898 and 1946 have affirmed the acceptance of a liberalized democratic and capitalistic system, based on North American methods. Thus an already richly hybridized Malay base has been profoundly modified by the readiness of the Filipino population to absorb some of the most dynamic elements from both the colonial and the tutelary periods. It is this permeability and a readiness to take on such foreign-born institutions to its heart which have characterized the present way of life of the country.

In the early days of the Philippines, outside the then newly established Moslem sultanates in the south, there were no kings, no rajahs, and no rulers as we know them or as the Indians, the Chinese, and the South American peoples knew them in their time. The first Filipinos to stand out amongst their fellows were the heroes of the nineteenth-century nationalistic movement.[2] Near to them, in the people's minds, is a galaxy of Iberian names: men who braved the elements in little ships to bring Christianity to South-East Asia; Magellan, Legaspi, Father Urdaneta, and those earlier soldiers and sailors who are still remembered with a certain affection and gratitude, as are the missionary priests of the first hundred years or so of Spanish rule. Outstanding Governors-General, like Anda, who led resistance against the British after the capture of Manila, and Basco, the economic developer, also have their place in Philippine history and esteem, and although the great men of the nationalistic movements, José Rizal, Padre Burgos, Bonifacio, Aguinaldo, and Apolinario Mabini, are doubtless cherished the most, this island people remembers those *conquistadores* who brought the Faith and the culture to which they are so attached. In addition, two intensely patriotic and politically able senior statesmen, who led the still American-dominated Commonwealth of the Philippines, Manuel Quezon and Sergio Osmeña, hold pride of equal place with any of the remainder. In such circumstances, it is not possible for any nationalist to ignore the wealth of the past and limit his moral acceptance to those who were native Filipinos working to expel a foreign presence. The Philippine Pantheon is as multiracial as the nation's ethnic make-up.

Today, the Philippines is emerging from decolonization processes which are not strange in this late twentieth century. After twenty-six years of titular independence, there still remain areas where practical sovereignty is incomplete; but there are very few countries which enjoy anything like a complete liberty of action and the Philippines does possess considerable moral and material advantages to assist her in the struggle for that political and economic balance which she so much requires to become a wholly viable unit.

Although her population is, ethnically speaking, strongly hybridized and speaks a number of mother tongues, the majority, some 95 per cent of the whole, is amazingly monolithic in its culture and in its deep-rooted loyalty to country, constitution, and democratic procedures which, since 1935, have slowly become a part of the life of these islands. The republic's material assets are equally as reassuring: the human base is adaptable, willing, and already rapidly absorbing modern education and training, and the usable land area is at present not only adequate to produce sufficient food staples for over 40 million Filipinos, but can also contribute valuable export crops: mineral riches complementing the organic production of the soil. The problems ahead for the present administration and its successors are generally those of maintaining political stability, continuing the struggle to improve law and order, and formulating and executing plans to rationalize the economy in face of a population explosion.

At the time of writing, government by exception exists in the Philippines, martial law having been proclaimed by President Marcos on 22 September 1972. As a result, the effects of party politics with all their dynamic but often disturbing influences have been considerably diminished in everyday life, and with this and the beneficial character of the present government by exception, have come improved urban security conditions and a partial check in inflationary movements. Materially, this strange régime is holding its own in the struggle to improve social conditions and is using simple but authoritarian methods which could well lead to a better way of life for the less privileged classes, whose standards have not overmuch improved over the years.

Nevertheless, despite this promise of social improvement, it is doubtful whether, with so fundamental an attachment to democratic practice, normal political activities can be stifled for too long. A new parliamentary system, based on a recent revision of the constitution and promulgated in accordance with the officially interpreted wishes of the Citizens' Assemblies,[3] could once again bring a diminution of Presidential power and a return to some form of party politics. A rapid evolution in this sense is not considered favourably in Philippine official circles: here it must be conceded that there is much to be done and time is against the governments of underdeveloped countries; in the case of the Philippines, a return to a parliamentary system might well be a delicate operation, bearing in mind the often destructive political rivalries which were fostered by service to the earlier 1935 Constitution. In addition, the current security situation, with both increased Communist activity of a Maoist tendency in the north and violent religious partisanship, engendered by an Islamic separatist movement in Mindanao and the Sulu Archipelago in the extreme south, has produced calls for strong, if not exceptional, powers, particularly within the specified areas. In such circumstances, President Marcos and his close collaborators will need all their political acumen, maturity, and expertise to make a sensitive appreciation of the majority's real aspirations so as to select the right time to guide their country back to democratic normality.

This book has been written in three interwoven sections: the first has been planned to give the reader a broad description of the stage on which the events described in the second and third have taken place; the second aiming to outline the heritage which, in the Philippines, has so strong an influence on the present. The last section deals with the independent republic, its history, its social problems, and its economic fortunes. The whole may well assist the reader in his understanding of the real character of this singular people, whose problems of underdevelopment are aggravated by population increase and whose living standards seem, for 90 per cent of the community, to be unchangingly low and unrewarding in a world where so much social improvement is promised. Against this, the Filipino faces and has always faced the future with optimism, good humour, and a determination to succeed somehow. Where this buoyancy exists, faith in human nature is generalized and, when misfortune is encountered, an individual is rarely alone in his attempts to combat it.

[1] Wood was used almost exclusively for building in pre-Hispanic times and the Spanish priests who came in at the end of the sixteenth century included those skilled in masonry. In such circumstances, earlier evidence seems to have been destroyed by the elements.

[2] In Chapter 4 below, some detail is given of the earlier Philippine dignitaries who received or fought with the Spaniards. These men are known from the Spanish chronicles of the time, but despite later attempts to give these admirable persons a national image, they were little more than local chiefs who did what they thought was best for the small communities which they ruled.

[3] This form of consultation, which had no place within the structure of the 1935 Constitution, is explained below (pp. 189–94), as are the events which led to the present system of government by exception.

PART ONE

The Islands and Their Early History

Chapter 1

The Islands

NEARLY ALL THE LAND MASS of the Philippines is contained in eleven of her 7,100 islands. The superficial area of the Archipelago is 299,404 square kilometres (115,600 square miles): these eleven largest islands cover 272,900 square kilometres (106,935 square miles). There are only 450 other islands of general importance, the majority of which are more than 4 square kilometres in extent. The remainder are islets and scattered rocks above water.

A little larger than Great Britain and Ireland and a little smaller than Spain, the Archipelago, with its enclosed waters, lies along the western limits of the Pacific Ocean, running through seventeen degrees of tropical latitude. The islands of Luzon in the north and Mindanao in the south make up two-thirds of the land area. Between lie Mindoro and Palawan to the west and the Visayas in the centre; the whole enclosing large internal seas. From Mindanao, the Sulu Archipelago strikes south-west. All form a cohesive block, shouldered to the north by Formosa and to the south-west by the lay-back position of the great island of Borneo (Kalimantan). Cut off from mainland South-East Asia by the South China Sea, these islands, together with those territories which now constitute Malaysia, Singapore, Indonesia, and Timor, make up a region which has, for centuries, been described as the East Indies. In any geological summary, it is impossible to divorce the Philippines from her East Indian neighbours and this is also true where ethnic origins and flora and fauna are studied.

Originating physically in continental South-East Asia, the East Indies arc swings firstly south-east and then changes direction in the area of the Sunda Straits to divide into north-east and due east spurs. In this island chain, there are now large water gaps, but it is over the existing land masses, probably more or less coherent in ancient times, that animals and plants passed, giving the East Indies the real regional character which, with surprisingly little dilution, it retains to this day.

The former land connections between Borneo and the Philippines are comparatively easy to visualize. The structural lines originating in mainland South-East Asia, either in prolongation of the Arakan Yomas or running down the Isthmus of Kra, through Malaya to the Sunda Straits, sweep upwards into Borneo to concentrate at its north-east. They then divide to pass through the Philippines, either along her western edge by way of Palawan, Mindoro, and the mountains of north Luzon, or take a more easterly course through the Sulus into the Zamboanga Peninsula of Mindanao. Robequain, in his work on the region,[1] describes this inheritance and gives details of the whole East Indian geological profile. His opinion is that earlier Philippine land connections northwards (by way of what is now the Luzon Strait between that island and Formosa) seem to have been severed during the Oligocene and that none were left by the Pleistocene era.

In the shallow seas, the Pleistocene era saw dramatic changes to the land profiles of the region. Although in more ancient times a cluster of islands existed in these waters, the Ice Ages caused the sea-levels to rise and fall in a range from 20 to 30 feet above the present marks to between 250 to 400 feet below them. For long periods, Palawan and the Sulu Archipelago formed part of mainland Asia which extended over the South China Sea to the south-east shores of Borneo and Java, where the vast depths show the former limits of this partially drowned continent. But if Palawan and the Sulu Archipelago formed part of a more or less coherent land mass, no recession of the seas during this era would have been adequate to bridge the gaps between Formosa and Luzon, Luzon and Mindoro, and the Sibuyan Islands or Palawan and the Visayan-Mindanao complex. With the final withdrawal of the ice, some eight thousand years ago, the seas were left at a higher level than they appear today. But the islands showed much the same outlines as they do now, the flora and fauna which had migrated from the north-west and the north were well established and from then on, plant and animal life could only travel to and from the region as they do in our times – as passengers aided by the wind and the currents.

The chaotic folding which occurred during the Miocene period lifted the eastern spine of the Philippines well out of the sea and coraline formation is now found at heights of nearly 2,000 metres. In contrast, the pressure created great ocean valleys of incredible depth, the most dramatic example being the Philippine Deep, reaching down to 5,900 fathoms, off east Mindanao. But the existing outline of the islands is of a relatively recent origin. Although stratified secondary rocks (mainly shales) outcrop frequently in north Luzon, Mindanao, and Panay, in any analysis of soil formation, the more recent rocks tend to point to the true geological character of the islands. Volcanic deposits amount to over 20 per cent of the parent materials, and coraline limestone of the Tertiary Period or later makes up an estimated further 13 per cent of the whole.

As we have seen, Luzon and Mindanao are the giants of the Archipelago and, here, there are extensive plain areas, drained by major rivers. On Luzon, the Great Central Plain to the north of Manila and the Cagayan Valley, lying between the massifs of the Cordillera Central and the Sierra Madre, are most valuable agricultural areas and are heavily populated. In Mindanao, the Agusan River and the Rio Grande de Mindanao have also formed significant plains of real agricultural worth.[2] But despite the existence of these large areas, which are only found within the more important insular masses, a dominant physical character prevails throughout: much of the land area is composed of mountain or spiny hill; coastal plains vary in breadth, are really nowhere extensive, and are often narrow and discontinuous; there is a sparseness of re-entrant features, although rolling uplands are sometimes found between plain and hill; alluvial lowland is uncommon outside the favoured agricultural complexes and one further exception, the Jalud Basin on the Visayan island of Panay which is laid down to rice paddy and sugar-cane.

It has never been easy to divide this Archipelago into physical groupings to assist detailed study, and researchers are confronted with varied boundaries, each enclosing land and sea complexes of a fairly coherent nature. But if the Philippine government's normal method is followed, both geological and geographical factors are best provided for and the main cultural divisions are easier to follow. Thus, Luzon and the islands along the western limits, Mindoro and Palawan, are normally considered in a single grouping. In the south, Mindanao and Basilan with the Sulu Archipelago form an entity and, between these, the Visayas, which are divided into western and eastern, complete an outline similar to a diviner's rod. But to the north and to the south of the major land formations, the picture is frankly discontinuous, for the scattered Babuyan and Batanes Islands extend northwards three degrees from the Luzon coast and the Sulus, although much denser in character, cover much the same area, running from the south-west tip of Mindanao at Basilan to north-east Borneo.

Despite discontinuity in the north and south-west, the Philippines is a real physical barrier for much of her length. The Luzon Strait, which runs clear through the island province of Batanes, is a broad sea corridor, but it is strategically overlooked from Luzon itself, from Formosa, and from continental East Asia. From the north coast of Luzon to the Celebes Sea, which separates the Philippines from Indonesia, the only transversal passages are those of the San Bernardino Strait between the islands of Luzon and Samar, and the

Surigao Strait between Leyte and Mindanao. These major seaways lead from or debouch into narrow internal waters dominated on all sides by Luzon and the Visayas and the Visayas and Mindanao respectively. The decisive naval battles between the Japanese and Allied fleets in 1944 were a struggle for the domination of these vital routes and they took place within or adjacent to the internal seas and their two straits, the only exits from the Indian to the Pacific Ocean over some fourteen hundred kilometres. Even in an era dominated by air movement, territorial sovereignty in its most liberal context could restrict overflight considerably, and, if applied in a more exclusive sense, might well impose either solutions more or less favourable to a Philippine government or costly and onerous diversions on the operators.[3]

The maps (below, pp. 235–8) show, respectively, the general position of the Philippines within the region and the layout of her main physical and administrative components. But to complete the picture, a brief description of the major local groupings is necessary.

Luzon, Mindoro, and Palawan

With the rocky Batanes and Babuyan islands, much of volcanic origin, Luzon is the largest land mass of the Archipelago and its centre of government and industry. It is also the greatest food-producing area. The island is divided by three mountain ranges: the Sierra Madre, running with its southern extension for the whole eastern length of the island; the Cordillera Central, constituting a massive core to the north; and the Zambales in the west. Apart from the Great Central Plain and the Cagayan Valley, other important features are the Laguna de Bay, a shallow but extensive lake south of the Central Plain; the Taal escarpment, with its active volcano to the south-west of the Laguna; and the narrow Bicol Peninsula which extends the Sierra Madre feature down to the extreme south of the island in a series of hilly promontories and volcanic mountains. The culmination is reached in the most southerly promontory, overlooking the San Bernardino Strait. East of the Sierra Madre feature, the coastal plain is narrow, but the importance of Luzon lies to the west. Here there are considerable areas of exploitable land.

Mindoro, despite its nearness to Luzon, is strikingly under-developed and underpopulated. Comprising a broad eroded mountain backbone with often generous coastal plains and rolling foothills, the island supports an undercapitalized, traditional subsistence economy, hardly sufficient for its own modest needs. Palawan is narrow and long (410 km.) in comparison with its breadth: it is a rugged high ridge of mountain with flat or rolling coastal plains on the east and west seaboards. Associated islands to the north and south are of much the same character and the whole constitutes a land bridge which not only served as an axis for organic matter in earlier times, but, even in present days, greatly influences physical conditions in the Visayan islands and the interior seas to the immediate east. Both the Palawan chain and Mindoro are the natural overflow areas for Luzon's growing population, and the indigenous peoples, who largely belong to ethnic and cultural minorities, are now outnumbered by Christian Filipinos, speaking Luzon dialects as their mother tongues.

The Visayas

The major islands are Samar, Leyte, and Masbate in the east and the Romblon Group, Panay, Negros, Cebu, and Bohol to the west. Physically they are generally characterized by spiny backbones, narrow coastal plains, and a non-existence of navigable rivers, the majority being torrents filling seasonally. Samar is the Philippines' third largest island and, with Leyte and Mindanao, it forms the bastion against the Pacific Ocean. Samar and Panay are exceptions to the general Visayan pattern. Not truly mountainous, Samar's elevation is moderate, with much of its relief rising in high rolling countryside capable of supporting cultivation of some sort, although the coastal plains remain narrow and are often strangled. Panay, as well as possessing narrow coastal plains in the west, north, and north-west, is divided sharply by two north–south mountain chains and a broad, transversal series of hills, plateaux, and intersecting valleys, stretching across the island, roughly parallel with the north coast. But these higher features contain wide, well-watered areas which are found in the basin of the Jalud River and its tributaries. These, and the plateaux and valleys within the transversal feature, are planted with rice, sugar-cane, and maize. Negros in the west has a relatively broad north-east coast plain running up in cleared rolling country to a series of volcanic peaks. This area, with its fertile, volcanic soil, is used to produce sugar-cane in large quantity. Except for the Pacific coastline of Samar, and south-east Leyte, the Visayas are surrounded by a group of internal seas, the Sulu, Sibuyan, Visayan, and Mindanao. Two ports, Iloilo in south-east Panay and Cebu on Cebu, are of international importance. The seas still provide the most natural local communications and are a valuable source of food.

Mindanao and the Sulu Archipelago

Mindanao, the second largest land area, has four satellite islands of immediate importance: Camuigan, Dingat, and Siargao to its north and Basilan in the south-west. From Basilan, the associated Sulu Archipelago runs towards Borneo. Mindanao is dominated by four main areas of high relief. The first follows the old structural line coming in from Borneo, through the Sulu Archipelago, rising into the mountain chain which passes north-east along the whole of the Zamboanga Peninsula. The second and the third run south–north and are believed to be linked in origin to the Indonesian Celebes and Moluccas features, but with the evidence at present available, this theory remains extremely hypothetical. These ranges, the eastern coast Diwata, with its extensions towards the south, and the Apo in the centre, running the length of the island from the Davao Gulf to Camuigan Island, are both formidable barriers for most of their length, although there are sections of low rolling country within the eastern coastal range (the Diwata). But the importance of these barriers is considerable for, except along the coastal corridors, the Apo Range is at present unbreached by surface communications and the Diwata Range is only pierced by one lateral, although a second transverse corridor exists and is even more exploitable. A fourth range, the southern Cotabato Coastal, of volcanic origin, effectively encloses much of the coastline of south Mindanao and, in this area, there are no lateral communications as yet. Contained within the framework of this mountain relief are the high plateaux of Bukidnon and Lanao and the two major lowland areas, the Agusan River and the Rio Grande Valleys, which have been noted before. The Bukidnon and Lanao plateaux run westwards across much of the centre part of the island from the Apo Range; the latter contains Lake Lanao, which is extensive, situated at high altitude, and volcanic in origin. These uplands, with their extinct and eroded volcanic features in the west, continue as far as the junction with the Zamboanga Peninsula at the strikingly narrow Isthmus of Panguil, only 25 kilometres wide and lying between the Moro Gulf of the Celebes Sea and Panguil Bay, an inlet off the Mindanao Sea. Because of great depth and the precipitous slope of the shores around Mindanao, anchorages are both sparse and indifferent along the north and east coasts.

The Sulu chain strikes off towards Borneo and is some three hundred kilometres in length. In the Pleistocene era, an almost continuous causeway probably existed, although the Sibutu Passage, just off the north-east coast of Borneo, an important strait for deep-draught navigation today, would have represented an important break. But now there is a complex group of islands, islets, and reefs of varying origin. Jolo and Tawi-Tawi are the major formations, but there are hundreds of smaller features sharing the same characteristics: a volcanic core and a subsequently built-up coraline surround.

In contrast, there are more than an equal number of more recent origin: these are low-lying and formed from young reef limestone. Uplift and subsidence are features of the Sulus and a particularly Southern Pacific character exists in this coraline area with its scattered volcanic core; its generally low-lying profile covered by palms; its islets and its reefs surrounded by seas which are narrow, often shallow, and hazardous to navigation.

Fragmented as the Philippines is, the sea has always carried the major part of her surface communications, and this is common to much of the East Indies. In the historic past, during the times when the region was being populated, but when the land bridges were already down, people came in boats: a strong seafaring tradition persists today in most of the rural and semi-urban communities. The proliferation of small ports and anchorages, the majority natural and well sheltered, is common to the western seaboard and to the interior seas. The eastern coast, along the limits of the Pacific Ocean, is everywhere less favoured and landfalls are strikingly few. As a corollary, where ports or negotiable coastal corridors are sparse, the area tends to be more or less underdeveloped, despite the efforts of over four hundred years to open up lateral ties from west to east. Even today, development is inconsiderable in these physically isolated places. Here and even in the most favoured areas, round-the-island communications are incomplete: there is still a lack of capital to open up hitherto unexploited lateral corridors and to punch holes through strangled coastal plains. As in the past, anchorages and small ports furnish the means to move men and material. Even on Luzon, by far the most developed of all Philippine islands, there is no circumferential road and there are only five west-east laterals built through the Sierra Madre and its southern extensions. Of these, only the Manila South Road, carried over the rump of the mountains into the Bicol Peninsula, is used as a true highway. The remainder seem to be of minimal importance today, although the physical corridors they use would be of a real potential value if east coast development carried any priority in planning. The other major islands facing the Pacific are even less well endowed and where the rare lateral has been built, its usefulness is restricted by the endemic underdevelopment of the narrow eastern coastal plains. Thus, land communications are frankly inclined in a south-north direction and both the transportation and industrialized infrastructures are concentrated away from the Pacific seaboard. Sea and land movements are complementary and multiple handling a tradition. The results of such technical inefficiency are palliated by the modesty of the wages structure in these less favoured places and a genial acceptance of conditions which have existed since man's first occupation of these islands.

The relief, which continues to inhibit material progress, massively influences the climate, which is equally as varied as the physical character of the Archipelago. Basically, the whole is tropical and monsoonal and much is visited regularly by cyclonic storms. Temperature is probably the least changeable of all natural phenomena: not only are ranges for a single station narrow but, except in the mountain features of north Luzon, there is little mean variation throughout the islands. At sea-level, readings of as little as 16°C (60°F) are rare and even at altitudes of 1,600 metres (approximately 5,000 feet) it is uncommon to observe less than 10°C; the highest temperatures, for practical purposes, not exceeding 38°C (100°F). But strong air currents and their generally related rainfall incidence provide marked variation and it is here that the islands' physical relief influences their climate. Most air currents are regular features and the Trade Winds and the north-east and south-west monsoons cover singly or severally the whole annual cycle, although their effects are greatly modified by geographical position and high-relief barriers. The north-east monsoon blows from October to January and the south-west from April to October. The north-east Trades maintain strong pressure over the east coast throughout the months of February to April and are continuous, in some degree, throughout the year, often striking the Pacific coastline with considerable force during the tropical winter. The south-east Trades cross the Equator and reach the southern Philippines during the summer months. To this generally ordered pattern are added the cyclonic movements, arriving sporadically from the low-pressure systems in mid-Pacific and producing westerly and north-westerly tracked tropical storms and typhoons which often turn northwards up the South China Sea. These bring with them strong air disturbance and widespread heavy precipitation during their peak season, which generally occurs from July to November. The relief adds almost permanent modifications to seasonal rhythm and for this reason climatic conditions over the Archipelago are markedly zonalized. A classification into four divisions is described in the *Philippine Economic Atlas*[4] and a map (below, p. 235) shows a climatic breakdown in accordance with this theory.

In a predominantly agricultural country, climate is always a factor of primordial importance: in the Philippines the physical divisions described produce more than normal micro-conditions: not only is their influence wider in geographical terms, but the amalgam of this and the constant wind pressure produce long periods of strikingly varied climatic conditions over the islands. In addition, atmospheric disturbances in the form of cyclonic movement bring with them heavy rainfalls which not only greatly increase crop yields but also cause widespread destruction and dislocation. The island province of Batanes and much of the north-west part of Luzon are particularly vulnerable. Central and south Luzon and the Visayas are less frequently visited: the remainder of the Archipelago very rarely suffers from this phenomenon but comes under the influence of the south-west monsoon and the Trades which bring a more constant and less destructive rainfall.

Life has been and still continues to be influenced by volcanic activity. Eruptive rock, eroded and brought down the slopes and valleys, increases fertility, although areas enriched in this way are scattered. Volcanoes which have continued active into historic times are few in number, but, for the relative size of the land surface, are of some importance, although no real widespread damage has occurred for many years. Recent activity has been of the explosive type and there is comparatively little lava flow. But there is a further natural phenomenon which causes damage from time to time. This is the earthquake, which did so much destruction during the seventeenth and eighteenth centuries. Tremors are felt regularly, but the epicentres are generally situated away from the land masses and, latterly, the intensity of such movement has been less. Effects are minimal, as most buildings, including even the peasant's hut, are designed to withstand shock.

The climatic profile, with its air current rhythm, has been described. Crop cycles, the capacity of the land, and the manner of husbandry are as varied as the wind, the relief, and the influences of the interior seas. But basically, the indigenous vegetation is marked by its solidarity with that of the region, having found its way to the Philippines along the land corridors from the North and the north-west, building up against entry from the South-West Pacific. There has been some exchange here, nevertheless, but any dilution by species originating from the latter region is strikingly small. We shall see later that completely foreign families of flora and fauna have been introduced during the last four hundred years for economic and dietetic reasons – plant life and animals of European and American origins have become fully acclimatized over the centuries and are now of untold value both for environmental and economic reasons. This man-made modification to natural selectivity in no way varies the strong affinity which exists within the plant and animal communities of the East Indies, and Robequain estimates that 62 per cent of the East Indian flora and fauna species flourish in the Philippines.[5]

Despite the comparatively rugged outline of the islands, the elements have been kind to the Philippines and land suitable for at least some useful cultivation amounts to about 40 per cent of the total. But there are factors which make almost a third of this cultivable area intensely marginal in the economics of even subsistence farming and not more than 25 per cent of the whole land area of 30 million hectares is in regular use,[6] and of this favoured element, half a million hectares are covered by domestic-type forest, often of a secondary-growth type. Despite this, the land available is generally adequate for the needs of the population – even during a period of rapid increase. How long this situation will obtain depends on both future population growth and the ability of the Filipino farmer to increase his efficiency so as to augment yield on currently cultivated land and to bring marginal land to profitable exploitation. These marginal lands offer an example in comparative technical progress, for they are marginal for reasons of current expediency. The main factors which the farmer must contend with are gradient, which can be conquered by crop selection and suitable agricultural methods; soil composition, which requires much the same treatment; and remoteness of the land itself, which calls for resettlement or better communications. A large percentage is influenced in a greater or lesser degree by all three of these major factors.

In addition to these producing and non-producing areas, there is a very large part of the country still covered by forest. 30 per cent of all the land area was under commercial forest in 1960.[7] We shall see later that this forest area is decreasing in size and that indiscriminate felling is causing natural adjustments which are often detrimental to man's environment.

The Philippines has attracted visitors from all over the world – particularly from North America. Much has been written to assist them in their travels and in their studies. It is from these writings, sometimes overemphasizing the singularity of certain of the country's characteristics, that erroneous conclusions are drawn. Thus, there *are* approximately 7,100 islands and islets in the Archipelago, but the real importance of this cluster physically is not to be found in its number but in its position at the western limit of the Pacific, its enormous length, penetrated by only two narrow seaways over fourteen hundred kilometres, the extent of the enclosed inland seas, and the economic value of eleven islands only. Again, the great Christian Hispano-Filipino culture which, even today, is a vital thing, joins with a borrowed North American way of life to obscure the real origin of the Filipino peoples and the living world about them which are respectively overwhelmingly Malay in ethnic origins[8] and emphatically East Indian in character. Less ill-treated in descriptions has been the climate, but here again, simplification has given an incomplete picture. A division into four main climatic zones, all of which are in some way regularly modified by cyclonic movement, must be retained. Tropical and volcanic conditions producing ready media for easy food and cash-crop cultivation are often cited as an incalculable natural advantage, precious to an indolent people living in a warm climate. But this again is a simplification and a quite incorrect picture is often retained. Volcanic soils are an exception rather than a rule: climate and gradient have joined hands with the destruction of natural forest cover to produce widespread erosion. Much of the cultivated land has been tilled for centuries and lacks natural elements and traces: as elsewhere, such lands require expensive fertilizers. Long dry periods in Western areas impose strict cycles and extensive irrigation to obtain more than one successful crop annually. Finally the great extent of the country's forests continues to hide the dangers of indiscriminate felling without replanting and of the destruction of large areas by primitive forms of cultivation.[9] Erosion, already noted, is often the worst evil following from these practices, but the extension of unfavourable micro-climates, the destruction of natural fertility within and adjacent to the uncovered areas, and the extension of rampant secondary growth do not assist in the production of the ever-increasing amounts of foodstuffs necessary to support the rapidly growing population of this predominantly Roman Catholic country. In these well-favoured islands realities must be faced as elsewhere, and science, learning, and hard work are required to keep their peoples provided for.

[1] Charles Robequain, *Malaya, Indonesia, Borneo, and the Philippines*, translated by E. D. Laborde (London – New York – Toronto, 1954).

[2] The Great Central Plain and the Rio Grande basin are the country's rice granaries. For traditional reasons, much of the Cagayan Valley is given over to tobacco cultivation. See below, pp. 88–9.

[3] Use of the internal seas by non-Philippine vessels is generally governed by the Rules of the Sea which the Philippine government contests. See below, pp. 127–8.

[4] *The Philippine Economic Atlas*. Program Implementation Agency (Manila, n.d.).

[5] Robequain, op. cit.

[6] Even this is somewhat of an overstatement, as the 1960 Census figures compounded the accounting where more than one crop per year was raised.

[7] Census of the Philippines 1960.

[8] As will be seen below, pp. 38ff.

[9] Burn, dig, sow, and abandon after two or three years.

Chapter 2

The Ethnic and Cultural Base

THE MAJORITY of modern Filipinos are brown-skinned, generally well proportioned, of a medium if somewhat slender stature with regular features, dark straight hair, and a flat nose. There are, of course, many exceptions and the most striking of these is the curly haired pigmy. His community is negroid, grouped into tribes, and his characteristics have been bequeathed widely through interbreeding over the centuries. Again, in remote areas, many non-negroid communities show physical characteristics of slightly differing strains to the majority; sometimes more Caucasian in facial profile, sometimes closely resembling the hill peoples of mainland South Asia. On the east coast and in some parts of the Palawan group, Papuan and Melanesian traces can be observed. Despite this variety, the population of the Philippines has much in common with that of the remainder of the East Indian world, although alien ethnic additions to a basic Malay stock are probably more apparent in the Archipelago than in the neighbouring parts of the region. Evidence of a considerable dilution of the majority group with Chinese, Japanese, Indian, Arab, and with European or American Caucasian, blood is easily discernible in both urban and rural communities.

The Filipino is both genetically and geographically a member of the widespread Malay world which stretches from Madagascar and the neighbouring east coast of Africa in the West to the Banda and Timor Seas in the East, and whose outposts have long been implanted in New Guinea and Papua and as far as the South Pacific islands. But this delimitation does not assist us in answering three questions of ethnic importance. Where did the Filipinos originally come from, at what period of history, and what was the nature of their culture at the time of their arrival? Answers to these questions have been given, often accompanied by a wealth of detail. Unfortunately, there is very little real concrete evidence with which to prop up these theories. The most acceptable is arrived at from a comparative study of tribal characteristics, as discernible today inside and outside the Malay world. This, at least, does provide useful indications.

In any population resettlement, the facilities available for movement to new lands are primordial. Thus, when small and flimsy craft were the only means at the disposal of a primitive people, all but the slightest of water obstacles were real barriers to progress. Even before the flimsy craft, man was moving about, searching for new food supplies, increased opportunity, and greater bodily comfort. It is in this context that we must consider the population of the region. As the sea rose and fell through the Ice Ages, opportunity fluctuated, but the inventive spirit of our ancestors brought methods to conquer the obstacles which climate, vegetation, and water cast across their path.

There are theories that prehistoric man had established himself in the area which we now know as the Philippines some 250,000 years ago. This may well be so, but there is nothing conclusive to prove it and even less to reveal anything of his character. The earliest traces of *homo sapiens* do not date to earlier than 50,000 years ago and may well be no more than 40,000 years old. These traces show clearly that a cave-dwelling community existed on what is now the island of Palawan, which, at that time, was in all probability a southern spur of the Asian continent. Occupation of the Philippines may well have been more widespread, but there is at present little to support this theory. Professor Robert B. Fox, after analysing all the available archaeological evidence, concludes, *inter alia*, that by the third millennium B.C., a wider occupation of the neighbouring islands had taken place, that in the last thousand years of that era, boats with sails were used and, by A.D. 1000, most of the Archipelago had been occupied.[1] Even with all the means at the disposal of modern archaeology, nothing conclusive has been found to determine any point of departure of these primitive settlers, nor is there any evidence to prove that subsequent immigration waves came in from outside.

Nevertheless, there have been many theories as to the origins and the movements of peoples into the East Indies and for many years now students of regional history have been considerably influenced by the 'successive wave' theory of the distinguished American anthropologist H. Otley Beyer, who lived in the Philippines for most of his life. Beyer was a great traveller, field researcher, and collector who combined analysis of tribal ethnology with the collection of evidence from excavations and other sources. His theories, expounded in a number of documents and papers published and circulated in the Philippines during the first half of this century, were seized on by the academic community in Manila and incorporated in many books used in teaching establishments at all levels. Beyer's theories travelled, for we find echoes of them in many well-circulated, internationally known works. It is true to say that they have become the basis of what is generally believed to have been the true origins of the Philippine people.

The 'wave' theory is an attractive one and it seems to solve many problems where purely archaeological findings have failed. Discarding the earliest ancestor, the individual of 250,000 years ago whose ethnic line is ended, the negroid Aeta (negrito) himself is a living example of prehistoric culture. Beyer believed that the Aetas arrived in the islands now known as the Philippines some 250,000 to 300,000 years ago, that their culture was Paleolithic (Old Stone Age), and that they lived by hunting and collecting. There is fair evidence to support his ideas relating to the Aeta ways of life at that time, for among the remoter groups living today this primitive culture persists. Pygmies still hunt and collect, have no agricultural methods or formed religious beliefs, live in shelters made of branches and leaves, and use bows and arrows and blowpipe weapons. On average, they measure 1.20 metres and some individuals as little as 1.10 metres. Dark-skinned and curly haired, with thick lips and flat noses, they must even now look much the same as their distant forebears who could well have arrived in the Philippines when the land bridges still remained more or less intact. Their influence on the community is slight, but, as we have seen, considerable interbreeding has taken place, often initially with members of other remote tribes. In modern Filipino blood there is an important negroid element. Their bare existence today is threatened by a low birth-rate, high infant mortality, and a seeming inadaptability to modern life. Only about 20,000 individuals of pure or of predominantly pure negroid stock are thought to exist, and these earlier peoples can still be found in the Zambales and mountain areas of the northern part of Luzon, and scattered in the remoter parts of the Visayas; seemingly left behind at the peak of the tide.

If we can identify a majority Malay stock in the plain areas of the Philippines, two additional communities are also apparent. The first is a widespread group, fragmented into tribes all over the remoter parts of the country. The second is far more concentrated and seems to have remained in the northern mountain areas of Luzon for nearly two thousand years. With the Aetas, these tribes compose the ethnic minorities of the Philippines and they and the Moslem populations of Mindanao and the Sulus form 99 per cent of the cultural minority, for the ethnic and cultural majority is Malay, Christian, and, by environment, plains dwelling.

The first of these remaining two ethnic minorities has been named Indonesian or Proto-Malay. Because of its physical characteristics, it is sub-classified A and B, the first being a tall, light-brown complexioned, fine-featured genus and the second a short, stouter and darker, heavier-faced type. Bearing in mind these physical attributes and the nature of the still undeveloped ways of life in their communities, extensions have been made and it is now believed that the Indonesian A and B 'waves' arrived in the Philippines from outside some 5,000 and 3,500 years ago respectively. The modern physical characteristics of these peoples show a Mongolian origin tempered with certain Caucasian elements; dosages differing from one widespread community to another. As this implantation probably took place in relatively recent times, it could only have been by maritime immigration and from comparative studies it would seem to have brought with it a Neolithic (New Stone Age) culture including the use of stone implements and a knowledge of seasonal agriculture. In contrast, in the hills of north Luzon there live groups of a Malay type whose ancestors in all probability arrived long before their more culturally advanced cousins who now occupy the lowlands. They show a more marked Short Mongol identity than the latter and, although they are close to the mainstream ethnically, have kept a purer blood stock than their neighbours who live on the more accessible flat ground. To include this third element with the ethnic minority is perhaps contentious, for the group is of a different strain and environment has added a very strong case for setting it apart. These Malay-type highlanders are now famous for their agricultural practices which include the construction, maintenance, and cultivation of extensive rice terraces on their high mountains, their pagan cultures with long-established community institutions, and their unique marriage and death customs.

But it is the final geographical position of the four groups, the Aetas, the Indonesians, and the early and later Malays, which adds weight to the theory that the present population arrived in the Philippines in fairly cohesive emigrations. When this and their physical characteristics are examined against a background of Asian prehistory, dislodgement of more primitive groups by higher-evolved and more dynamic later arrivals conforms to a known pattern. Man lived in Palawan 40,000 if not 50,000 years ago. Circumstantial evidence is available to support a theory that the Aetas also arrived at a time when the long journey was probably made dryshod. At some period, probably during the last thousands of years before our era, these Aetas were pushed up into the less accessible areas, the same areas which they use today for collecting and hunting – the hills of north-east and central Luzon, the Bicol, and the Visayas. In contrast, the people who are now called Indonesians seem to have been more numerous and, it is believed, possessed a more varied and developed culture, including some farming skills. As they, in their turn, moved away from the plains, they took a multitude of routes, for the physical profile of the Philippines with its broken relief would have allowed a million, not a few thousands, to make their way from the flat ground, up the river valleys and re-entrants, to gain peace and liberty there while time passed them by. Although the majority of these groups have been confronted with some Christian or Moslem missionary penetrations and other alien sociological influences, a number still remain isolated and comparatively untouched by our civilization. Interbreeding with other remote communities has taken place, often with the two opposing ethnic groups, the Aetas and the true Malays, and it is from these tribal concentrations that much of the Aeta-type hybridization stems.[2] The Malay-type highlander seems to have followed much the same tradition as his Indonesian predecessor, but the migratory groups were probably more concentrated along the coastline of north and central Luzon at first and their culture was more advanced. They may well have sought the hill regions more or less voluntarily rather than been dislodged, for their special agricultural traditions and the use of the mountain environments for defence could already have been inborn. So we now see large tribal groups high in the mountains, more or less concentrated and distant from and foreign to the seas around.

Where did all these people come from? The consensus of opinion today favours the southern part of the Asian continent where population movements have continued up until modern times. But here we lack any written record and we are once again faced with comparisons as the only aid. Whether the Palawan cave-dweller came due south or from the north-west is, of course, indeterminable. When the last land bridges were down, after the great thaw some 8,000 years ago, island hopping could only have been possible along that graceful East Indian arc running from Kra to Timor, with the alternative upward sweep from the Sunda Strait to Borneo and the Philippines. If the 'Indonesians' came from outside, as their genetic make-up and culture suggest, and their immigration was made in two separate waves, respectively some 5,000 and 3,500 years ago, as Beyer believed, it would probably have been over this route from mainland South-East Asia that they walked and paddled. The first Malays, those who are now highlanders, probably did much the same, but would have been aided by small sailing craft. Between the first arrivals of all these peoples in the East Indies and the establishment of the Malay majority, there must have been almost continuous movement into and around the region, some influences being also felt from Oceania. In contrast, a study of the mainstream Malay expansionism shows a clearly maritime culture and the growth of its influence far to the west and to the east. The initial point of departure for these people is equally as unproven and, once again, the cradle of their civilization is believed to have been South Asia.

The overwhelming majority of the population of the Philippines is basically Malay in origin, although there is a wide disparity in anthropological make-up within groups, and interbreeding with other communities and other races has already produced a hybridized stock. Although people of the same mainstream inhabit much of the East Indies, only residual movement, little more than adjustment, now takes place. This is slight, for even in such loosely knit states as Indonesia, the Philippines, and Malaysia, immigration is controlled and generally discouraged. Any large-scale movement towards the Philippines seems to have been completed by the time the Spaniards arrived in the first part of the sixteenth century and most of the Malay distribution over the East Indies took place during our era. A seafaring man and a farmer, in earlier times the Filipino was often a pirate. He is a bold and resourceful fisherman and today, living in the lowlands and generally not far from the coast, he combines agriculture and in-shore activities, planting his food crops in season and using the nearby sea both to augment his family's staples and for transport.

As the country was progressively populated, communities were founded, with leaders and councils. Later some interdependence grew up and, helped by the implements obtained from coastal trading, a more efficient and settled society came about, generally self-supporting, evolving slowly as the years went by. This Malay culture has remained the base of Philippine life over the centuries but, more than anywhere else in the East Indies, powerful alien pressures have forced it to broaden in character. Although Christianity may be said to have complemented it, the effect of Chinese, Indian, Arab, and European presence has enriched it. In its comparatively short history, evolutionary forces from within have been of far less importance than the consequences of these external pressures: the other indigenous cultures have had little to offer and, in any case, these latter peoples were effectively isolated from the majority until the twentieth century.

Although the Chinese had explored parts of the East Indies well before the birth of Christ, any lasting influence was contributed at a much later period, with the arrival of traders who left parties ashore to buy and sell for a later expedition. From the twelfth century onwards a more or less permanent Chinese presence is known to have been maintained in the islands, but earlier trading calls must have been made. Separately, some Japanese parties are believed to have reached Luzon, but evidence here is insufficient to give an accurate picture of their impact at the time.

To the west and to the south, on the Malay Peninsula and on the islands of Sumatra, Java, and Borneo, southern Indian expansionism, initially in the form of coastal trading, had commenced before our era. With the growth of the Pallavas dynasty, which was founded in south-east India during the second century A.D., movement around the Indian Ocean increased and by the fourth and fifth centuries, colonies had settled along the coasts of Malaya, Sumatra, and Borneo. These prospered and trade reached a peak by the seventh century. The traders brought with them their Hindu religion, improved implements, and a more evolved, better-organized way of life. Within and adjacent to their settlements, pockets of Indo-Malay culture grew up, the arts thrived, and small communities were fused with others to form larger units. As the years went by, whole areas were dominated and, by about A.D. 650, the Sri-Vishayan Empire was founded, centred on south-east Sumatra. This empire, with its maharajas and rajas replacing the loose-knit system of Malayan clan chiefs, became the strongest political unit in the East Indies and maintained considerable influence as far north as the former Indo-China states. As the centuries passed, Sri-Vishaya was weakened by internal struggle and was replaced by its natural offshoot, implanted in neighbouring Java, the Madjahpahit. By A.D. 1400 Madjahpahit had grown to its full glory and its sphere covered all of what is now Indonesia and Malaya, and its suzerainty had reached as far north as Formosa. Thus, Indo-Malay temporal power, centred firstly on Sumatra and then on Java, with tentacles reaching east and north, was maintained during most of the period from the mid-seventh to the end of the fifteenth centuries. China and Islam began to erode its fabric during the fifteenth century and Madjahpahit was finally assaulted by Moslems from Malacca in 1478. At the beginning of the sixteenth century, little was left of it and Java was almost wholly converted to Islam by the end of that century. Today nothing coherent remains of its culture outside the island of Bali, where the last remnants of Hinduism are still kept alive, isolated within the boundaries of a state which professes a liberal Islam. It is extremely difficult now to assess the impact on its northerly and less-evolved neighbours over eight or nine centuries of this Indo-Malay culture. In particular, expeditions from Madjahpahit called in at the small ports along the coasts of north Borneo and the Philippines, penetrating the interior seas as far as Panay and north-east Mindanao. Some sovereignty was loosely claimed over these lesser-evolved territories, but authority over either the whole or part of a remote Archipelago, the islands of which were separated politically by water, could never be a real thing unless a permanent administration was landed, maintained, and effectively guided from the parent country. This was never the case with either Sri-Vishaya or Madjahpahit, and although officially organized expeditions explored the Philippine coasts and seas, it was generally the normal exchange of local East

Indian traffic, often from neighbouring Borneo, which brought with it the colour of this more evolved culture. It was a substantially diluted way of life which came ashore to confront these coastal peoples, living their lives in more or less isolated communities and, even if more than one community came together to receive or repulse the visitors, the impact was never more than fragmented. Nevertheless, these centuries were long enough to leave their mark, even if intercourse was irregular and transitory. We shall see later that the Spaniards systematically destroyed most of the native records on their occupation of the Philippines and, for this reason, we are forced to look for traces and signs of this Indo-Malay culture in later writings and in modern life. Anthropologists have estimated that interbreeding between the Indian and the Malay has contributed visibly to the hybridization of the Philippine stock: the old pagan religions were enriched by emanations from the Brahmin Pantheon: local dress described by Spanish writers in the sixteenth century was akin to the Indian and, even now in the Moslem areas of Mindanao and in the Sulu Archipelago, remains much the same. Dialects are riddled with Sanskrit words, but some of these and an element of the other influences may well have been brought in later by the Gugrati Moslems who, in particular, came to Sulu as evangelists. Literature, folklore, and metalwork still bear strong marks of an Indianized culture.

The great expansion of Islam eastwards changed the course of the East Indian world. In the first and second centuries after Christ, Arab traders had already explored much of the Indian Ocean, had reached China, and had touched at numerous East Indian ports. But those who pioneered were sailors and merchants, and Islam was yet to be born. After Islam, this Arab merchant enterprise continued and, with expeditions fitted out in the neighbouring Moslem area of Gugrat, they engaged in the spice trade. It was then that vessels from Arabia and from Gugrat were to be found over most of the Indian Ocean, but southern India and the East Indies were the most profitable areas in which to choose places of call. Even then the spread of Islam in the Malay countries was inconsiderable, mainly because of the strength of the Hindu expatriates in Sumatra and Java. Only later, in the thirteenth century, was a firm foothold established in Malacca and the faith taken eastwards.

From Malacca, Islam conquered Sumatra and Java, gaining converts throughout the Indonesian islands. By the end of the fourteenth century, it had reached Sulu, and by the sixteenth century, southern Luzon and Manila itself. With what is now Malaya and Indonesia in their hands the evangelists were within an ace of converting the whole region. In less than three hundred years, a new culture had become paramount, much of the Malay folklore and ways of life had been profoundly modified, and almost all the Hindu veneer generated by Sri-Vishaya and Madjahpahit in Sumatra and Java had disappeared. The Islam introduced was generally brought by the Gugratis and was Indian and Sunni in character. Although considerable efforts have been made to purify teachings, it is an Indianized faith which has remained. In this form, it was probably more acceptable to the easy-going Malay than the stricter Arabic teachings and it blended with and was superimposed on an indigenous folklore which, earlier, had never succumbed completely to Brahmism. Thus, women walk in public unveiled and many of the tenets of the faith, fiercely maintained in more westerly countries, are most liberally interpreted. Only some pockets of fanaticism have appeared and one of these, Sulu itself, probably owes its devoutness both to the former presence of Arab teachers and to the centuries of aggressive militarism inherent to an isolated Moslem community within a Christian state.

To complete the narrative, mention must now be made of later and increased Chinese presence in the Philippines. Like the Arab traders who came at the beginning of our era, the Chinese were sailors and merchants, and their interests were secular and primarily materialistic. They did not seek to convert, nor was much of their culture passed directly to the relatively backward Malay. Later, petty officials accompanied the ships and, where a trading post was established, some sort of political organization came in with it.

A *modus vivendi* grew up; near extraterritoriality for the Chinese with a growing interest on their part in the commerce and organization around them. Grouped as they were with more or less individual native communities around them, a system of preference, protection, and (mainly for prestige reasons) the collection of small amounts of tribute followed. From the eleventh century onwards, this foreign presence was built up and by the Ming Dynasty (*c.* A.D. 1368) it was firmly implanted. The Chinese officials who had been landed drew the firm conclusion that they were masters of the small area in which they found themselves and that the islands were tributaries of their emperor. They reported back this implantation of authority, although their trading posts could only have been widely scattered at the best and real political power ashore was extremely tenuous. In time, the idea of Chinese power in the Philippines was accepted on mainland Asia and, during the early part of the Ming Dynasty, China claimed suzerainty over both the Philippines and part of Madjahpahit. At the turn of the fourteenth century, she attempted to enforce her authority and naval squadrons were despatched to the East Indies. Although tribute missions from native chiefs arrived in

China, her authority was never more than fragmented and localized, and even this loose claim was abandoned after less than fifty years. What has been permanent since those times is the presence of Chinese merchants, firstly in their trading posts and later in more or less coherent communities living in Philippine towns. For more than a thousand years Chinese manufactured goods and works of art have been traded and some of the Chinese way of life has entered into the day-to-day habits of the Filipino. Perhaps more important is the considerable contribution of Chinese blood resulting from interbreeding with Malay women over the centuries. There are very few urban communities in the Philippines today where this genetical dilution is not apparent.

To sum up, the people who are now described as Aetas, Proto-Malays, and Malays filled the whole region, probably settling during well-separated periods. There is no real proof of their origin, but it has been generally accepted that they did come from the North and north-west and that their movement was common to much of the East Indies, the most recent, the Malay penetrations, fining off towards New Guinea and Papua. Basically, therefore, the inhabitants of modern Indonesia, the Philippines, and Malaya are blood brothers. Where small differences in basic culture occur, it is where the Proto-Malay has occupied a more or less important area, although time has been adequate to allow a fairly similar distribution. In contrast, quite foreign influences have greatly changed the evolution of culture in the three main East Indian countries and time, distance, and historical events have produced a wide disparity during the last 1,500 years. During the sixteenth century, three European countries, Spain, the Netherlands, and Portugal, each conquered and annexed part of the Indies for herself, but even before this period, foreign intervention, modified by both time and space, had caused a profound effect. Thus the Indo-Malay empires, with their centres in what is now modern Indonesia, never held sway over the more remote Philippines. Islam, brought to Malacca from the western limits of the Indian Ocean, was launched eastwards from that town, travelling along the traditional Indies arc; but it did not turn northwards to penetrate the Philippines until a later period. It was, in the event, too late to obtain the religious control which it now enjoys in Indonesia and in Malaysia, for in the Philippines less than 4 per cent of the population profess that faith. Again, because of the relative proximity of the mainland, Chinese pressure ashore in the fifteenth century was probably more pronounced in Luzon than in any other part of the region. For these simple, physical and historical, reasons the character of the Filipino people already stood apart from their neighbours, even at the time when the Spaniards arrived in the Visayas with their own avowed colonial intentions.

The majority stream, whether Christian or Moslem by faith, has forged the overwhelming part of Philippine culture and its way of life: in this book it is only natural that the main thread is followed and emphasis placed on this heritage. Nevertheless, today the ethnic minorities continue to exist, but for centuries they stood aside, away from History, generally scarcely changed by Spanish rule. When the Americans took over the islands, integration was commenced, accompanied by the subjugation of the recalcitrant Moslem communities. The situation of the minorities at the end of Spanish rule is described below (pp. 102ff.) and this is updated by an examination (below, pp. 135–7, 162–3) of the situation since independence.

[1] Robert B. Fox, *Prehistoric Source Materials for the Study of Philippine History* (Manila, n.d.).

[2] Despite the seeming inadaptability of the Aetas in this modern world, hybridization bears witness to a domination of Aeta physical characters in the majority of cases of interbreeding.

Chapter 3

The Philippines at the Time of the Spanish Discovery

By the sixteenth century, a comparatively static ethnic situation had established itself. The only real population movements still taking place were relatively small and mostly from within the Malay world itself. These were adjustments prompted by religious or political pressures. In the mid-thirteenth century, some immigration from Sri-Vishayan Borneo into the Visayas had probably taken place, but by then Malay lowlanders were already well established all over the Philippine plains and valleys. Residual movement in the fourteenth and fifteenth centuries was mainly impelled by Islam. Moslems from the newly converted territories came up from the South to conquer and settle the Sulus and western Mindanao. Malays like the Filipinos themselves they brought with them, despite the Indianized character of their faith, a partially secular Arabic culture, ancillary to the religious teachings of the saids (Islamic missionaries) who accompanied them. Arabic law, architecture, and the adaptation of Islamic epics became current in the Sulus and polygamy and concubinage with the harem system were introduced. These Moslem settlements were to become local centres of instability: a mixture of religious fervour and a disregard for the traditional agrarian *status quo* degenerated into militarism and violence in the name of the Faith. Piracy, never absent in these waters, increased and prospered. Coastal forays against the settled but pagan lowland communities were made under a quasi-evangelistic guise. Until the mid-nineteenth century, peace and security within the internal seas and as far north as Manila Bay itself were threatened. In the worst times villages and towns were pillaged and men and women from the non-Moslem areas were abducted to slavery. A facet of this violence is the ethnic variety of the Sulu population which is descended from chaotic interbreeding.

In the first years relatively peaceful conversion had taken place, but from evidence given by the first Spanish colonists, the faith adopted by the hitherto pagan and settled coastal peoples was only skin deep and no real Islamic tradition had had time to establish itself outside the Sulus and western Mindanao. In the more recently converted pockets, traditional culture was still maintained and the Filipino lowland people followed a way of life which, although varying from area to area, continued to have much in common, as life remained based on the coherency of its physical environment with its wet agricultural traditions.

But not all the inhabitants of the Philippines lived in the lowlands. The Proto-Malays or Indonesian tribes drove the Aetas (negritos) from the plains to be, in their turn, usurped of the more fertile lands by the Malays. This process was re-enacted during the later movements of the true Malays. Earlier settlers, Malays who probably arrived at the beginning of our era and during the two or three centuries before, do not share the comparatively heterogeneous culture of the later arrivals and, at the time of these larger movements, were also dislodged. Early Malay-type groups have also inhabited remoter areas for centuries and still remain pagan and relatively under-evolved, although they follow a settled life, often employing highly complex methods of crop cultivation. Additional cultural variety has been caused by the physical profile of the Philippines, described above (pp. 25ff.). The main plain areas are extensive but few in number. Everywhere else, coastal corridors are narrow and strangled river valleys and re-entrants are widely separated. During the mobile period, a group moving from the coast or from the jealously guarded flood areas might well have crossed an obstacle on a coastal plain or struck up a river valley or deep re-entrant to become isolated for generations and, during this isolation, strong divergences in culture were imposed by both environment and relations with neighbouring, less evolved communities. The tribal groups of lowland Malays who live on the plains and on the linked corridors are large and closely related in their ways of life: in the physically chaotic areas, communities are smaller. It is the lowlanders who form the bulk of the population and it was they whom the Spaniards were to meet at the time of their first arrival in the Philippines. For centuries the colonists had few relations with other communities because of the remoteness of their tribal areas.

The lowlander outside the Moslem areas had already an old, fairly evolved culture before the Spaniards' arrival and in any study of the Philippines, some description of this simple civilization is essential. The Spaniards modified it, but did not destroy it, although to their discredit, much of its literature and written records were burnt by the priests or on their orders. Their culture is still an essential part of modern Philippine life and is often a stabilizing factor in a country torn by conflicting currents and influences. The lowlander was generally a farmer and he had long specialized in wet grown rice: he was, as we have seen, often a sailor and a fisherman, and he hunted to supplement his diet. On the land he used a wooden plough and harrow drawn by a water buffalo: many of his other implements were made of iron as were his weapons, but the sling, the bow and arrow, and the blowpipe were also employed. Gunpowder was not unknown at the beginning of the sixteenth century. Many of these people could read and write their particular dialect, and all dialects, which were and continue to be closely related, were set out in the Malayan alphabet of seventeen letters formed by fourteen consonants and three vowels. Men and women dressed differently. The men wore a short jacket and a waist cloth and the women a jacket and a short skirt, generally with an apron (*tapis*) tied around the waist. Ornaments of beads and precious and semi-precious stones and metals were worn by both sexes. Their staples were rice and, when this was in short supply, root vegetables of the yam variety. They added other commodities, depending on the geographical situation of the community, the season, and the social position of the family. These adjuncts were fish and shellfish, game and pork, and chicken and water-buffalo meat. Coconuts also contributed to variety as did bananas and indigenous citrus fruits, all generally mixed with rough sugar obtained from cane. Fermented toddy was brewed from palm, sugar, and rice.

Social organization was based on the family unit where men and women were considered equal, women sometimes assuming the highest responsibilities. Families were graded as of the ruling, free, or slave class, but slaves could obtain their freedom from what was often no more than a debtor condition and freemen could rise to the highest rank, if they showed outstanding virtues. Families were formed into villages called *barangays*, named after the sailing vessels which had been used by the Malay settlers. *Barangays* were of varying size – a hamlet to a small town, a chief or *datu* ruling with the aid of an elders' council. As time went by, a higher echelon of organization evolved, a *barangay* group. Here, to further defence, family tie, or materialistic gain, two or more *barangays* would fuse in a federal unit, the leadership often passing naturally to the strongest, whose chief became overlord, although each unit retained its own leader and identity. Legislation in these communities was often written down, but our knowledge of this facet of sociology has been narrowed by the early destruction of documents by the Spaniards. Civil and criminal cases were judged in public, before a council of elders. Fairly rudimentary punishments were meted out, including death and slavery. Outside the *barangay* or the grouped community, relations were not always peaceful and the traditional Malay hot temper and pride was at the root of much violence. But day-to-day contacts were made easier by 'parleys' where representatives talked out their problems until friction had lessened and some sort of compromise could be reached.

From the earlier social organization stemmed two factors of considerable importance. The first, that fragmentation of communities with the largest only amounting to an association of villages, produced a lack of cohesion which, in its turn, resulted in a real dearth of anything more than a local leader and a complete lack of any large-scale military resistance to the Spanish colonizers. To the latter this must have seemed strange after their earlier campaigns against the great indigenous empires which they had to destroy to rule in both Mexico and Peru. The second factor strikes directly at a continuing source of malaise, even today: this is the land-tenure system of the time, the character of which bears a striking resemblance to that which still exists. It is true that formal serfdom is no longer practised and, in the event, did not continue into the colonial period, but a landowning class was already established, share-cropping was a normal system, and usury was widespread. The latter, in its final stages, brought with it the serfdom to which we refer earlier. In a study of such social inequality later in this book, echoes of this already well-established structure will be found in the continuing political unrest throughout the colonial period, brought into the twentieth century in the form of Communist-sponsored revolt and civil disobedience.[1]

The environment of these rural people has not much changed over the last four hundred years. The coconut palms and the paddy-fields are more numerous and the methods of cultivation have been improved marginally, but only the introduction of maize (Indian corn) has altered the staples and, except for a few strains of vegetables and fruit brought in from America, the dietetical additives remain much the same. The dwelling-houses of wood, built up on stakes or poles, roofed with palm fronds, are almost unchanged and these shelter large families in one- or two-room areas.

Outside the materialistic part of their life, the Filipino Malays had inherited a broad, evolved, but disorganized religious tradition, a strong sense of music and poetry, and a rudimentary heroic literature. The pagan forms of worship were most complex and deities and lesser immortals numerous. Over the Archipelago, no real uniformity existed, although in one or another form, natural virtues and evils were individualized, animism was practised, and sorcery and innumerable superstitions thrived. Afterlife was expected and the dead were buried with ceremony and grief. Welded to these beliefs, which had been amassed within the ancient communities, was the fragmented veneer of the Sri-Vishayan and Madjahpahit culture which enriched and formalized the non-animist Pantheon and had reinforced the number of superstitions. Music, verse, and dancing form a major part of the Filipino's life today and are sometimes the only escape available in a life of toil and poverty, often aggravated by difficult climatic conditions. They may be married together as a unit within tribal folklore and have now become remarkably advanced. Even by the middle of the sixteenth century, these relaxations had evolved and the Spaniards, who fostered the whole considerably, built on the firm foundations of a real artistic tradition.[2]

In the context of modern history, permeability was probably the most important of all comparative weaknesses. The way of life was basically sound and just, but Malay civilization had evolved in backward areas and was not to be subjected to the more dynamic influences until later centuries, and as we have seen, much of the movements within the remainder of the East Indies had passed the Archipelago by. Its pagan religion was a loose marriage of tradition and superstition, lacking the strength generated by the more decisive beliefs (particularly Brahmin Hinduism and later, Islam and Christianity, with their one god only) which were coupled with strong and recorded codes of secular morals and conduct. On the materialistic side, the technical level of these peoples was strikingly backward in comparison with Central and South American, European, Arabic, Indian, and Chinese civilizations of the time.

By the mid-sixteenth century, Islam had already obtained a real hold and was moving rapidly northwards. The Malay culture of the Philippines was threatened with the same fate as had already befallen it in the Peninsula and over most of what is now Indonesia; and mainly because of a lack of religious and technical sophistication, it had little with which to defend itself. This seemingly inevitable current of events was sharply checked and almost immediately reversed by the Spaniards who, although they were never able to bring the Moslems of the Sulus and western Mindanao to the Cross, stopped Islamic evangelization to the north and, outside the traditional Moslem areas, converted the lowlander Malays to Christianity. Thus an East Asian civilization was partially replaced by a Mediterranean culture, firmly reinforced by the authority and way of life of the Roman Catholic Church.

1 The Spaniards, as we shall see, introduced their own refinements into the system, but this only served to emphasize its basic inequalities.

2 Much more can be written of this indigenous culture which the *conquistadores* discovered on their arrival and in the Bibliography (below, pp. 231–2) reference has been made to assist further reading.

PART TWO

Western Domination

Chapter 4

Iberian Expansionism

PORTUGUESE SHIPS are believed to have visited the Philippines at the beginning of the sixteenth century, but there can be no dispute about the dates, the character, and the size of the two Spanish expeditions which, in 1521 and 1565 respectively, arrived in the Archipelago and were followed by over three hundred years of Spanish colonization. The first, headed by Ferdinand Magellan, a Portuguese in the service of Spain, consisted initially of five vessels, the largest of 120 tons. Magellan left Spain in 1519, crossed the Atlantic, and probed along the coast of South America for a way around the continent so as to reach the Indies from the East. He succeeded and, after both mutiny and desertion had cut his small squadron to three, cleared the straits which are now named after him and gained the Pacific Ocean in November 1520. After considerable privation and a landfall at Guam, Magellan touched at Samar on the Philippines' eastern seaboard in March 1521 and here he received friendliness and hospitality from the inhabitants. With their help, the squadron sailed for Cebu in the western Visayas and, as in Samar, was welcomed by the local chiefs. In both Samar and in Cebu, conversion of Filipino Malays to Christianity took place. Magellan, however, seems to have made a singular miscalculation in Cebu. In this loose-knit and independent society, he attempted to consolidate his own position by trying to increase the strength and standing of his benefactor, Humabun, the chief of the *barangay* complex of Cebu itself. In this context, a skirmish took place with a neighbouring chief on the shores of the small island of Mactan, immediately across the straits, and here Magellan and eight of his men were killed. With this loss of prestige, Humabun turned on his guests and killed a further twenty-eight of them. The squadron left in haste but continued exploration in the interior seas, abandoning a further ship owing to manpower shortage. After many adventures the two remaining arrived at Tidore, an island in the Moluccas, opposite the Celebes. There the decision was made to continue the journey home separately, the *Victoria* (85 tons) sailing westwards around the Cape and the *Trinidad* (110 tons) returning eastwards via the Magellan Straits. The *Victoria* arrived in Spain in September 1522, the first ship to have been sailed around the world. The *Trinidad* was forced back in the Pacific and was given up to the Portuguese in the Moluccas: later four of her survivors reached Spain.

The *Victoria* brought back a cargo of oriental commodities, including those much-coveted items – spices. These goods, and the knowledge that a route existed westwards to the Indies, provided the impetus for further exploration. Spain despatched squadrons in 1525, 1526, 1527, and 1542, but all failed in their attempts to gain a real foothold in the Archipelago, although the first and the last of these touched briefly at points on the Philippine coast before sailing southwards to the Moluccas, despite the hostility of the Portuguese, who were already strong in that area. The 1542 expedition, which continued its explorations through to 1549, was commanded, during its first years, by Ruy López de Villalobos. It was Villalobos who gave the name 'Felipina' to a single island of the Archipelago, in honour of the Spanish crown prince, who later became Philip II. Subsequently, the whole of the island chain became known by the same name.

In 1564, a new expedition was fitted out, this time in Mexico, and the command was given to Miguel López de Legaspi, a Spanish magistrate of what is now Mexico City. His immediate subordinate was Father Andrés de Urdaneta, a most competent navigator, former soldier, and sea captain, but for some ten years an Augustinian missionary priest. The squadron consisted of four ships. They sailed with sealed instructions from the *Audiencia*[1] of Mexico to colonize the Philippines for Spain. One ship very soon deserted Legaspi, but the remaining three, after calling at Guam, reached the Philippines and anchoring off Cebu, were treated with considerable hostility. The squadron immediately left and after touching at Samar sailed on to Leyte, where it was well received at Limassawa. Exploration of the Visayas then continued and contacts were made in Bohol: from there, Butuaan (now Butuan) in north Mindanao and, once again, Cebu itself were visited. Cebu was chosen as an initial firm base by the colonists, but the hostility of the local inhabitants had first to be overcome. It took an armed assault over the coast, aided by the ships' guns, to obtain favourable conditions by treaty. The first Spanish settlement in the Philippines was built there in 1565 and, with its fort, provided the centre from which colonization and conversion extended, firstly to the local island of Panay in 1569 and then to islands in the Sibuyan Sea and to the south-east tip of Luzon itself.

In 1570, parties were sent against Moslems entrenched on Mindoro and these were cleared. In the same year, Manila, which had been partially converted to Islam, was visited and attempts were made to colonize and re-convert the area, already a place of entry for regional trade. These attempts were met with armed resistance, but the Spaniards attacked the town and partially reduced it before leaving once again for Cebu. In 1571 a second expedition was prepared and it was decided to move the main centre of Spanish power to Manila. With the help of Visayans and reinforcements from Mexico, the Spaniards occupied the Manila area and consolidated their position around the mouth of the Pasig River: systematic colonization of Luzon followed. At the same time expansion over all the Visayas and parts of north Mindanao was initiated from Cebu.

This half-century of courageous effort to discover part of the prized Orient and hold it for Spain was part of a far greater expansionist movement. The more advanced Eastern peoples, the Arabs, the Indians, the Chinese, and the Japanese, had navigated the Indian and Pacific Oceans since the first millennium A.D. and trade, which included the purchase of slaves, had flourished along the southern coasts of Asia as a result of voyages to the South.

During this same period, the Europeans and North Africans had moved in a more restricted fashion. The Dark Ages had had their due effect, and the Mediterranean, with its more evolved cultures, had generally been sufficient for trading needs: where longer journeys were necessary, these were primarily along the European and the neighbouring West African coasts. There were few exceptions to this, although the Greek expeditions under the Persian kings in the sixth century B.C. and under Alexander the Great, and their colonization of parts of North India, had also been accompanied by maritime exploration down the Indus and to the shores of the Indian Ocean around its delta. From there, probes northwards probably reached the Arabian Sea and the Persian Gulf. Later the Scandinavians sailed west to find Greenland and may well have reached north-east America. It was not until travellers on land had penetrated as far as mainland South-East Asia and China and the exchange of commerce with Asia through Middle Eastern trading houses had become considerable that a desire to explore and participate more fully in financial gain became stronger. Then, two factors provided the catalyst which transformed wish into action: the seaman's art, with his instruments and the vessels necessary to brave an Atlantic passage, evolved rapidly and Saracen conquest, fatal to the free movement of goods from Asia to Europe, gained the whole territory of the Middle East and the coast of North Africa.

Portugal was the first country to move out of Europe. Expeditions along the west coast of Africa at the beginning of the fifteenth century were followed logically by the discovery of the passage around the Cape in 1487 and Vasco de Gama made his famous voyage to India during 1497 and 1498. Portugal's establishment of her Indian colonies only preceded by a few years probes as far as China and Japan, and a hold was obtained in Malacca during 1511. Infiltration through the East Indies followed, although no real attempt was made to force northwards towards the Philippines by the mid-sixteenth century. But she did guard her already acquired treasures jealously and strongly reacted to any Spanish move in her sphere of influence. To the west, in the Indian Ocean, she was the undisputed mistress for nearly a century.

The Moorish invasion, with the ensuing long wars and the slow retreat of Islam to the south-west of the Iberian Peninsula, inhibited earlier Spanish expansion. But while Portugal headed south and then eastwards, Spain explored to the west, Columbus reaching the Caribbean in October 1492. Considerable activity ensued and in 1513 it was realized that another ocean, the Pacific, lay west of the Americas.

Neighbours in south-west Europe, Spain and Portugal were both gripped with the desire to expand, colonize, and prosper from trade monopolies. Both Christian and Catholic, the Cross accompanied their expeditions wherever they went. Conversion of the native populations was a logical corollary to colonization and, if anything, in the formative years, Spain was more vigorous in her drive to evangelize than her neighbour, whose glory was relatively fleeting; her empire shrinking rapidly by the end of the sixteenth century. But at the end of the fifteenth century, the desire and the force of each were well matched; both were equally jealous of their acquirements and the confrontation of overseas interests had already resulted in violence and death along the African coasts where any Spanish attempt to move towards the Indian passage was countered vigorously. In this acute situation, Rome intervened in an attempt to keep the peace by a division of the world into two spheres of interest: Portuguese and Spanish. But after the recognition of Portugal's conquests in Africa and her right to expand eastwards, and Spain's claims to the west and south-west, papal decisions became partisan and, finally, at Tordesillas in June 1494, the two countries agreed by treaty to a demarcation line running from Pole to Pole, 370 leagues west of the Cape Verde Islands. This decision gave rise to loose interpretation. The Cape Verde Islands cover a lateral area of over 300 kilometres and here there was already an inherent inaccuracy, although by far the most important differences were those of opinion: the forms and positions of the various land masses remained conjectural, the charts of the day reflecting this ignorance of geography;

in addition a longitudinal position was still difficult to plot. Exaggeration of these problems was compounded by Spain, who claimed far greater areas westwards than even the most liberal interpretation of the agreement could have allowed. According to the agreement, the Moluccas fell just inside the Spanish sphere of interest, while the Philippines were clearly within the Portuguese. Father Urdaneta, on reading Legaspi's sailing instructions to colonize the Archipelago for Spain, was convinced of the illegality of the order, but it is interesting to note that these same instructions confirmed Portuguese sovereignty over the Moluccas and restrained Legaspi from challenging it. This mixture of ignorance and guile operated at the limits of the two worlds and it was in these circumstances that Spain filled a vacuum which Portugal might never have been able to occupy, let alone maintain effectively against strong Moslem pressure for over three hundred years.

Thus, Legaspi's successful expedition fell within the great Iberian movement to control the Indies from whence precious metals, jewels, silks, and spices were obtained. For the Spaniards, this foothold in Asia was both the fulfilment of their desire for a presence in the Orient and an extension of their occupation and colonization of Central and South America. Already well entrenched there, but excluded from the Eastwards Route by the Portuguese, their mercantile problems were at first aggravated by the long haul around the Horn which both Magellan and Legaspi had experienced. But the privations and delays imposed by this route were almost immediately removed. As a part of the Spanish plans, the charting of a return route eastwards, towards the area where the Pacific was seen for the first time in 1513, was to be undertaken as soon as possible. The same Father Urdaneta piloted the *San Pedro* out of Cebu, arriving at Acapulco on the Pacific coast of Mexico in October 1565. This voyage of a little over four months was to lay the pattern for all communications between Spain and her colony for the next two hundred years.

The news of Legaspi's success, brought by the returning explorers in 1565, was followed by the despatch of reinforcements from Mexico to the Philippines. This first sailing westwards out of Acapulco towards the new colony foreshadowed a long tradition of Philippine dependence on New Spain, as Mexico was named at that time. Any trade with the mother country was through this colony and, although much of the exchange was confined to relations between the Philippines and her American advance base, movement between the former and Europe was via trans-shipment points on either the Pacific or Atlantic seaboards, over the passes to the opposite coast, and then to resume the long sea voyage west or east.

New Spain from her own resources also provided much of the men and materials to assist the colonists in the Philippines: in larger ships, this advance base could be reached from the Philippines in a little over six months and, during the sixteenth and seventeenth centuries, the effects of the Portuguese denial of the Eastwards Route were minimized.

Legaspi's task of colonizing was assisted by his gallant immediate subordinates. Outstanding among this small band were Martín de Goiti and Juan de Salcedo, Legaspi's grandson. These two campaigned in Luzon in the years immediately following the occupation of the Manila area and the majority of the western plains and the southern Bicol Peninsula had been subdued by 1580. With a foothold solidly established in Luzon and the Visayas and some exploration of Mindanao already undertaken, the Spaniards started on the long task of settling down in a country separated from Spain by over nine months' journey at the best of times. The first explorers were given titles to the control of land; grants of this nature were called *encomiendas* and the recipient assured, under certain regulations, the control of not only land, but also of its people and of its resources. The system was a general one in these first years of Spanish colonization and it did provide a reward for those men who had braved so much to live, in most cases, the remainder of their lives so far from their native land. But if the individual was rewarded for his labours in this way, what was Spain's share in the advantages of the colonial system? There is no doubt that her satraps in Central and South America provided considerable economic gain and that the riches of New Spain not only gave incentive to her own colonizers and assistance both fiscally and commercially to the mother country, but also provided the backing necessary to maintain Spanish presence in the Philippines. The annexation of the Archipelago brought no such financial return, and, although the Portuguese, and later the Dutch and the English, were able to extract considerable riches from their possessions and trading posts in the Indian Ocean and the East Indies, the Philippines was a continued drain on the exchequer of Spain and New Spain until the introduction of the Tobacco Monopoly in 1782. Spanish rule in the Philippines was maintained in the teeth of opposition at home and then only because of the pressure exercised by the clergy, whose fears for their converted flocks were continuously voiced in the highest circles.

[1] An *Audiencia* was the viceroy or government of a territory under Spanish rule in Council. See also below, p. 72.

Chapter 5

Spain and Christ

LEGASPI'S INSTRUCTIONS, prepared under the authority of the *audiencia* of New Spain, laid down a number of quite separate clauses as guidelines for the conduct of his expedition. He was ordered to explore the 'Islands of the West, near the Moluccas', the Moluccas themselves being expressly excluded from his sphere of action. He was ordered to make for other islands 'such as the Philippines – within the demarcation of His Majesty'. This was patently a breach of treaty agreement with Portugal and it was against this clause that Father Urdaneta's conscience rebelled. In priority after the preamble were that the territories be converted to Catholicism, that a return route eastwards be explored, and that all legal means be taken to enrich the Spanish Crown by the procurement and despatch of 'spices and other riches'. Legaspi was also ordered to send back useful intelligence: details of ports, of the inhabitants, their character and way of life, the resources of the country, the local cost of spices, and the value which the island peoples placed on goods brought in by the Spaniards. The instructions then recommended the expedition to pursue local trade relations and to found a settlement in the most favourable area. In the context of Iberian expansionism and Spain's past colonial conduct in America, the *audiencia*'s phrasing seems extremely well balanced, particularly when we consider the scanty knowledge of the area available at the time. And so, despite Portuguese hostility, Spain was to claim possessions in Asia and find a return route back to Europe through her American colonies. A permanent settlement was to be made and Christianity brought to the inhabitants. Trade, particularly the procurement of the precious spices, was only mentioned later in the text. It is indicative of the character of the expedition that five missionary friars were included in its number, among them the navigator, Father Urdaneta. All were of the Augustinian order.

By the end of the sixteenth century the Spaniards had occupied much of both the great island of Luzon and of the Visayas. On Luzon itself, the progress of the colonizers was, understandably, limited by the formidable geographical barriers which exist. Thus, after the capture of Manila and the establishment of the seat of government there, the rich, well-watered areas to the north and south of the capital formed the hub of both the administration and of the economy. Very rapidly, other expeditions fanned out. To the north, the whole of the western plain was reorganized under colonial rule and, soon after, the bleak Ilocos and Cagayan coasts, facing the Luzon Strait, were occupied. Progress then continued southwards up the broad valley of the Cagayan River as far as Isabela. Only the massive central mountain area and the Sierra Madre, with its thickly forested coastline, were outside Spanish influence for some time. To the south, the Bicol provinces of Camarines and Albay were as quickly explored as the north and garrisons left there to continue the work of colonizing. In the Visayas the major islands of Samar, Leyte, Panay, Negros, Cebu, and Bohol were all explored and garrisoned at much the same time. Only Mindanao, the Sulu Archipelago, and Palawan remained outside Spanish rule, although missionary work had already begun by the beginning of the sixteenth century in north-east Mindanao and was to be followed soon after by settlements further west and in the Zamboanga Peninsula.

This very rapid progress over a very wide area did not at first mean complete domination of the territories which the Spaniards claimed to have occupied. Garrisons were established at focal points, local officials or the holders of *encomiendas* began to move into the surrounding countryside, and the priests, few in number at first, but considerably increased by the end of the sixteenth century, looked after the souls of the Filipinos. A more detailed study of the state of the colony at the close of the century will confirm the continuation of the religious nature of the occupation: in those days, the early history of Spain's new colony was largely made by the first *conquistadores* and members of five religious orders, only very occasionally supplemented by secular clergy. Within the structure of colonial rule, missionary fields were allocated on a geographical basis. The Augustinians came in with Legaspi: the Franciscans arrived soon after. Jesuits and Dominicans were in position by the end of the sixteenth century and the Recollects' first mission arrived in 1606.

Until 1821, the administration of the Philippines was marked by the titular dependence of the colony on the authority of the viceroy of New Spain. This dignitary, in the name of the Spanish Crown, ruled through the monarch's appointed local representative, the Governor and Captain-General.[1] As was the case of all Spanish colonies from 1524 to 1836, the monarch was advised and assisted administratively by a Madrid-based body, the Council of the Indies (Consejo de Indias). The Council also served as the highest court of appeal for cases coming from Spain's overseas possessions. But in

Manila, the Governor, as Captain-General, had himself almost vice-regal powers. As a direct appointee of the king, his personal status was quasi-absolute and when distances are considered in conjunction with the breadth of his chartered responsibilities, he had the widest administrative powers coupled with a command of the armed forces. His character and conduct could affect local conditions almost as much as those of an absolute monarch in Europe. In addition, he was president of the Manila royal *audiencia*, the colony's supreme judicial body, and possessed fairly summary local powers of decree reaching over a very wide field. At his executive disposal, to a greater or lesser degree, depending on the character of the senior clergy at the time, were two hierarchies, one temporal and the other spiritual. As the Governor-General, he had absolute control of his administrative subordinates: he also had considerable titular powers over the local ecclesiastical organizations and, if relations were good and co-operation between the temporal and spiritual powers prospered, much could be done. If the contrary was the case, as was very often so, progress flagged, for the official Establishment relied considerably on the priests who had not only assumed wide *de facto* temporal powers within their parishes, but were also a considerable reinforcement to the overall Spanish presence in the Philippines, where the number of Europeans outside Manila was restricted and was to remain so until the nineteenth century. Administratively the islands were divided into provinces or, where Spanish power was tenuous, politico-military districts. A provincial governor (*alcalde mayor*) and a military district commander (*corregidor*) held a province and a politico-military district respectively. Subdivisions into town areas (*pueblos*) were made and elected municipal officials (*gobernadorcillos*) were responsible for their administration: villages (*barangays*) with a local chief in charge, formed the last link in the executive chain. Spiritual power worked side by side with this temporal administration. The Philippines was formed into an archdiocese at the end of the sixteenth century: the archbishop continued to exert direct authority over the diocese of Manila, but administered the remainder through his bishops at Cebu, Nueva Segovia, and Nueva Carceres.[2] Dioceses were divided into parishes and, in addition to these, missions were established in the less stable areas. Superimposed on this spiritual authority was the presence of the local superiors of the five powerful religious orders to which the country was entrusted for the major part of its religious enlightenment: if the archbishop of Manila was sometimes out of line with the Governor-General's wishes, the religious orders were very frequently at variance with the expressed desires of the highest prelate in the country.

Despite a provision for some temporal authority over the Church's functions in the islands[3] the strong presence of the friars outside the capital often made it necessary for travellers to obtain the missionaries' authority for their journeys in the countryside. Neither could the executive establishment of the archbishop nor of his subordinate bishops assist greatly in areas where the orders were all-powerful and secular clergy non-existent. Nevertheless, this seeming intransigence on the part of the priesthood was generally the result of a genuine desire to protect its flocks. The priests were often the only persons to whom the Filipino peasant could turn, especially where the petty officials, or worse the holders of *encomiendas*, became too brutal or grasping. The parish priest was the only Spaniard for many kilometres: in early times it was he who had explained his faith and had made conversions. He and his successors, in the eyes of most parishioners, typified both the religious and executive authority of Spain. To the credit of these early priests, it must be said that they generally did all they could to protect their converted flocks: the superiors of the religious orders showed the same concern as their subordinate brothers. To assist both state and Church in their aims, the physical layout of the countryside had been slowly modified after Spanish conquest. The *barangay* or village, as we have seen above, was left in its basic environmental position, the villagers having to remain on the land or by the sea to cultivate or to fish. But power was quickly concentrated into those larger settlements which the Spaniards first occupied, fanning out later to additional focal points, each having both a temporal and spiritual character. In these, the *pueblos*, the people were grouped 'under the bells'. The church, often the only 'hard' construction, with its incorporated or adjacent bell-tower, formed the central point of the *plaza*. Around the *plaza* sprang up the municipal seat of government, the school, and the dwelling houses of the more influential inhabitants. Thus, this simple basic organization, which remains much the same to this day, at the time embraced the majority of the country's inhabitants. As now, the larger towns and cities were of relatively small size, and, although their basic requirements for some degree of autonomy were recognized by the Spaniards from the earliest times, the number of people who lived outside the *barangays* and *pueblos* was small. The simple Christian culture of the Philippines evolved in the rural areas, in the agricultural and fishing communities, welded together by the nucleus under the bells, the parish priest and the local *principales* heading this subordinate but all-important hierarchy.

Into a backward Malay life were injected certain aspects of Mediterranean culture and science. In early times, considerable impetus had been provided by the *conquistadores*, but most of the logical developments in the seventeenth century were initiated by the friars. From their missions and from the garrisoned points, they pushed out into the countryside, themselves founding the first townships and building roads, bridges, canals, and even strongpoints against the destructive Moslem forays from the south. Within the environment of their new life, these men, often of considerable ability, introduced the flora and fauna strains from the Americas and Europe which have already been referred to above (p. 33). The most important of the plants which still remain as part of Philippine life are maize, tobacco, cacao, sweet potato, pineapple, and some fruits and vegetables used as semi-staples or dietetic additives: papaya, tomatoes, marrows, etc. Domestic animals were also brought in, cattle being the most important. Of these introductions, maize, tobacco, and pineapple are now of immense value, the first as a staple for the majority of people of Visayan origin and the other two as cash crops. In all such advances and in improvements to both the strains and the culture of traditional crops, these early priests were devout pioneers. But if materialistic factors were pioneered by the clergy, the artistic life of the people was not forgotten. Traditional folklore was largely assimilated, Malay-type art was fostered, and the local song and dance repertoires enriched by Iberian influences. The Latin alphabet with the Spanish language had been introduced officially, but local Malay dialects were now written down in Latinized script. Primary education became a facet of local religious life. The establishment of the basic prerequisites for learning was also achieved within the colony: books, almost all of a religious nature, began to be produced locally; libraries were established within the walls of the religious institutions and foundations for a Christian Filipino literature laid down. From Europe also came simple teachings of science, again the prerogative of the priests. In earlier days, these were often modest, tended to be of the 'natural' type, and more generally inhibited by clerical conservatism. Perhaps the boldest of the priestly scientific endeavours in this context was the planning and construction of their own stone-built churches and monasteries, which followed closely the European designs of the period.

For some time after the establishment of Spanish rule, the dynamic character of official expansionism was still intact and from this foothold in the East Indies, Portuguese monopoly of penetration into Asia was challenged, particularly in the furtherance of Spanish-type Roman Catholicism. Before the end of the sixteenth century, missionaries had already embarked for China and Japan, but they were generally received with official hostility. In both these countries, Spanish missions were at variance with the already established Portuguese Jesuits who, with papal authority, claimed a territorial monopoly there for missionary work. But this foreign penetration into East Asia was short-lived and during the seventeenth century, Iberian missionary presence was almost eradicated in both countries. Elsewhere Spanish expansionism into sovereign Asian territories was also brought to a halt. Thai control of Cambodia at the end of the sixteenth century brought hostilities on a reduced scale – and much intrigue. By 1630 all had settled down once again and, except for some frustrated attempts, Spanish expansion northwards was limited to a short occupation of Formosa.

Despite its alien nature, Spanish rule in the Philippines held firm, although, as will be seen in the next chapter, periods of real peace during the first eighty years after conquest were few. Consolidation took place in all those areas which were not too remote for satisfactory occupation or which were still not under Moslem control. Soon afterwards, however, the energy of the colonizers flagged noticeably until, by the mid-seventeenth century, the character of both secular and religious endeavour had modified considerably and an atmosphere of torpidity had penetrated almost everywhere.

During these essentially formative years, Spain had extended her colonization across the Pacific and, in the teeth of natural difficulty and both Portuguese and, later, Dutch opposition, had maintained and improved her hold over much of this scattered Archipelago. As we have seen, her attempts to increase political and religious influence to the north and south had been less fortunate and, by the mid-seventeenth century, she had reached the zenith of her power in the East. At this same time, the single-mindedness of the priestly hierarchy had made it possible for the foundations of Catholicism to be laid firmly in this culturally alien environment. It is this latter influence, dating from the earliest period, which remains the most alive today. Despite official Spanish disenchantment with her new colony, the moral pressure of the Church maintained her presence in the teeth of a constant drain on the treasury of New Spain and the physical difficulties of the most time-consuming lines of communication ever used by a colonizing power. The Filipino today owes much to these missionaries who, in those days, came so far to work, and almost always, to die in the land which they had adopted. It was during these years that Philippine life was modified and moulded into the Malay Christian culture which has been strong enough to withstand much of the alien pressures of late twentieth-century politics and philosophy.

[1] The title was shortened to Governor-General. Because of the distances involved, the Manila Governor-General's position, as we will see later, was almost unchallenged and the monarch's delegations to the viceroy of New Spain mostly concerned themselves with the questions of financial and material aid. The

viceroy's powers were apparent at the end of a Governor-General's term of office, when a clearance had to be given (see below, p. 72).

[2] Now Naga City in Camarines and Laloc in Cagayan. The Nueva Carceres bishopric was later transferred to Vigan.

[3] The Governor-General, in addition to his considerable temporal powers, was also delegated some of the royal powers of ecclesiastical administration and patronage.

Chapter 6

Consolidation and Defence

THE FORMATIVE YEARS of the colony's youth stretched from the 1570s to include much of the seventeenth century. During this long period, the world was changing rapidly. European nations established settlements in the Americas, Africa, and Asia. China, the giant of the East, had been visited and traded with and was becoming more and more uneasy on account of the alien missionary activities being pursued within her frontiers. Japan cut herself off from the world in 1639. Portugal, whose hostility to Spain's first ventures in the East Indies was violent, had scarcely been reconciled to them in the context of the Spanish Succession to the Portuguese Crown in 1580 when her overseas possessions were faced with growing pressure from both England and Holland.

If these first years after the Spanish conquest were relatively quiet, they were never ones of complete peace. Challenge came both from inside the country and from Asians around. All attempts made to push further into Mindanao and the Sulus were failures and the Moslem Filipinos[1] retaliated sharply, attacking the settled villages to the north and in the Visayan area. In 1574, a strong Chinese pirate force under Lim Ah Hong made a flamboyant raid on Manila itself and, although defeated, held out for some months in a coastal stronghold in central Luzon. A Japanese attempt to secure a foothold in the extreme north of that island was countered by force and, after a violent skirmish in 1582, the invaders withdrew to their boats. Already a number of Philippine rebellions had been put down and these were to continue spasmodically throughout the colony's history.

Portugal's weakness overseas and, after the Spanish Succession's solution of the two countries' colonial problem, the inability of Spain to reinforce it satisfactorily in the Indies, was to cause the colony considerable problems early in the seventeenth century. The Dutch began to infiltrate through the East Indian arc and, by 1610, had succeeded in dominating both Amboina and Ternate in the Moluccas, the area 250 miles due south of Mindanao which had become a focal point for European trade in spices. Despite aid from the

Philippines, this Dutch domination grew, firstly in the militant, commercial field and then as a political venture within the operations of the Dutch East Indian Company. Thus to the immediate south, the Spaniards in the Philippines were no longer the neighbours of Catholic fellow-Iberians but of a hostile, dynamic, and Protestant nation whose commercial acumen was as sharp as it was ruthless and whose aspirations were centred on the East Asian segment.

Dutch hostility escalated to colonial war and for some fifty years fear of attack was constant in Manila. The first came in 1600 and was followed by three more. They were all just about within the scope of the colony's own resources to repel and only the last, in 1647, caused any land threat to Manila: then a small force was landed on the Bataan coastline in the northern part of Manila Bay, but the intruders were beaten back to their ships after causing damage and loss of life. Although far from Europe and maintained by quite separate lines of communication, one westwards and one eastwards, the two antagonists were fairly matched, the Spaniards practising a continental-type system of defence, with the Dutch relying strongly on sea-power based on their new possessions. Despite the Spanish success in keeping hold of their colony, Dutch action in the seventeenth century was a real threat and might have caused a serious dislocation to the political and religious consolidation of colonial power in the Philippines. Even today, these earlier battles are still remembered, mainly as a challenge to Roman Catholicism, and a religious thanksgiving, 'La Naval de Manila', continues to be celebrated to thank the Holy Virgin, the protector of the Spanish squadron (two old galleons) which in a seemingly miraculous fashion defeated a more numerous Dutch force in 1646. It was fortunate at the time that British maritime interests were largely concentrated in the Indian Ocean and were generally at variance with the Dutch. Occasional hostile British acts took place, generally the plunder of a galleon. Spanish European and world power had been damaged by the destruction of her Armada in 1588.

To combat the internal and external threats to the colony, the government raised Filipino forces to reinforce the small numbers of peninsular and insular Spaniards who, with Mexican troops, formed the nucleus of the army and navy. In addition, quite substantial militias existed in the settlements all over the country and the local people themselves, led by Spanish officials and priests, turned out to parry some of the hardiest threats from the Moslem raiders. With the small Spanish presence in the Archipelago at the time, it is doubtful if the colony could have survived without the goodwill of the majority of its people. And this goodwill was reinforced by positive acts: the armed assistance of the population in time of need and the enlistment into the forces of men who were of good basic military material.

Thus, with the administrative and spiritual base laid down and the majority of the people in the settled areas living in peaceful communities dominated by the local priests, Spanish rule strengthened, helped by the Filipinos themselves, who had already something to say as local officials or elders of congregations. This time of consolidation was, however, punctuated by trials of strength between the state, as represented by the Governor-General, and the Church, represented by the ecclesiastical hierarchy and the superiors of orders. Nevertheless, over the large expanse of the islands, these differences were generally considered as urban problems and, outside Manila and the one or two larger towns, life went on in a humdrum fashion dominated by a policy of *laissez-faire* and a tolerance between local representatives of the two factions. After the first flush of conquest, which had its moral as well as material aims, pioneering spirit gave way to a certain laxity. Small fortunes were made by Spanish officials and traders, often at the expense of the people and of their own government. Priests were accused of leading a life of comfort with some disregard for certain of their vows. But in the Malay world, especially that influenced by Spain and the Catholic Church, there was and still remains a built-in safety valve. The grasping official was countered by the priest whose flock was threatened with poverty: the immoral act or the idleness of a priest was reported by the official and, if things became impossible, the hot blood of the Malay erupted into an act of local violence – often of short duration – and things settled down again to the humdrum life which had evolved from the Spanish graft on to a primitive, pagan-cultured stock.

[1] The Spaniards called them *moros* (Moors), a word which is, today, considered pejorative.

Chapter 7

The Colonial Order

FROM THE TIME of the Spanish conquest and until 1834, the Philippines was officially closed to foreign trade and only very limited transactions actually took place. Despite the efforts of a handful of individuals, the majority French, to penetrate the country, the only non-Iberian European influence during this period was experienced at the time of the short British occupation of Manila from 1762 until 1764. Nevertheless, throughout Spanish rule there was a constant alien presence widespread over the Archipelago: this was Chinese, exercised from within, commercial or artisan in character, but reaching out beyond the normal world of trade to add some of its ways of life to the communities adjacent to the permanent enclaves and settlements which had been established over the centuries. These settlements also existed in the unconquered Moslem-dominated areas of Mindanao and the Sulus even before the Spaniards were able to venture more than a few hundred metres from their fortified encampments which were occasionally maintained there. The Chinese brought into the Philippines considerable quantities of goods which were exchanged at relatively fair rates and, in turn, were exported back to New Spain and Europe. Outside this regular trade relation, some local commerce existed between the colony and its neighbours, particularly Thailand and Cambodia. Also within this community of interests were the Carolinas, the Marianas, and the Pelews, which had been annexed by Spain and were administered through Manila. Thus, at the end of an extended line of communication, this little world of the Spanish Indies followed its limited interests.

The Governor-General ruled over the king's subjects, who, unless they lived in the less settled districts, were often tied to the *encomienda* system. Here there was minor abuse, although it must be said in fairness that many of the *encomenderos* attempted to administer their estates justly and, in any case, as we have seen, natural safety valves existed. Within the system, the majority of Filipinos were subjected to the payment of tribute and to the provision of personal labour for public works. During the early period, tribute levied on a family amounted to 10 *reales* per annum. Labour was compulsory for all Filipino males of working age and amounted to forty days a year: this period could be compounded in either part or whole at a rate of 1½ *reales* per day. Certain other small taxes and dues were also collected within the system.

Spanish-administered law in the Philippines was, as in her other colonies, mainly derived from the Laws of the Indies (*Leyes de las Indias*), a code of great value for such early times. But, although these laws were adequate for the first century of occupation, reform of this essentially colonial statute failed to keep pace with political evolution and it was not until late in the nineteenth century that the more liberal metropolitan code was in part authorized for the colony. Rule by a Governor-General continued from the time of Legaspi, the first incumbent, until the United States seized power. There were in all 122 Governors-General and the majority either died in office or before they could return to their native country. Quasi-absolute as their powers appeared to be, they were, for most of these times, in some measure both advised and restrained by the royal *audiencia*, a legal body whose responsibilities went far beyond those normally entrusted to a group of trained jurists. With the Governor-General as president, its composition varied over the years, but generally consisted of four or more senior justices, an attorney-general, and a number of subordinates. It acted as a supreme court, but also had executive, financial, and administrative powers. In the absence of the Governor-General it also ruled during an interregnum.

The *residencia* was a peculiarity of the Spanish colonial system which applied to the Philippines. This was the retention in the colony of both the Governor-General and certain categories of the highest officials who had served there, to answer complaint and grievance arising from their tenures of office. This retention period could last for more than six months for a Governor-General: it was naturally unpopular with the executive class. Nor was it very efficient, for claim and counter-claim had to be deliberated and, as in principle any citizen could have his say, there was much that might be irrelevant – if not completely false. Perhaps it did in some way restrain the abuse of office, but on account of its retrospective character, it could often only act on evidence which had been eroded by time.

Manila, the capital city, was the centre of both government and commerce. Here in 1570, Legaspi's able subordinate, Martín de Goiti, made a landing at the mouth of the Pasig River and here a first battle was fought between his small forces and those of Rajah Soliman, the Moslem chief of the south bank. No permanent settlement was made until May 1571 when Legaspi himself arrived to establish the focal point of Spanish colonization on the lower Pasig.

He had abandoned Cebu and his choice was sound: adjacent to the fertile river areas of central Luzon and the volcanic soil of the Taal and the Laguna de Bay depressions, it was well placed within the Archipelago's largest land mass and was the richest and most populated area in the islands. In addition, although the people spoke different dialects and were grouped into communities whose ethnic make-up differed marginally, one from another, they did possess a majority of common characteristics, being lowland Malays, living in a region where communications were relatively easy. The Spaniards built their city on the south bank of the river where the great sweep of Manila Bay has provided one of the largest of the world's natural harbours. The central area was walled and fortified, and was called 'Intramuros'. During two centuries, the greater part of the Spanish population of the Philippines lived within this bastion: here were also the government offices, the official residences, the commercial centre, and a cathedral and churches.

At first Intramuros was built of small timber and palm frond, changing rapidly to plank and pole. But in 1583, much was destroyed by fire, and with the priests taking a leading part, construction in stone began. Across the bay at Cavite was the Arsenal, and a shipbuilding yard. Surrounding the capital, to circle Manila Bay, were roads linking small towns, which became more important as Manila grew. As we shall see, this circle and the shallow hinterland of the Laguna de Bay almost constituted a prison in themselves and it was in Manila and generally in Intramuros that the dramas and crises of colonial life occurred. The more influential Spaniards, both officials and merchants, lived in some style, surrounded by the goods of life which made their stay in the islands as pleasant as it could be. These classes never intended to remain for long periods in the Philippines. The Church's hierarchy also lived comfortably in large, half-empty religious institutional buildings. Even the lower ranks of expatriates kept up a fair standard in relation to contemporary conditions. There were, however, poor whites and poor near-whites, and around the urban centres *mestizos* (peoples of mixed blood) tended to live at a level not much removed from that of the native Malay-Filipinos themselves. Yet even the best of the expatriate families could fall on bad times because of the fickleness of the commercial system, and these individuals could well lead the lives of paupers, relying much on loans and charity until their fortunes changed. A further category of expatriate must also be mentioned. This was the American-born soldier or adventurer, generally a citizen of Mexico or Peru, who lived a less formal existence not necessarily confined within the walls of Intramuros itself.

Just outside the gates was the Parian, a ghetto-type suburb in which the Chinese settlers in Manila, with rare exceptions, were forced to live. This colony numbered over eight thousand and, in addition, there were enclaves at Cavite where they worked as artisans in the shipyards and where they carried on their maritime trade. Adjacent to the Parian, at Dilao, was a small Japanese colony: a second area, further up river, was occupied by the latter in the early seventeenth century; Armenians and Indians made up the bulk of the remainder of the non-Filipino population.

Spain maintained her colony with the minimum of force and this often led to most difficult situations. At first, with the help of Mexican and locally enlisted soldiers and sailors, sufficient troops and vessels of the line were kept in the Manila area, both to beat off external attack and to cope with the internal situation. But as the seventeenth century wore on, power ran down considerably and for much of the period until the British attack in 1762, there was no naval force of any size and the military establishment was limited to one regiment (the King's Regiment) in Manila, with local militia in the provinces. The Spanish presence was ludicrously small – eight hundred to a thousand in the capital and a handful of officials elsewhere. The priests provided a solid reinforcement to the latter, but they tended considerably to encroach on temporal rule because of their advantageous position throughout the islands. Ruled by this small minority was a population of a little over a million and the dynamic and often hostile Chinese numbering between thirty and forty thousand, of whom over half lived in or near Manila.

In the capital, the small ruling community led an enclosed but often eventful life. Church and state were continually at loggerheads and, within the ecclesiastical establishment, the orders were extremely sensitive to any authority of the archbishop and his staff, whose sway outside Manila and the immediate areas of the three bishoprics was slight. Despite this, relations between the state, the hierarchy, and the orders were much better in the provinces and it is probable that neither colonial rule nor evangelism suffered over-much from the quarrelling which was endemic on the banks of the Pasig. Despite the original concepts of Spanish conquest, an incredibly narrow life was led by an extremely materialistic society.

With the Philippines closed to most of the world, the Chinese provided the link with their own country and foreigners – often of hostile nations – flying flags of convenience, managed to bring in goods from India and elsewhere. A little traffic was allowed between Manila and the neighbouring East Indies and the mainland South-East Asian states. But the vital link with the outside world was the famous Manila Galleon, sailing regularly to catch the seasonal winds and connecting the Philippines with the Pacific coast at Acapulco in New Spain. The route was generally that pioneered by Father Urdaneta: from Cavite it led through the northern Visayas, via the San Bernardino Strait and out into the Pacific, striking north-east with the monsoon to as far up as the thirty-ninth parallel. With a heavy ship, the voyage took between six and eight months at least and, except for experiments using the Bashi Channel to the north of Luzon, there was little change of routine until the mid-eighteenth century, when a French navigator shortened the journey by turning into the wind between 31° and 33° N. With the current and wind well behind her, the Galleon made the return journey in two and a half to three months.

The contemporary Spaniard in the Philippines took little or no interest in agriculture, was actively discouraged from journeying in the provinces, believed that he was well with God if he did not fall foul of the Inquisition, and showed an incredible lack of initiative. To be fair, it must be said that certain factors played an important part in his conduct: both state and Church made regulations to discipline initiative and the climate, the diet, and the conditions of life were not conducive to energetic action. So this ideally placed seaport of Manila witnessed little of the commercial and social activities which Batavia, Calcutta, Bombay, and even Canton enjoyed. The lives of its most influential inhabitants were ruled by the periodic sailings of the Galleons and when a Galleon failed in its mission, through either loss at sea or hostile attack,[1] financial disaster faced both the colony and the families who had invested in that particular venture. The Galleon was of such paramount importance that some detailed description of its commission will explain much of the capital's way of life.

So as to allow a more or less direct commerce with the outside world as a complement to the enforced isolation of the colony, the Galleons took aboard goods collected in Manila for sale in Mexico and Peru – and even for onward shipment to Spain itself. With the revenues obtained converted into silver dollars, they returned, carrying, in addition, the colony's annual subsidy of 110,000 dollars, passengers, and freight. The passengers were mainly officials, their families, and priestly reinforcements: the freight was made up of semi-luxuries: flour, oil, wine, salted fish, etc. This commerce was itself restricted so that neither Spain herself nor her colonies in America would be flooded with cheap goods from the East which could both endanger Spanish exports and cause too great an outflow of silver from the Spanish group of states towards China and India, from where the majority of the Galleon's goods generally originated, as only very small amounts of indigenous produce were ever shipped.

In 1593, to effect this control, a ceiling was placed on the value of the merchandise allowed for shipment: 250,000 pesos (the standard Philippine currency, retained under the Republic) outwards and 500,000 inwards. In 1702, the restriction was raised to 300,000 and 600,000 pesos respectively, and in 1734 to 500,000 and one million pesos. At first, two ships a year were permitted, but later they were cut to one sailing annually. Although the latter regulation was honoured, the value restrictions were generally flouted, and when a Galleon was captured, it often had double the freight value allowance aboard. Freight generally consisted of Chinese silks, damasks, porcelain, and silverware; pearls, precious stones, and cinnamon from India and Ceylon; spices from the neighbouring East Indian islands; and a wide range of piece goods from the surrounding areas. The freight space aboard was divided into a number of *boletas* (space tickets) which were allocated by a board presided over by the Governor-General. *Boletas* were allocated to the Governor-General himself, members of the *audiencia*, officials, clergy, and Spanish residents, of whom widows and retired persons were the most favoured. As the goods despatched often sold for more than twice their Manila values in Acapulco, the importance of these *boletas* can be appreciated. After allocation, many were sold, sometimes to Chinese merchants, sometimes to persons already holding an insufficient number. So the colony lived and in this environment of constant bickering between officials and priests, the semi-isolation of the Philippines from her neighbours and the capital from the provinces, small fortunes were made and lost. Large-scale corruption accompanied the construction of a new Galleon and, with each voyage, because of facilities for shipping personal allowances in addition to the *boleta* allocation, the posts of General of the Galleon and of certain of the ship's officers were only obtained by the payment of a handsome sum into the pocket of the Governor-General. When the Galleons returned, there was much rejoicing: festivities took place and money was squandered. Because of this thriftlessness it was often necessary to borrow against the next voyage, both to live during the interim period and to obtain the capital for the purchase of goods for the next shipment.

Natural calamities often occurred in Manila: typhoons destroyed dwellings and craft; the fire of 1583 almost cleared the city; and in 1645, an earthquake brought down the majority of the buildings. Violence and feuds were endemic. In September 1668 the Governor-General, Diego Salcedo, was kidnapped by the Inquisition and, on trumped-up charges, was shipped to New Spain, dying *en route*. Another Governor, Alonso Fajardo de Tenza (d. 1624), is said to have killed both his wife and her lover; and a third, Fernando

Manuel de Bustillo de Bustamante y Rueda, was assassinated in October 1719 by a rabble, reputedly encouraged by the orders. Murder and duels occurred frequently and all classes and conditions of European or Asian knew violence as a method to solve social or commercial problems. Against all this, the work of certain of the orders and of the Brotherhood of Mercy (*obras pías*) stands out. The orders maintained the few medical facilities available: the Dominicans and the Jesuits established universities. The Brotherhood of Mercy, a lay order, combined the first merchant banking system with a large network of practical charity. A replica of a Portuguese institution founded by Queen Eleanor, widow of John II of Portugal, in 1498, it was headed by a superior, a number of deputies, and a secretary, all of whom came from leading families in Manila. The order's methods were an amalgam of the prudent investment of monies left to it in legacies and the use of the income from these investments for charitable purposes. Investment was made on a highly materialistic basis, sums being lent for the Galleon trade or even for trade to the provinces. Money obtained as income was used to maintain orphans in regular institutions set up for the purpose, to assist in cases of extreme poverty, and to relieve suffering in times of calamity. Considerable sums were expended on well-chosen charitable acts and the Brotherhood itself personally ensured that these were correctly used, despite frequent attempts by officials and clerics to expropriate them. Moreover, small and more personal acts of Christian charity were undertaken. A person who, for political spite, had been mauled and left to die was often spirited away and, in the worst cases, corpses which had been refused a Christian burial by the priests were taken away by the Brotherhood and disposed of as decently as possible.

Upper- and middle-class life among the expatriates was not easy, despite good stone dwellings and numbers of servants. Diet was mediocre and the climate difficult for the European. The Galleon brought in the semi-luxuries of life and, to some extent, others came in from China and the surrounding Asian countries. But although the priests had acclimatized a number of vegetables and fruits to assist their flocks, little effort was made by officials or merchants to bring in further varieties. Food was relatively expensive for those days, lacked variety, and, in many cases, was of poor quality. There was no butter, little milk, and lard was used in the place of cooking oils. Coffee was imported (it is grown extensively in the Philippines now), as was wine, which was expensive and scarce. The best items were the local fish, pork, and poultry; beef was of poor quality. Culinary preparation, according to European visitors, was also mediocre and there is little doubt that the meals were heavy and greasy, and not well adapted to the humid tropical climate. The luxury dish, as now, was the roasted sucking pig and at entertainments given in houses, this was the normal *pièce de résistance*. To keep face, the leading families entertained on a scale which often brought them to ruin. Balls were given and such invitations had to be reciprocated. But as the official was never too well paid and the merchant was a prisoner of the comparatively sluggish commercial world around him, recourse to corruption was essential and, even then, thriftlessness often caused eventual poverty. Intrigue among the families and among the priests often bedevilled the little community. Everything depended on the fortunes of the Galleons and the colony ran at a deficit.

It is true that the Filipino did not require the Spaniard to instruct him in vying with his neighbour on the question of entertainment. Like the Spaniard, he is generous, hospitable by tradition, and will spend his money freely among his friends. On a level which often makes malnutrition a possibility, the Filipino would place money on his own bird[2] at cockfights, would spend it on fermented rice wine, and would invite guests to his house, however humble it might be. When the money ran out, as it often did before the crops were brought in, he borrowed or lived within the larger economy of the greater family, for as in Spain and in many Eastern countries, the greater family consists of the uncles, the cousins, and the in-laws; but, with a Christian twist to the practice in the Philippines, it also embraces godfathers and godmothers. To say that the colonists were always welcome in the countryside in those days would be erroneous. When the British invaded Manila, there was a wave of anti-Spanish feeling, both in Luzon and elsewhere in the Archipelago. Nevertheless, Iberian rule was fairly loose and easy-going, and the stricter Anglo-Saxon administration soon became more unpopular with the inhabitants of the Philippines than its predecessor. Essential to continuity in the provinces, where the British scarcely penetrated, was the now well-ingrained tradition which joined Catholicism to the Spanish-infiltrated Malay customs of the country. Even in the towns, which at the time were hardly more than overgrown villages, the handful of European officials and merchants was so small that its moral and social impact was shallow. Spanish might be spoken in the few areas where officials and merchants dwelt, but elsewhere the priests learned the language of their flocks, bringing further difficulties to the outsider who wished to learn facts first hand. Schools existed in every little community and some educational instruction was added to the religious teaching which seems to have taken up much of the time.

If the seventeenth century saw the adoption in Manila of an imported and somewhat stagnant way of life, it was decidedly less formal and more flexible in character elsewhere. The turmoils and scandals of colonial existence seem to have been essential to what dynamism remained from the first days of occupation. But these incidents were mainly confined to the capital, to the string of little towns around Manila Bay, and to Cavite, where the ships were built, where the Galleons were laid up, and where the Chinese based their maritime activities. Only occasional echoes of this mundane life reached elsewhere, although there were sometimes fleeting penetrations: the arrival of a new *alcalde* bringing with him unpopular changes; the attempts of officialdom to gain a greater hold on the rural populations; the grasping methods used by one or another tax-collector or settler. For the people, the sun, the rain, and the winds were the most important elements in their lives and after these came the simple things of home and, in the majority of cases in the lowlands, the house was near to the church, which in turn added its own influence to bring about the most powerful change of all in Philippine life. So arrived the eighteenth century and all seemed to continue as before. Even the occasional revolt, loosely organized and poorly led, originated from much the same social grievances and the other two centres of disturbance, the Chinese and *moro* communities, produced the same threats as they had done earlier.[3] Despite an already lengthy period of occupation, the Spaniards had been quite unable to establish themselves in the Moslem areas. Elsewhere, where a primitive and pagan culture existed, in the central mountains of Luzon, no successful settlement took place before the mid-eighteenth century. In the more remote areas of Mindanao, where the non-Malay tribes lived an even more primitive life, very little contact was made throughout Spanish rule.

This isolated and materially underdeveloped colony was maintained in sharp contrast with the world around it. Under such conditions there were many worthy local chiefs as well as men of goodwill who, seeing themselves or their neighbours exploited, led revolts and died as heroes. But in this Philippine world, there was no Tipoo Sahib or prince of a long and powerful line, enjoying before Spanish conquest the fealty of large masses, who could lead powerful, well-equipped forces to further his own policies. When the British arrived, they found an introverted, weak, and lax Spanish yoke over a leaderless Malay people, whose traditions and customs had been evangelized and dressed in European clothes. The material advantages of the better-off often coming from corruption or the Galleon trade must have seemed almost ludicrous, if only because of the narrowness of these activities. The Spaniards had done little to further the exploitation of the natural wealth of a comparatively rich country: they relied on an entrepôt trade to recompense them for the rigours of life in this tropical and humid climate.

[1] Many were lost; poor design and heavy seas were the main contributory factors. The British had a go at some of them with spectacular success. Drake, Cavendish, and Anson were the leaders in the game.

[2] Cockfighting is widespread, especially in the rural areas. A large proportion of Filipino adult males keep a fighting bird and are extremely proud of it, carrying it with them, caressing it, and, in a social gathering, launching it against a neighbour's bird in a friendly mêlée.

[3] The Spaniards attempted to counter the often hostile Chinese presence by expulsions. Some took place in 1596 and on three occasions during the eighteenth century. Because of the hold which the Chinese merchants enjoyed over Spanish officials, enforcement of the expulsion orders was lax and the community continued to increase and prosper. The last Chinese revolt against the Spaniards took place in 1762 after the British capture of Manila.

Chapter 8

The British Intervention and its Aftermath

THAT THE PHILIPPINES was unprepared for any attack by a well-equipped force from outside had been obvious since the rundown of her military strength later in the seventeenth century, but a period of comparative peace after the Dutch attack in 1647 seemed to justify a policy of saving money on defence. A sharp reminder of the colony's weakness was, however, given in 1735 when a small Dutch squadron appeared before Manila to liberate a ship and crew which had been confiscated off Mindanao for trafficking with a local Moslem leader there. Because of the unpreparedness of the Spanish forces, the Governor-General, Fernando Tamón Valdés, had to accede to the Dutch demand. But what was probably more serious was the constant lack of suitable sea-power to counter the incursion of the *moro* pirates, and this unstable situation continued well into the nineteenth century.

The British intervention was a small incident of the Seven Years War, with Britain opening hostilities against Spain in 1762. The French and Spanish possessions in America and Asia were obvious targets for British maritime strength and the Manila invasion was mounted from India. Although the authorities in that city had been informed both of the hostilities and of a possible threat to the colony from India, no official news of the outbreak of war had been received, either from Mexico or Spain. The colonial leadership was also compromised owing to an interregnum, the last Governor-General, Pedro Manuel de Arandía, having died in 1759, his place being filled, as was the practice, by the then archbishop of Manila, Manuel Antonio Rojo del Río. Although Rojo well combined priestly virtues with administrative ability, he was no military leader.

The British arrived off the Pasig in the late afternoon of 22 September 1762, having assembled their small fleet at the entrance to the bay during the week preceding their appearance. This force consisted of thirteen ships with some 2,000 soldiers and marines embarked. They included two batteries of artillery, the remainder being infantry. A third were Indian sepoys but, in addition, a labour force of some 1,400 Indians also accompanied the combatants.

Manila was defended by less than 600 troops of the King's Regiment, the remainder of that unit being on detachment at Cavite and elsewhere. Attached for fortress duties was a handful of Filipino gun-crew members. Immediately the emergency was perceived, four militia companies of sixty men each were raised from among the inhabitants.

On the morning of the 23rd, Admiral Samuel Cornish and Brigadier-General William Draper, the joint commanders of the expedition, sent an ultimatum to the acting Governor-General demanding 'the surrender of Manila, its fortifications and its territory'.[1] This demand was rejected and on 24 September, a landing was made on the coastline of Manila Bay, not much more than 2 kilometres south of Intramuros and the mouth of the Pasig. The British took up positions which were well protected by the stone constructions of three churches and it was from here, after an exchange of gunfire, probes, and sorties between the two sides, that a final attack on the city, supported by a bombardment from the ships, was delivered on 5 October. Almost as soon as a breach had been made, the British made themselves masters of Manila with its fortifications and main buildings. After a lull in the fighting, an ultimatum was delivered to Archbishop Rojo and the Spaniards capitulated on 6 October. There could have been no real alternative to Rojo's decision, for the British commander had informed him that he would put the place to sword if his demands were not met. The terms of the capitulation included an immediate payment of 2 million pesos with a follow-up payment of a similar sum by the treasury in Madrid.[2] Manila, Cavite, and the surrounding areas were to be surrendered; the Spanish administration, including the *audiencia*, left in place; religious and commercial freedom was to be guaranteed.

This is a bare narrative of the most important events which led to a twenty-month occupation of the area, but it in no way describes the real character of the little war. The brief hostilities were often bitter, although from the records available, the Spanish garrison with its civilian volunteers often fought gallantly and a number of bold sorties were made, but with little avail. The unreadiness of the fortifications and of the fortress artillery, little appreciated before the emergency, was frustrating to the defenders and when they were beaten back into the city, the British spared few of the combatants. An aggravation on both sides was the use of non-European troops, for the city's garrison was belatedly reinforced by levies from Pampanga, poorly armed but in no way lacking in courage. The barbarity of the skirmishes in front of Intramuros increased and atrocities were perpetrated on both sides. The military use of the three churches[3] was also greatly resented and the pillage, which took place after the successful assault, was prolonged and violent. Despite it being well within the custom of the times, it did the British commanders no credit. Fear and resentment was naturally widespread. After two hundred years of comparative tranquillity, with its leisurely and corrupt way of life, Manila was jerked into the eighteenth century and its religious dissension, colonial rivalry, and force of arms.

British rule over Manila and its immediate territories ceased on 31 May 1764, fifteen months after the Peace of Paris, which ended the Seven Years War. During those months of occupation, concurrent events of much interest took place in the countryside. Within the terms of the surrender it was – and still remains – difficult to judge the extent of Manila's then dependent territories. In practice during this period, despite expeditions mounted along the Laguna de Bay and directly south and north of Manila, little further territory was ever occupied between the main inhabited area and the lake. The difficulties encountered by the British were largely the result of the determination and vigour of one man, Don Simón de Anda y Salazar, the junior member of the *audiencia*, who left Manila on the eve of the final assault, taking with him a commission of lieutenant-governor and instructions to maintain the provinces loyal to Spain. Proceeding at once to Pampanga, he set up an interim government, rapidly becoming the *de facto* ruler of all the settled part of Luzon outside the enclave which the British had occupied. In his action he was loyally supported by the local Spanish officials and by the priests who had so much control in the countryside. The Philippine revolts which, in the northern provinces of Ilocos and the Cagayan Valley, attended Spanish defeat, were ruthlessly put down by him, as were those which erupted south of the British-occupied area. He succeeded, for the first time since the early days of Spanish rule, in introducing a strict but generally just régime, putting his domains on a real war footing, even initiating the exploitation of the country's natural resources. Almost immediately he brought strong military pressure on the occupiers, for he maintained a force which included not only Spanish soldiers and French deserters[4] from the British, but also the militias raised in the Pampangan provinces north of Manila, who had great military potential when well officered. His containing action considerably hampered the British, who brought pressure on Rojo to declare him a rebel. By that time Rojo had decided that peace and prosperity could only be brought back with British help. He agreed to do so and the *audiencia* endorsed his decision. Anda immediately reciprocated, proclaiming himself Governor-General, stating that Rojo was a prisoner and that he, Anda, was the only member of the *audiencia* who still enjoyed his freedom. Despite military expeditions against him, Anda maintained his position. There is little doubt that his material strength greatly assisted his determination to continue to exert this pressure. Able and well endowed as an administrator, he not only enjoyed the support of his Pampangan soldiers and of the priests, who raised money and bands for him (often leading them personally), but also possessed ample funds to wage war. At the time of the British attack, two galleons were within or near to Philippine waters. The *Santísima Trinidad*, returning from Acapulco with between 2 and 3 million pesos-worth of silver coin and bullion aboard, made harbour at Palapag on the east coast of Luzon. From there the treasure was moved up the coast and then west to Anda's headquarters. From all accounts this fortune was expended wisely and honestly, for on a subsequent investigation of his term of office, the accounting was proclaimed satisfactory in every respect. Anda's position was also strengthened by the escape of three other members of the *audiencia*, Francisco Leandro de Viana, the attorney-general, a vigorous and intelligent commentator, and two juniors. For the British, military operations outside Manila became a stalemate.

After the capitulation, the British East India Company had assumed the administration of the occupied territory and had appointed an officer, Mr Dawsonne Drake, as governor, the archbishop as Captain-General and the *audiencia* taking orders from him. This situation continued even after the termination of the Seven Years War, for Anda, refusing to believe the news of the Treaty of Paris, maintained hostilities. Archbishop Rojo died on 30 January 1764 and the British, recognizing Anda, then opened negotiations to restore the Spanish administration. Anda entered Manila on 31 May[5] and the British left during the first fortnight of June.

The *status quo ante* was soon re-established. During their occupation, the British had maintained a commercial system designed to their advantage. The port was opened to foreign trade and, despite Anda's containment, local produce was exported and free trade with the exterior operated. They also brought in Indian currency to compete with the peso. Despite their administrative strictness, for which they were hated, they had impressed the merchants by the broadness of their commercial interests. In particular, the temporary cessation of the Galleon trade with its traditions and attendant preparations, highlighted the flexibility and wider interests of their more liberal system. This was not forgotten, particularly by Viana, who later made recommendations for the refounding of the economy. But for the moment the old practices returned; Manila was once again closed to foreign ships; the Galleon trade was resumed; and stagnation returned to the shores of Manila Bay and the banks of the Pasig River.

[1] *Journal of Archbishop Rojo* as related in Le Gentil de la Galasière, *A Voyage to the Indian Seas* (Manila, 1964).

[2] The document executed to cover the second sum was rejected on presentation and never honoured. Draper was severely criticized on his return to Britain from Manila on account of his failure to obtain the whole of the 4 million locally.

[3] Arandía had been a strong and able official. He had attempted to diminish clerical interference in temporal matters. In an appreciation of Manila's defences he rightly saw that two of the three churches masked both surveillance and fire from the city. He proposed that they be demolished, but was quite unable to put his measures into execution.

[4] Rojo's journal states that the British forces included 350 Frenchmen who had been forced to enlist in India. The number is disputable, but deserters from the contingent did join Anda.

[5] An interim replacement for Arandía, Francisco Javier de la Torre, had been nominated in Mexico. Torre arrived at Anda's headquarters in March 1764, but graciously stood down until Anda had retaken Manila for Spain.

Chapter 9

Peace and Commerce

ALTHOUGH ITS FIRST eighty years had had their vicissitudes, Spanish power in the Philippines, when challenged, generally reacted positively to external and internal threat until about 1650. From then until the British success in Manila, there were few governors who were able to maintain true authority; especially as they were well compromised from the start of their tenures by corrupt practices. Some tried hard and, of these, Francisco José de Obando, marqués de Obando, and Pedro Manuel de Arandía stand out. They held office in the period just before the capture of Manila. From 1764 onwards the situation was very different. Anda was replaced by Torre, whose appointment was provisional. In the little time he had before the arrival of a permanent successor, Torre showed himself able and astute. Viana submitted his memorandum on the economy to him in 1765 and Torre himself believed in that strong centralized rule which Viana advocated at the expense of priestly methods of isolation, the material reliance of officials on corruption, and the savings of the treasury on defence. Further development of the colony's inherent riches was also advocated, as was the liberalization of trade. Torre's competent contribution was to restore Spain's broken authority after a severe moral and material defeat, at the same time preparing the ground for his successors.

Anda's interim government had been the first set up outside Manila since Legaspi's arrival in Cebu. Essentially a by-product of British occupation, it was the first lay executive organization to be welcomed by the priests in the provinces and, during its brief life, those Spaniards who were exiled from Manila were able to observe the true state of events outside the capital. What they found most significant was the friars' adherence to a traditional economy of staples – fishing and a restricted range of cash crops. The liberalized trade in occupied Manila and the temporary ending of the Galleon voyages were at the same time complementary to Anda's need to use the colony's own resources to the full. The germ of a new system had been implanted.

Torre was followed in July 1765 by José Raón, a vigorous but exceedingly corrupt man. His term yielded little, but in 1770 Simón de Anda y Salazar, who had left the Philippines in 1767, returned to replace him. His new task was a much broader one than that of the resistance leader. During this transitory period he was an honest Governor-General with the intelligence to appreciate the basic weaknesses of the society he headed. He was no economic expert, but, in the face of great opposition from the conservative hierarchy and the Galleon-bedevilled society of Manila, progressed marginally in his efforts to found a system which could compare with those in the overseas possessions of other European countries with their great capital investments. He insisted, not always successfully, on the integrity of officials and merchants. The slack he was able to take up by his attacks on the misuse of public monies resulted in an increase of revenue, which in turn made more funds available for public works and defence: at a time of reconstruction this was of great importance. His policies ensured his unpopularity with the clerical community, whom he had constantly attacked for their restraining and intimidating policies and actions. He died in 1776, while in office, the object of calumny and social ostracization. Anda himself had submitted a memorandum to King Charles III. The conduct of the orders and their members was his main target, but he also made recommendations to strengthen government and to liberalize trade, both of which had been significant points of his colleague Viana's submission. It is interesting, therefore, that the appreciations of these two, steeped in Philippine problems as they were, should now be taken so seriously by the next Governor-General, José Basco y Vargas, a product of the metropolitan middle classes, a sailor by calling, but a firm believer in a professionally based commercial society. Basco, like Anda, almost immediately had his difficulties with the civil and clerical establishments in Manila. But time was running short and he struck in the first months of his term (1778–79). His opponents, who, as was almost traditional, had advocated violence against his person, were removed and banished. For the first time, the Governor-General was relatively untrammelled by gross pressures and Basco had the work of Viana and Anda to assist him in his task of building a viable economy.

That redoubtable pillar the Galleon trade was at last being forced out of business by the growing interest of other European nations in the products of China. Although the Galleon had never held a monopoly of trade with that country, the laws of Spain had been designed to exclude the introduction of Chinese merchandise brought by other means into her metropolitan and colonial areas; these laws guaranteed a sellers' market in Acapulco. Moreover, to force up prices, some of these goods filtered farther than the Spanish territories and sold in both Europe and America. This system was now challenged. Basco's philosophy was based on the growing exploitation of colonial products and a liberalization of foreign trade. His opponents were the clergy, highly suspicious of non-clerical persons in the provinces where natural riches existed, and the privileged citizens of Manila, outstanding among whom were the members of the *audiencia*, who profited most from the restrictions inherent in the Galleon trade. But Torre, Anda, Viana, and even the corrupt Raón had already broken the ground and Basco's own firmness with his early opponents, including some in the *audiencia* itself, made the execution of policy somewhat easier.

Probably his first concrete step was the founding in 1781 of the Economic Society of Friends, whose aims were the promotion and encouragement of local enterprise. He saw that many crops and products could be of real value in international trade and that, where there was a domestic market for these, advantage could be taken of their relative cheapness to levy forms of indirect taxation. Those commodities which he remarked upon and which have stood the test of time were spices, hemp, timber, rice, maize, cocoa, sugar, and tobacco. Others, successfully promoted for a limited period, such as indigo, cotton, and tea, were forced out of production by external influences. He also advocated an increased activity in mining, in particular for iron, copper, and gold, all of which, with their by-products, are now important items in the Philippine economy. The first of the society's experiments, a project to produce raw silk, was a failure, but Basco's policies at last bore fruit. In 1781, a tobacco monopoly recommended by him to the king was approved. The effects were startling. Almost as soon as the scheme was fully organized, the colony was transformed from a deficit to a surplus area.

The monopoly was a brainchild of Viana, approved by Basco and vigorously pushed into operation after royal assent. It changed the colony's economic character, although it was undeniably a suspect social step, for it placed too much emphasis on the disciplined and inflexible use of comparatively limited areas of the Archipelago: large parts of the Cagayan Valley, the Ilocos coastline and valleys, Nueva Ecija, and the island of Marinduque. Here, in the lands considered apt for the cultivation of tobacco, the production of other crops was forbidden, notwithstanding the domestic requirements of the smallholder. Thus all land was turned over to a single cash crop which was bought by the government at its fixed rates, laid down from time to time. As a result, unless land was also owned outside these fertile areas, the family had to buy staples on the open market. A small fluctuation in the fixed rate for tobacco leaf or of the market prices of staples could well bring hardship. Glut or famine could bring a rapid domestic disaster. Although the monopoly produced the revenues necessary to transform the economy, it was never a very efficient instrument. It brought with it a bureaucracy of its own and a corruption based on extortion, theft, and professional dishonesty. But the subsidy from Mexico could now be discontinued and in its turn the surplus earned was remitted back to Spain, who not only received large sums in bonds on the Manila treasury, but in time began to anticipate revenues from her colony by the issue of bearer bonds on annual crops.

The close of the eighteenth century not only saw an increase in the production of local goods, which in turn both widened the Philippine domestic market and provided commodities for export, but it also saw, for the first time, the modification of the well-established shipping route initially imposed on Spain by her agreements with Portugal in the sixteenth century. In 1766, the *Bueno Consejo*, a frigate of the Spanish navy, arrived in Manila, having proved the Cape route on the orders of Charles III. It seems ludicrous when we think that, despite the disappearance of Portugal as a serious colonial rival before the beginning of the seventeenth century, no real Spanish effort had been made to prospect this route before. Even at the end of the eighteenth century the move was highly unpopular in Manila, for any change in the Galleon's track (and the Galleon was by tradition the official contact between Spain and the Philippines) would endanger the trade between Manila and Acapulco. On the purely practical side, although the Portuguese had disappeared from the scene nearly two hundred years before, there were serious rivals in the Indian Ocean, for the British, Dutch, and French maintained large forces and the Pacific route, despite the occasional action of privateers, was more secure. So the Galleon sailings to Mexico continued.

The Galleon trade took a long while to die. The market in Acapulco was becoming more and more disadvantageous on account of unofficial trading relations between Spain's colonies and ships plying the American coasts. At a certain point, the profit margins became too small to maintain a suitable schedule and, on occasions, the ships returned to Manila undischarged. In addition to the new permeability of the Spanish colonies in America, a trading innovation, linking Spain and the Philippines direct, aggravated this deteriorating situation. Based on the use of the Cape route, which had been followed by royal frigates carrying despatches from 1766 to 1783, a Royal Company of the Philippines was established in 1785. Its aims combined direct trade between the Philippines and Spain with a scheme for capital investment in the colony, so as to develop its natural resources. Although the Royal Company was a monopoly and enjoyed exclusive rights to move goods between the Philippines and other Asian countries, this in itself was a liberating move, for not only was the company to compete with the Galleon, but at least some trade between the colony and its neighbours was at last authorized. Thus the reliance on an inefficient and corrupt entrepôt trade, which had effectively hindered local development, was broken after two hundred years. The Royal Company provided an interim solution, but it was a fairly inefficient instrument whose life was less than fifty years. Nevertheless, during its operations, it invested large sums in the economy and, after its winding-up in 1834, the Philippines was officially opened to foreign trade. The Galleon predeceased the company by some eighteen years, the last ship clearing her cargo in 1815.

Basco resigned in 1787. He had governed the Philippines for over nine years and, often in the teeth of opposition, had introduced and followed up reform policies: organizing the tobacco monopoly; strengthening Philippine military preparedness and conquering the Batanes; improving the schools system and judiciary. His success in tightening up moral and social conditions was considerable and, for the first time for generations, defences were strengthened, increased forces maintained, and Spain's sovereignty extended, for the mountain areas and the Batanes Islands of north Luzon were occupied and the fortifications in the Visayas and Mindanao were made good after so many years of neglect or abandonment. He left the Philippines under repeated attack for his policies and personal integrity, results of jealousy and factionalism.

In the fifty years following British withdrawal, the commercial aspect of the Philippines had changed dramatically, although it would be wrong to overemphasize the importance of the occupation. The lessons learned by Viana and Anda in the provinces were the by-products of both their exile and the concurrent British exploitation of their prize. Of greater importance was the influence of new ideas held in Europe, which eroded the narrow protectionist policies and made Torre and Raón receptive, and Basco positive, to reform. There was, moreover, a real need to restore the finances and the infrastructure of the Philippines after the war and the only commercial undertaking of importance, the Galleon trade, had already been found wanting. The Governors-General after the British withdrawal cast around for any viable alternative. The riches obtained by other European nations from their colonies contrasted sharply with this conservative and precarious entrepôt trade which, with the annual subsidy from Mexico, was the only means of balancing the books.

But if, in contrast to many of their predecessors, Torre, Anda, and Basco were men of both intelligence and integrity, the same might well be said of their successors, Félix Berenguer de Marquina (1788–95) and Rafael María de Aguilar (1795–1806)[1], whose tenures of office brought the Philippines into the first years of the nineteenth century. They contributed to both economic thought and deed: progress was favoured by their attempts to make the colony prosper in a changing world. It was also during this period that the number of Spaniards in the Philippines increased considerably. For the first time minor administrators, overseers, and technicians came in a quantity sufficient to allow both the expansion of projects and their surveillance. Unfortunately, with the Royal Company came persons holding sinecures. The company, in its turn, had its own share of corruption.

The nineteenth century brought educated men, both European and Filipino, who believed in principles rather than in practices. After British withdrawal the foundations of a new colonial society were laid. Although in no way excessively liberal, the establishment of a régime which cared for the population as human beings fostered a less materialistic spirit among the Spanish ruling class. The emergence of Philippine nationalism within this intellectual revolution changed the character of opposition to minority rule from a distant country and for the first time, groups calling for political and social reform enjoyed wide attention among the intellectual classes of the country. The birth of this informed Philippine nationalism was belated, but so was its evolution which had been effectively retarded by the priests who controlled the only centres of secondary education.

[1] Marquina recommended a number of reforms to the home government, but none seem to have been authorized. Aguilar greatly improved external and internal security. Besides administering ably and honestly, he reformed the medical services and encouraged local production of spices and cotton. He also put down irregular whoring.

Chapter 10

Philippine Nationalism and the Katipunan Revolt

PROFESSOR GREGORIO ZAIDE has calculated that more than a hundred revolts were organized against Spanish authority in the Philippines during the colonial period. He divides them into four categories: those prompted by the Filipinos' desire to win back their lost freedom and happiness; those caused by colonial oppression of various kinds; those of an economic nature; and the purely religious uprisings resulting from priestly intolerance.[1] The first group embodied the natural wish to return to the loosely organized Malay–Filipino society of pre-Spanish times and to shed the authority of an alien race which sought to impose a strange culture: as colonization matured, this type of unrest became less intense. The nearly-always spontaneous rising caused by oppression has already been discussed: It was when neither the friar nor the official took unilateral action, one against the other, that this last safety valve blew. The third category, the result of economic dispute, was and continues to be a constant factor where no redress through suitable legislation or bargaining is possible. The uprisings prompted by religious deviation were an essential by-product of earlier Catholic authoritarianism and, even in the nineteenth century, the Church remained strikingly intolerant. Understandable as most of these incidents are when they are examined today, those belonging to the economic group seem to have the deepest roots, for they generally involved disputes over land tenure or some other agrarian grievance, which, in a predominantly rural country, strike at the very life of the community. The leadership of the earlier Philippine uprisings has already been touched on and, despite the often very considerable qualities possessed by one or another local chief or factional head involved, neither the basic Malay society of the Archipelago nor the colonial structure of the Spaniards fostered any wide power for a Filipino. This contrasted sharply with the authority enjoyed by individuals in both the Indo-Malay and the Moslem societies of the more southerly East Indian islands, and brings clearly into perspective one of the most important reasons why the Mindanao and Sulu chiefs were able to maintain their political and religious integrity during three hundred years.

Although much of Philippine unrest in colonial times showed need for some reform or another, the seeds of nationalism, as opposed to a desire to modify, were never far from the problem, although they were often latent. Thus, the first type of revolt contains a good dose of this element, as did the risings which attended the British victory and which were put down by Anda's administration-in-exile. Even if this nationalism was latent throughout much of the seventeenth and eighteenth centuries, its political embodiment had to await both the appearance of an educated indigenous middle class and a suitable climate in which to develop fully. In the event, the climate was introduced from Europe rather than springing from local sources. The period of materialistic progress at the turn of the century ran its full course before the colony was formally opened to foreigners and before a real national conscience evolved from the diverse social currents which were becoming reconciled as the result of contacts with the outside world.

Before these events are examined, a return to the third reason for unrest, economic impositions within the colonial society, will be of much value, as it can assist in an appreciation of the basic flaws within that hidden and isolated world outside Manila which, at the time of Basco's governorship, was only just being opened up. Here the principal actors were the officials, the friars, the landowners, the farmers, and the Chinese. Land and the revenues from it were the most important material factors. Religion and clerical ubiquity were never absent. The official, in the routine of daily life, was probably the least important, although it was he who collected taxes and administered the regulations for compulsory labour. What constituted the stage was the land, with its cultivators and economic manipulators always on the scene. The clergy not only provided a solid social–spiritual reassurance, but were also integrated into the scenario by their wide material interests in land tenure.

In pre-Hispanic society, land was owned by individuals and families who could work it, lease it, or dispose of it. By nature free spending and hospitable, the Filipino often uses more money than he possesses and, in those early days, after running into debt, he forfeited his land and could ultimately be reduced to slavery; this condition might also be extended to his family. After the colonization of the Philippines, the Spaniards abolished slavery and, despite contemporary customs, never countenanced it in the Archipelago. But the rat-race of man chasing commodities and money continued and, as society stabilized, the pattern of landownership became sharply defined. Certain religious orders owned large parcels; these they had either inherited from the faithful or had taken over against debts; and they depended on these dowries, called 'friar lands', for the income necessary to maintain their missions. It must be stated here that this land was normally leased out to farmers at reasonable and fair rates and, if not sub-let, could provide a living for both parties to the agreement. In addition to the orders, there were a few individuals of Spanish nationality who maintained estates, often farming themselves and leasing small tracts for domestic exploitation to their permanent employees. In contrast, by far the greatest area of good land was owned either by Filipinos or by *mestizos*: this group began to constitute a class of its own. These, the *caciques* as they are called, were not always so considerate towards their tenants, and if they combined ownership with an additional leasing of friar lands for eventual sub-letting, they were in the business and the margins left for the working farmer could be small. The village farmers also owned parcels, but in the late nineteenth and early twentieth centuries they were generally diminishing in size on account of indebtedness. The normal pattern was for the better-off villager to possess enough for his domestic purposes, adjacent to his home: this would include small gardens within the *barrio* itself.

But if the Filipino villager was slowly being dispossessed to the benefit of the orders and of a new landowning class, the need for capital to work the land he farmed was a continual problem. Over-spending was endemic and liquidity had never been helped by the overriding interest of the *caciques* in the acquisition of property. Recourse to the Chinese merchant who acted both as a usurer and as a shopkeeper was therefore necessary. It was he who, at the same time, provided credit in his shop and the money to help the family through the most difficult periods. Never liked nor respected by the Malay Filipino, he, as today, contributed massively to the economy of the country. The landowner did have his traditional role, for in many cases he produced the rice seedlings raised under suitable conditions and, in favoured areas, he also provided irrigation. Not all peasant farmers were so lucky: many had to retain or purchase their own seed which they sowed themselves. If purchase was necessary, any advance of monies against a future crop was made at rates which were often penal and the cost of seed was always at a premium.

In and around Manila and the handful of towns, urban development at that time was negligible and, except in a few well-filled suburbs, problems of detribalization and a complete reliance on a non-agrarian economy were rare.

The late eighteenth century saw the end of the impermeability of the Philippines to foreign influence. Officially, trade relations were freed at the time of the winding-up of the Royal Company. In practice, there had been a local tolerance by Governors-General, and for many years ships of all nations had been able to trade with Manila and some merchants were even able to set up establishments ashore. Regulations attending such trade were tediously formal and the ability of a new class of *compradores*, essentially drawn from the *mestizo* population, added to the influence which these people of mixed race had already obtained from the growth of their holdings, particularly in Luzon. It was essentially a facet of this period of transition; the French, the British, the Scandinavians, and the North Americans coasted in the hope that entry would be allowed: the Indians and the Chinese traded as they had done for so many years. The presence of these aliens brought with it the seeds of a challenge to Spanish authority, for the liberal ideals of Europe began to be discussed in the port. When national movements appeared later in the century, their protagonists were as often as not educated men, many drawn from well-to-do, influential families. They were the products of a Philippine-based educational system, although some had had the advantage of study or travel in Europe and elsewhere. Education in the colony was almost exclusively priestly until the Americans took over the Philippines, but it did produce a certain liberalism. Throughout the Spanish period, the primary schools were essentially religious, but within the 'Services of Both Majesties' as Father de la Costa has called it,[2] a more advanced instruction had appeared in Manila during the earliest days of Spanish rule. The Dominicans and the Jesuits were the forerunners. At first, their colleges and universities only served the Spanish population, but a certain back-door entry was allowed and *mestizos* were first admitted into the Jesuit college of Sant' Ignacio and later freely into Santo Tomás (Dominican) in the seventeenth century. As time went on, this practice was generalized. In addition to the universities of San José (Jesuit), Santo Tomás, and San Juan de Letrán (Dominican) some colleges giving secondary education were maintained by the priests. Institutions for girls were also set up, but these gave a restricted course of studies, understandable in the spirit of those days. From these establishments, and sometimes direct from primary schools, came candidates for ordination and both the hierarchy and Spanish policy, although changing from time to time, encouraged this practice. The history of the Philippines' secular priesthood before the arrival of the Americans is not a happy one and a direct result of the frustration of these men in their calling was the impetus they gave to the first nationalistic movements during the nineteenth century. These Filipino priests were less well instructed than the members of the orders. They were also suspect for moral reasons, the nature of the Malay being incompatible with the priestly calling, according to the friars. It is probable that the Filipino–Malay character was and still remains antipathetic to the discipline of the celibate and unworldly structure of a priestly life. It is also true that the majority of these candidates was poorly prepared for the task owing to an indifferent education and a thoroughly subjective and limited formation. When, for political purposes,[3] ordinations of locally born candidates increased considerably, standards lagged sadly behind. But among these, throughout the period, were efficient and devout secular clergy whose personal lives were exemplary. Even they were obstructed by the friars and the Jesuits (the latter expelled in 1767, but allowed to return in 1859) and there were few posts open to them: a curacy, a minor administrative post, little else. No wonder that the more liberal and better instructed often discussed their mutual frustrations. They became at once politically and clerically suspect.

Outstanding among others were two further classes of Filipino influenced by emergent nationalism: the subordinate officials and the soldiery, people who mixed a good deal with the Spanish cadres. They, with the priests, provided the backing necessary to govern. The conditions of their material and social life were often so inferior to those of their colonial masters that, despite the many advantages which they enjoyed, comparison in this regard could only bring bitterness. Yet, before the emergence of a Filipino professional class, no real leadership existed and, even then, the nationalist movement was initially reformist, both in character and by manifesto. The Spaniards had adopted the old, tried method of ruling their colony by dividing the people: the priests had helped by their isolationist policy and the geographical fragmentation of the Archipelago, cut as it is by water and mountain barriers, had made tribal grouping almost natural. Thus a Filipino today still retains a recognized identity as an Ilocano, a Pampango, or a member of one of the other groups, all of whom have their separate dialect. It is difficult to say when a national identity began to gain ground in the minds of even the more educated, but it was probably at some time in the early nineteenth century that a consciousness of being members of a Malay people grew, initiated by the conditions of life and the colour of the skin of the native on the one side and of the Spaniard on the other. Here, again, the process was made complex by the relatively favourable economic conditions of the time and the behaviour of the Spaniards themselves. We shall see later that the activities of liberal movements in Spain had important repercussions in the colony and on the Spaniards living there. But even before this, the numbers of Europeans living in the Philippines had increased considerably, to as much as 4,000 by the turn of the century and reaching nearly 35,000 at the end of Spanish rule. This dilution of the old type of colonial society had its effect and social relations between the Filipino and the opposing group, the *mestizos* and the Philippine- and overseas-born Spaniards, were easy and even some familiarity existed as both groups belonged to the same religious faith and, in any case, the Filipino by nature is no great respecter of persons. It needed outside influences to bring this latent national consciousness to a point where a real independence movement could grow from roots among the middle classes and those less favoured groups who spontaneously gathered around them for political purposes.

The Galleon trade and the titular sovereignty of the Mexican viceroy were brought to an end by 1815. Two conflicting influences were almost immediate. There was, at once, a dramatic realization of the meaning of independence rather than of liberalism and as a counterweight, an influx into the Philippines of a number of quite reactionary individuals arriving from Mexico, where their continued presence had been hostilely opposed by the revolutionary authorities. From then and until the end of Spanish rule in 1898, a stop–go situation obtained and it was within these conditions that the already evolved Philippine middle class had to live and react. This swinging policy continued to stir up the more articulate groups of both the intelligentsia and of the emerging urban population, whether the origins of the individual were Spanish, *mestizo*, or native Filipino. In a Spanish colonial society already buffeted by the Peninsular War and South American liberation movements, of which Bolívar's was the most flamboyant, even this less demanding colony was profoundly influenced by events which showed that power could be seized from rulers if the will to do so was strong enough. A short period of liberalized rule at home, motivated by the French occupation of Spain, resulted in the colony being represented in the *Cortes* of Madrid, the Spanish parliament. In 1812, the Cadiz Constitution was approved, but after the defeat of the French in the Peninsula, this was abrogated by Ferdinand VII. The stop–go movement continued and, intermittently, the *Cortes* was called and delegates from the Philippines were allowed to attend: in Spain itself, this usually coincided with periods when the authorities accepted some degree of reform, but these were usually terminated by repression and revenge. And so it went on, through the regency of Queen María Cristina of Bourbon and the unstable reign of her daughter, Isabella II, to the short-lived republic of 1868–70.

During this latter period, liberalism was even encouraged in the colony and, reinforced by the arrival during previous years of left-wing Spaniards from the mother country,[4] blossomed briefly in both

Manila and the provinces during the governorship of Carlos María de la Torre (1869–71). With the end of Serrano's regency in 1870, the authorities reverted to a policy of repression and gatherings which could be used for discussion of political ideas were banned.

Although some unrest arose from demands for agrarian reform during the earlier part of the nineteenth century, the first real incident marking the beginning of a struggle for change did not come until 1872. At the time, this event was not immediately the result of truly patriotic designs: a mutiny of Filipino soldiery and dockyard officials in the port of Cavite arising out of day-to-day grievances. Nor could this have been considered an outstanding incident, for mutinies in native regiments had occurred before. In this case, however, the Manila government decided to exploit the situation and they linked the actual uprising with the liberal activities of a number of priests and professional men whose names were already known in the informed circles of Manila. After the briefest of trials, which was held *in camera*, three Filipino priests (one of *mestizo* origin) were executed with the ringleaders of the mutiny. Overnight the Cavite mutiny of 1872 became a symbol of patriotic martyrdom, for Fathers José Burgos, Mariano Gomez, and Jacinto Zamora were transformed into national heroes and sufficient impetus was given to the young nationalist movements to constitute them into a real challenge to Spanish rule. As soon as the intelligentsia's determination was apparent to the authorities, repressive action was taken, local police measures strengthened, and deportation after the most summary of trials was frequently ordered. As is almost natural in such movements, repression encouraged the reformists and a crystallization of the nationalist sentiments of the middle classes was almost immediately to be found in the Propaganda Movement, which was to advocate equality between Spaniard and Filipino, both under the law and in day-to-day matters, but at the same time emphasizing the loyalty of the colony to the Spanish Crown. In particular a secularization of the religious organization in the country and a freedom of speech and the press were demanded within these general terms. The Propaganda Movement had in its ranks a number of gifted persons, the majority being professional men of well-to-do families, some of whom had studied in Spanish metropolitan universities where the germs of the movement were sown. Many were to continue their political activities well into the time of the American occupation of the islands, but one, whose name is now revered above them all, was destined to die, as were the three priests of the Cavite incident, a martyr's death, the outstanding symbol of Philippine martyrdom in those last days of Spanish rule.

Dr José Rizal (1861–96), a member of a wealthy family of

Calamba, a town a little to the south-east of Manila, was a physician and, latterly, a specialist in opthalmology. He had a brilliant if short career, studying at the Jesuit Ateneo in Manila and later at the University of Santo Tomás. At the Ateneo, he took his arts degree with distinction and his first medical studies followed at Santo Tomás. He left the Philippines in 1882 to continue his work in Madrid and only returned when he had graduated. It is very probable that, in the current idealization of Rizal, his qualities as scholar and as humanist have been exaggerated. He was, nevertheless, a giant among his peers and the first really national figure to emerge from this Christian Malay environment. Even in his teens, he was a well-known poet and, to his achievements in learning and medicine, he added a remarkable gift for languages and literature. A member of the Propaganda Movement, both his activities and his inherent challenge to Spanish authority had been remarked before he departed for Spain and the publication of his two famous novels, *Noli me tangere* and *El Filibusterismo*, both in Spanish, reinforced official opinion that he was a dangerous person to be allowed freedom in the colony. Action had already been taken against his family, but when he finally returned to the Philippines in 1892, he was almost immediately exiled to Dapitan, a small port in north-west Mindanao. In the short period before his exile, he had founded a new political society, the *Liga Filipina*, an instrument designed to preach solidarity among Filipinos. Although its proclaimed intentions were social rather than political, such a movement was equally as unwelcome as that of the Propagandists, for it advocated the organization of the people for a common social cause – and as such could easily become a more efficient instrument for action than the looser-knit reformist group of the Propagandists. In the event, with Rizal's departure the real impetus within this new cell ceased to exist. The remainder of Rizal's story is history. During his exile in Mindanao, a new political movement, the *Katipunan*, was founded by Andrés Bonifacio (1863–97). It was almost at once nationalist and revolutionary, the reformist nature of the Propagandists having had no real effect on conditions in the colony. Bonifacio himself was a man of humble origins. The efforts of the talented middle classes had been discarded and in their place emerged the planning and organization of a secret society directed by men who believed in action, but at the same time used much of the mumbo-jumbo and fantasy of clandestine groups. By 1896, the nucleus of an armed revolutionary force had been constituted and it was this that the Spanish authorities discovered on 19 August. Arrests were made throughout the Manila area, but Bonifacio and many of his followers had been warned and had taken to the countryside. Rizal had practically no part in this movement.

One of the *Katipunan*'s intellectuals, Pio Valenzuela, contacted the exile in Dapitan, who was then living on parole. Rizal refused to associate himself with the secret society, for he believed that the Filipino people were quite unready for armed resistance against their colonial masters. It is probable that he found radical suggestions repellent, for he continued to hope for an evolutionary solution to the impasse which faced the Filipinos and the Spaniards, whom Rizal admired and whose culture he had espoused. Rizal had already volunteered for military service as a surgeon in the Spanish army in Cuba. He was accepted and took ship for Spain. In a volte-face, initiated by the Manila authorities, he was arrested aboard on their cabled instructions and returned to the Philippines. He was tried on charges of sedition and was shot on the Luneta, outside the ramparts of Intramuros, on 30 December 1896. He was not the only one to die for his ideals: the three priests were the first in a long line and the execution of the associates of the *Katipunan*, arrested on 31 August, had already taken place. He was, however, one of the ablest of Filipino patriots and both his achievements and his character have gained for him the highest place in the esteem of his countrymen. It is ironical that, once again, the Spanish authorities had made a decision which could only bring severe repercussions on themselves. Rizal's part in active rebellion against them was minimal: an encouraging word here, advice there, and his ideas were reformist rather than revolutionary. He was executed on grounds which were legally non-existent, but his death strengthened the *Katipunan* and the struggle entered its final stage in a bitterness stemming directly from the execution of this most talented man.

After the *Katipunan*'s discovery by the Spaniards, Bonifacio had made his headquarters at Balintawak, then a village north of Manila (now a suburb). At a meeting of his followers, revolution was decided upon and a skirmish at San Juan de Monte, north of the Pasig River, took place on 30 August. The movement gained impetus and attacks against garrisoned posts occurred in Luzon and elsewhere. Rizal's execution was one of the immediate reprisals. Cavite province, south-west of Manila, then became the centre of the revolution and here Emilio Aguinaldo (1869–1964) led the *Katipunan* and managed to defeat a Spanish force at Bin-Kayan. In early 1897 further engagements took place in this area and a split in the revolutionary hierarchy followed after the Tejeros assembly in March. After a vote taken among the principal rebels, Bonifacio retired, but attempted to form his own government in opposition to the general movement. In a skirmish, Bonifacio was wounded and captured. Later he was tried by a revolutionary court-martial and with his brother was executed by Aguinaldo's men.

The revolution did not maintain its previous impetus: reinforced Spanish and colonial forces began the pacification of Cavite province and Aguinaldo's forces were driven into the mountains to the north and south of Manila, from where they continued to fight until a peace agreement was negotiated at Biaknabato between the then Governor-General, Fernando Primo de Rivera, represented by Pedro Paterno, a Filipino lawyer, and the Aguinaldo government which had proclaimed a republic in November 1897. The agreement provided for an indemnity of 1,700,000 pesos to be paid to the rebels in return for the exile of their leaders to Hong Kong. A general amnesty was declared: rebels other than the leaders were given the choice of living peacefully in the Philippines or departing from the colony. Aguinaldo and twenty-five of his followers sailed for Hong Kong at the end of December 1897 and the rebel forces surrendered their arms to the Spaniards.

When the Americans arrived in 1898, they found a country whose rebel chiefs were still in Hong Kong, but where unrest and armed incidents were endemic.

In a brief period of six years, the character of the Philippine opposition to colonial rule had changed from a desire for reform under the Spanish Crown to one for abolition of all alien control. Belated as it was, this desire was a real one and the Americans had to face it.

[1] Gregorio F. Zaide, *Philippine Political and Cultural History* (Manila, 1953).

[2] Horacio de la Costa, *Readings in Philippine History* (Manila, 1965). Referring to the sometimes differing requirements of the Spanish Crown and the Roman Catholic apparatus.

[3] From time to time the archbishop, often with assistance from the Governor-General, attempted to decrease the authority of the Superiors of Orders by ordaining local candidates. All moves to take parishes away from the friars generally ended in dismal failure.

[4] Napoleonic rule in Spain, with the often disastrously unstable intervention of the *Cortes* of the time, probably did much to encourage a middle-class reaction to traditional monarchical rule. The later 'blow-hot, blow-cold' policies of the restored Bourbon régime also resulted in the arrival in the colony of individuals whose political consciousness derived from the French Revolution.

Chapter 11

Outside Spanish Rule

Magindanao and the Sulus

IN THE MID-NINETEENTH CENTURY, Spain took steps to assert the sovereignty which she had claimed over the whole of Mindanao and the Sulu Archipelago since the first days of conquest. Until then, the Moslems of the south not only considered themselves independent, but for all practical purposes were independent. Further, their belligerent conduct took the struggle into their enemies' camp and, except during brief periods of colonial strength, they maintained control of much of the Visayan and Mindanao interior seas. This *de facto* independence was coupled with a traditional reliance on violence and plunder to maintain the separate economies of two powerful princedoms, Magindanao, with its capital at Cotabato on the Rio Grande, and Sulu, with Jolo as the seat of government. Each was a sultanate with long feudal traditions and with a well-implanted Moslem culture. The loosely confederated Maranao community living in Lanao and the Moslem settlements on the Zamboanga Peninsula were under the sovereignty of Magindanao, which also reached as far east as the Davao Gulf.

Early attempts had been made by the Spaniards to pacify these areas which, for nearly 300 years, were centres of instability adjacent to their evangelistic effort. The sultanate of Magindanao was attacked in 1596 and in 1639, but both expeditions were a failure. In Lanao, a force penetrated into Maranao coastal territory in 1637 and later pursued its way inland with some vigour. After this show of arms, impetus flagged and the area was for all intents and purposes abandoned to its previous way of life. On the Zamboanga Peninsula, Spanish settlements were founded in the seventeenth century and a fort built at Zamboanga itself in 1636. All was abandoned in 1662, only to be re-established early in the eighteenth century. Sulu was attacked intermittently during the first years of colonization and in 1638 a garrison was established at Jolo. Like Zamboanga, it was abandoned after a brief period.

No real attempt on the part of the Spaniards to subjugate the Filipino Moslems can be said to have commenced until they strengthened their naval patrol by steam gunboats in 1842. Davao at much the same time had been hived off from the sultanate of Magindanao in a purely commercial understanding. Before, in 1832, the garrison at Zamboanga had already been reconstituted. The sultanate of Sulu was attacked in 1848 and 1851, and in the latter year was finally placed under Spanish suzerainty; the sultan retaining considerable local powers. Magindanao was occupied after expeditions in 1851 and 1861, but Lanao, with its seaboards to the south and north, was not reached until the 1890s. Although politico-military districts were set up as this Spanish presence increased, their rule was never a complete one and the ways of life and lawlessness of the people continued, well implanted after so many centuries. All was immediately evacuated in 1899 after the American success in Luzon and it was not until the latter pursued a vigorous campaign of pacification in the twentieth century that the old sultanates, with their outlying dependencies, were finally brought under a central Philippine administration. The areas which have been described above are shown below (p. 238): these generally remain Moslem lands, although infiltration by Christian Filipinos has taken place and the Davao Gulf area, never a strongly held part of the sultanate of Magindanao, has passed over massively to emigrants from the north.

The Manila authorities, maintaining from the start that the Moslem south was part of the colony, always resented the presence of outsiders in that area and continually attempted to close the whole Archipelago to foreigners. In Mindanao and in Sulu this was impossible: at best they would occasionally apprehend a vessel trading direct with the sultanates, at worst they were chased ignominiously from the seas which they claimed as theirs. The south looked outwards, towards Mecca, towards India, Malacca, Borneo, and the remainder of what is now Indonesia. The sultanates had a particular economy based on the free use of the sea. Much of the traditional Philippine staples were produced, but copra, shells, pearls, and coral figured among their exports. The proceeds of piracy and coastal plunder augmented the gross product and captives from the Christian and pagan areas provided cheap labour in slavery and could be re-exported. The sultans were interested in friendly trade relations without the hated colonial and religious ties which the Spaniards had imposed further north. They approached other European nations, particularly the Dutch and the British, who were known to consider religious matters as of secondary importance. The Chinese, because of their materialistic way of life, were always welcome. The Spaniards had arrived too late in the Philippines to turn the clock back in this fervently religious community.

The Dutch were the first European power to assist the Moslems in their struggle. In 1645 and 1648 they attacked the Spanish forces which had succeeded in establishing themselves at Jolo. In 1764, after their evacuation of Manila, the British took with them the deposed Sultan Alimoud Din, who had had a chequered earlier career, having agreed to a Spanish presence in Zamboanga, been chased from the sultanate by his brother, and befriended in exile by the colonial power. The British restored him to his throne and, in gratitude, Alimoud ceded the sultanate's possessions in North Borneo, Palawan, and in the area in between to the East India Company: this gift was soon nullified by the hostility and treachery of the local *datus* (local notables with an Islamic feudal tradition). Magindanao was also attracted by the purely materialistic outlook of the British, but, after British assessment of local conditions, no agreement was reached and the sultan's propositions were never followed up. In 1844, the French, in their much-belated colonial drive, attempted to gain a hold in Basilan, the large island off Zamboanga. Because of political pressure in Europe, they were forced to abandon their interest. Nevertheless, the *de facto* independence of the two sultanates continued and a mission formed by British private interests, including Rajah James Brooke of Sarawak, visited Jolo in 1849 and a treaty was negotiated, but never ratified. Thus, when the Spaniards attacked Sulu in 1851, the Moslems had no real allies and the British, who were appealed to, refused aid, mainly on account of their European preoccupations, but partly because of the past history of treachery by the local Moslem chiefs during the former's earlier flirtation with the sultanate. Even at the time of the Spanish domination of the southern Archipelago in 1878, the sultan continued to deny Spain's complete sovereignty over him. In that year, Jamalud Alam ceded the Sulu possessions in Sabah to the North Borneo Company, in the persons of Gustavus von Overbeck and Alfred Dent. Notwithstanding the claims of the Spanish government at the time, in a protocol of 1885 between Spain, Germany, and Great Britain, the first power agreed to renounce

> as far as regards the British Government, all claims of sovereignty over the territories of the mainland of Borneo which belong or may have belonged to the Sultan of Sulu . . .

The independence of these lands is the basis of an outstanding difference between the Philippines and Malaysia.

There is no doubt that the Moslem territories were never effectively incorporated into the Spanish Philippines and that they maintained throughout the colonial period an administration and a culture entirely different to the remainder of the Archipelago. Government was essentially feudal and princely. Sultans and *datus* were generally related by blood and ruled, as a group, despotically. Depending on the times, the sultans' powers rose and fell. In strength, they dominated their peers in council; in weakness, the *datus* in council with the sultans gathered power to themselves and negated any practical centralized government.

This situation, often bringing chaos with it, continued throughout Moslem independence. It produced a hornet's nest in the region, with generally sterile, often barbarous, results. Nevertheless, it did conserve something of the Malay written annals which the priests had effaced in the Spanish-occupied parts of the Archipelago. But to the Malays it was basically as alien a culture as Christianity, although already well implanted in Indonesia and Malaya, where its way of life had been modified by the separate methods of colonization of the Dutch and the British.

It is here that a genuine attempt must be made to assess the character and weight of this particular community against world values at the time. Compared with the greater cultures, the Moslem Philippines group had little to recommend it. War, violence, and theft, when combined, are destructive and sap the resources of both the militants and their neighbours. In this case, the proceeds of such a way of life were squandered uselessly. Moslem culture had brought in with it a good part of its more worldly traditions; princely power, a centralized hierarchy of high officials, and some say for an electoral college made up of local notables. But in the warring and loosely knit groups of Sulu and Magindanao, there was factionalism which often negated the purposes of these excellent tenets. Thus, although the two sultanates had ample means to trade and to barter along the shores of the whole Indian Ocean, and possessed able scholars and leaders, material progress in both communities was slow. Internal feud and quarrel bedevilled normal relations within the groups and wealth was distributed to little purpose. In an international climate of growing political awareness and social consciousness, the Moslem Filipinos' conduct was continuously militant, sometimes treacherous. For the comparative defencelessness of their neighbours they had nothing but contempt and for the Spaniards they felt disdain and hatred. The arrogance of Spanish officers and officials was a source of constant hostility. Thus, even after the occupation of Sulu and Magindanao in the middle of last century, agreements formally entered into by the sultans were dishonoured and Spanish rule was flouted in every case possible. So the south remained archaic, almost medieval, at the time of the Industrial Revolution. When Spain abandoned her colony, she left the sultanates to return to a *status quo* intolerable in a region where peace and order were already becoming firmly established. In sum, the greatest successes of the Moslem south were the ability to resist, alone, all efforts of a major power to subject the territories permanently and the resulting conservation of a Philippine–Malay culture, albeit itself considerably diluted by East Indian Islam.

The Ethnic Minorities

Until the mid-nineteenth century, the widely scattered ethnic minority also escaped much of the colonists' attentions. Most of the earlier and more primitive settlers are believed to have moved away from the coastal areas long before the arrival of the Spaniards and, because of their isolation, they maintained their simple pagan cultures. In the north of Luzon, although much of the country is populated by the close-knit Ilocano group, the Tinggians and the Ibanags of the Abra and Cagayan Valleys respectively form two communities which have kept a coherence despite their proximity to Christian settlement. A percentage of the Tinggians were exposed to missionary activity, for, although the Spaniards did not attempt much penetration of the central mountains until the 1850s, some progress south was made from the Ilocano coastline where the Abra River flows through a mountain-dominated corridor into the sea. The Ibanags were more vulnerable to outside influence. They had concentrated in the Cagayan Valley, away from the coast and hemmed in by the great ranges of the Central Cordillera and the Sierra Madre. Ilocano settlers came south from the Luzon Strait coast to join them and the Spaniards found their way into the valley from the same direction. Thus the Ibanags constitute an exception to the rule of isolation and, although they maintain ethnic differences and some separate cultural traditions, they have been converted to Christianity and have absorbed much of the Spanish–Philippine culture of the lowland Malays. Elsewhere in north Luzon, the Central Cordillera hill tribes maintained their Late Stone Age pagan traditions and the Sierra Madre communities, such as the Gaddangs and the Ilongots, were little influenced by the colonists until their later days in the Philippines. The negroid Aetas, living in scattered communities over Luzon, the Visayas, and Mindanao, remained outside the Spaniards' cultural world and, in Mindanao itself, the numerous ethnic minorities were doubly isolated from European contacts as the Moslems added their own hostility to the remoteness of the tribal areas.

The political and cultural pattern in Mindanao at the end of Spanish rule was the result of the colonists' attempts to evangelize and occupy the non-Moslem areas, and the ebullient and warlike moves of the Magindanao sultanate and its vassal groups to counter any such expansion. The Moslems themselves had little or no direct influence in the north-east and eastern parts of the island and here the Spanish missionaries were able to gain some sort of foothold, although they remained extremely vulnerable to the continual raiding operations from Magindanao and Sulu. Spanish colonization also extended along the northern Mindanao coastline from Surigao at the north-east point, through Butuaan at the mouth of the Agusan River, to Cagayan de Oro in Misamis Oriental. As we have already seen in this chapter, some progress inland was made, but any move westwards into Lanao was countered by the Maranao communities. Despite this Spanish occupation of the coastline and of the valleys, the minority tribes, such as the Bukidnons and the Manobos, remained outside the colonial pattern. Later, when Davao separated from the sultanate of Magindanao, little penetration of the Atus, Bagobos, or Mandagas occurred. In the Zamboanga Peninsula, the large Subnunum tribe had been the target of Moslem missionary activities for centuries. As Spanish strength grew in the east of this feature, expansion westwards and southwards from Dipolog, Dapitan, and Ozamiz (Misamis) took place and some conversions to Christianity among the ethnic minorities followed. The Bilaan community in Cotabato and west Davao was also a target for Moslem missionaries and remained outside the sphere of colonial rule until the last.

If much of Philippine culture can be classed as basically Malay Christian with a definite Iberian timbre, this impact remains considerably lessened in those specific areas of the Archipelago where the Spanish administration had little or no time to gain a hold over the minds and material lives of the people. The first of these areas is the traditional Moslem part of the south. Next in importance are the mountain regions of north Luzon. Larger in size, but less thickly populated, are the interior parts of central Mindanao, the Davao Gulf, and the spiny Zamboanga Peninsula. Elsewhere, some parts of Palawan and of Mindoro also show characteristic signs of a physical remoteness which left ethnic minorities untouched over the centuries. But if the Moslem sultanates constituted a threat to the security of the other parts of the colony, the ethnic minorities, with no coherence between their groups, were no more than archaic reminders of a primitive culture. Although they were not always wholly benign (head-hunting was practised in some communities), they gave little or no trouble unless their areas were forcibly penetrated. Nevertheless, the almost complete exclusion of the colonists from these lands until the last years of their rule resulted in a series of minority situations which today bring with them both political and social barriers to the attempts of the Philippine government to build up a single nation.

Chapter 12

American Intervention

THE JEALOUSY with which the Philippines was guarded from outside interests until the first part of the nineteenth century is unique in this later period when most nations practised a vigorous policy of free trade. The complications inherent in unofficial mercantile transactions and illegal residence ashore of foreigners before 1834 were both tedious and costly for the operator. Nevertheless, in the end, it was the British and the Americans who succeeded in making the islands a remunerative trade area, despite an almost negative attitude of the Spaniards in commerce, for the latter still drew much of their revenues from the tobacco monopoly, which remained in force until 1882. Economic progress began to be felt after Manila was opened officially to foreign trade in 1834. Sual, also in central Luzon, Iloilo in the Visayas, and Zamboanga in Mindanao followed in 1855, as did Cebu soon after. With the opening of the Suez Canal in 1869, shipping time to the East was cut considerably and two further Philippine ports were cleared for foreign entry: these were Legaspi in the south of Luzon and Tacloban in Leyte. In this expanding society, the commodities exported from the Philippines were rice (through Sual), indigo, hemp, pepper, sugar, and copra. Rice was to become a deficiency crop because of the reliance on it as a staple by the rapidly growing Luzon population: indigo was soon eclipsed by synthetics and pepper could be produced more economically elsewhere. Hemp, sugar, and copra continued to grow in importance and much of this trade was in the hands of aliens, British and American. The Spaniards maintained a hold on the tobacco market after the monopoly was abolished and they continued to have considerable influence in general commerce, although the British and Americans came ashore to set up trading houses and branches of their own banks. To the indigenous operations of the *caciques*, their mixed-blood *compradore* colleagues, and the Chinese businessmen were now added those of the aliens, who brought with them capital and commercial drive, making common cause with these non-Spanish groups. Later, penetration into the primary sector followed and cane-growing and milling were organized directly by foreign trading houses; the cultivation of coffee and coconut palms increased and some of the factoring here was taken over by the outsiders. To complement expansion, communications improved both in the inter-island boat sector and in the road and inland ferry infrastructure. A railway was built by a British contractor, linking Manila and many of the larger towns of the central Luzon Plain.

The political weakness of Spain after the reign of Isabella II and the revolution of 1868 tempted both the French and the British to try to gain a foothold in those areas where the colonial administration was at its feeblest. In the event, the French, as we have already seen, had to bow to strong political pressure in Europe, but the British maintained their hold on the Sabah territories conveyed from the sultanate of Jolo to the Borneo Company and this transfer was formalized by protocol with Spain. In a world dominated by the maritime powers of Europe and North America, a climate had already been established for the ensuing United States adventure in the Philippines.

The growth of the United States as a world power and the distaste with which she viewed Spanish colonial conduct in her residual empire were matched by her vigorous worldwide commercial penetration and a sentimental desire to see all subjugated peoples free. Even before the outbreak of the Spanish–American War, United States politicians had considered the risks and the benefits of intervention in Spain's empire and relations between Washington and Madrid had already been worsened by the latter's growing impatience with American commercial infiltration. Thus, a serious explosion which occurred on board the USS *Maine*,[1] lying in the harbour of Havana on 15 February 1898, provided the opportunity for the United States to intervene. Public opinion in America contributed to the deterioration of the situation and an ultimatum was delivered to Spain demanding, *inter alia*, withdrawal from Cuba. On 24 April Spain declared war on the United States as the direct result of this exchange.

There is no doubt whatsoever that firm if somewhat loosely framed contingency plans had been drawn up for the American occupation of the Philippines on any outbreak of hostilities with Spain. In the event, the United States Asiatic Squadron, commanded by Commodore George Dewey, immediately received radioed orders to proceed from Hong Kong to Manila to destroy the Spanish fleet. The Battle of Manila Bay took place on 1 May 1898, six days after Dewey had received these instructions. This battle lasted some seven hours and on the surrender of the Spanish Admiral Patricio Montojoy Pasarón, all of his twelve vessels had either been sunk or badly damaged. Maritime power was not sufficient for the next logical steps: the invasion of Manila and the destruction of Spanish authority in the Philippines. It was necessary, therefore, to await military land forces. The first of these came from the Philippines itself. Aguinaldo, who had been in exile in Hong Kong, arrived in Cavite aboard an American vessel and immediately met Dewey. Aguinaldo agreed to assist the Americans and, disembarking, reorganized the forces which had laid down their arms after the Pact of Biaknabato in 1897. With weapons purchased earlier through the American consul-general in Hong Kong and supplied direct by Dewey, Aguinaldo soon dominated much of Luzon with about 12,000 revolutionaries, and by July he had encircled Manila and stood poised for attack. He was restrained by Dewey until a sufficiently large United States land force had arrived to command the situation fully, for Spanish strength in Manila was fractionally larger than that of the revolutionaries. By mid-August, an American force had been landed, having arrived during July in three separate expeditions. On 13 August, Manila was captured by American and Philippine forces: the day after, surrender documents were signed. The war continued to be fought all over the islands for another eight months,[2] but by the Treaty of Paris, signed on 10 December 1898, Spain ceded the Philippines, Guam, and Puerto Rico to the United States and abandoned Cuba. In compensation she received $20 million.

This short account of initial American actions in the Philippines shows the determination of the United States to remove Spanish power from the Archipelago. But military victory does not always bring the complete solution to problems. The Treaty of Paris provided for the cession of the colony to the United States, but in accordance with its clauses the political future of the Philippines was to be decided by Congress. To be reckoned with was the Philippine revolutionary movement which had already fought Spain and, in 1897, had accepted a compromise solution: here, in the persons of General Aguinaldo and his now numerous Philippine forces fighting alongside the Americans, there was a demand for almost immediate national independence. President McKinley made the decision and in a solitary analysis of the situation one night, accompanied by prayer and vigil, he came to the conclusion that the Filipinos were unfit for self-government (*sic*) and that evacuation of Manila would leave the islands open either to European intervention or to anarchy and indigenous misrule. The die was cast. American policy was clarified. The islands were to be completely occupied and pending the recommendations of a commission, a military government established. This was not the solution which Aguinaldo had wished or foreseen, as he had already constituted his own interim dictatorship, and where the revolutionary forces were in control, local government was organized on a universal suffrage under a provincial governor. A central revolutionary congress had met for the first time in September at Malolos, just north of Manila, and on 21 January 1899 a written constitution was formally approved, which is now referred to as the Malolos Constitution. A Republic of the Philippines was proclaimed two days later with General Aguinaldo as its first President. In the light of McKinley's decision of 21 December 1898, a collision path had been taken by both sides. Military plans to put into effect the United States trusteeship policy were promulgated on 5 February 1899 and full-scale pacification operations against the Philippine republican government and its armed forces continued throughout that year and only ceased officially after the capture of Aguinaldo in the remote town of Palanan on the north-east coast of Luzon on 23 March 1900. Taken to Manila, Aguinaldo almost immediately took an oath of allegiance to the United States. By doing so he was only being realistic and showing courage and dignity. Resistance against the Americans had generally been overcome by the beginning of that year. The Filipino people were tired of war, content to be rid of the Spaniards, and on the whole intrigued by the friendliness and easy-going manners of these new rulers. Aguinaldo's final action stopped useless bloodshed in the face of American determination to set up a protectorate.

Whatever can be said of latter-day American presence in the Philippines, the earlier years brought much that was benign, constructive, and productive. Despite the difficult days at the end of organized Philippine resistance when violence, often offered by criminal groups in the name of patriotism, was met by violence, pacification of the country went on until by 1902 the major part of a sound administrative and social system was completed. This firm rule was invaluable in a country whose own liberal movement had had few followers a quarter of a century beforehand. The single-mindedness of the American effort is not strange to observers; an area was first pacified, then assimilated; a political and social demonstration being made to convince the Filipinos of the merits of this new Western way of life. Despite fears and alarms, the Roman Catholic faith was maintained and even encouraged although freedom of religious belief was introduced, the Church formally separated from the state, and, for a time, numerous nonconformist Protestant movements from America concentrated on the country. The Catholic hierarchy prospered, switching its advance base from Spain to the United States, American priests coming in to work alongside and later replacing their Spanish brothers. In this liberalized religious world, the Protestants contributed considerably to the

social effort and the Philippine Independent Church, founded by a former Catholic priest, Gregorio Aglipay, a devoted nationalist, produced a valuable counterweight at a time of authoritarianism in this massively Catholic society. In the same vein, the re-establishment of teaching institutions, their buildings often devastated by war and the conduct of the revolutionaries in the provinces, was pursued by the new administrators. American soldiers, later assisted by their wives, often taught in the newly reconstituted primary schools, both urban and rural. These schools multiplied and a new generation of Filipino teachers in embryo appeared, young people who helped with the classes and later went on to the secondary establishments which began to appear in 1903. In much the same way, sanitary and medical conditions in the country were vastly improved, indirectly leaning on the school framework for the popular dissemination of ideas.

American military government continued to operate until 4 July 1901. This interim administration was well equipped legally to contend with events which took place during an essentially unstable period. It also provided the means to bring direct and often personal intervention to areas which were well populated but scattered and lacking communication. From the start, however, its status was that of a temporary expedient, the United States authorities depending on it to maintain peace and order while a more liberal and fitting pattern of government could be worked out. Thus, during its own lifetime, the military régime's replacement was being studied. A first Philippine Commission reported back to President McKinley in January 1900 and a second was constituted in April of the same year.[3] Working on the basis of the earlier commission's report, the second, which had executive powers as well as those of fact-finding, arrived in the Philippines in June and almost immediately began to reinforce the military government by planning and programming executive services into the administration. By the time civil government was re-established, a fairly adequate system of public and local services had already been set up and among these were the educational facilities which were so quickly organized as part of the territorial occupation by the armed forces.

The next step was the final abolition of the military régime and its replacement by a framework of government which was well advanced in character, considering that it was conceived for a comparatively backward Asian country in the year 1902. Working on the checks and balances of two contrasted bodies, the representative and the officially appointed, a legislative group of two chambers was set up under the Philippine Organic Act. But there was a delay in its establishment; first stability and peace in the countryside had

to be sufficiently implanted to allow elections to take place and a non-authoritarian government to survive; secondly a census had to be taken and an electoral roll prepared. In the event, elections to a Lower House of 80 members took place in 1907 and with the five-strong second Philippine Commission, broadened by the nomination of four Filipino members during 1908, acting as the Upper House, the first Philippine Assembly met in October of that year. The Governor-General retained wide powers during 1906–13,[4] an imperative in a situation which had to be carefully studied and where politicians had little experience of parliamentary rule. An interesting counterpart was nevertheless introduced from 1902 onwards. Two Filipino resident commissioners to the United States were elected and these officials represented Philippine views in American government circles and in the United States Congress itself.

Being faced with a requirement to enter politics and slowly progress by this path rather than fight for independence, the leading Filipinos took to the change like ducks to water, although protesting firmly all the time. They have continued to show their deep affection for the craft which over the years has widened from the choice of a national government to the elections of local officials in the smallest rural communities. Initially, however, it was essential to organize political groups and the first of these, after a period of transition, became the Progressive Party, whose platform was eventual independence within an American system. A more advanced group, which before the elections of 1907 fused itself into the Nacionalista Party, demanded immediate and complete independence. This two-party confrontation within the bounds of a semi-executive Lower House was of considerable value. Debate was fostered and the political apprenticeship which was served in the formalized structure of the Assembly produced a generation of men who were soon figures in public life.

A further facet of this political kaleidoscope should be mentioned. In the last chapter, the situation in the ethnic and cultural minority areas was examined and, as we have seen, there was little to base government on in these territories. The American authorities, therefore, removed the administration of these lands from the competency of the Assembly as a whole, vesting it wholly in the Upper House, the former Philippine Commission which from its arrival in the islands had made a study of the problems involved. A bureau of non-Christian tribes was established and two minority provinces set up. The first to be organized was the Moro province in 1903, with sub-provinces to fit the general configuration of the Moslem lands. The numerous mountain tribal areas of north Luzon were constituted into a province (Mountain province) in 1905 and here the tribal territories were separated enough for sub-provinces to be organized on an ethnic basis. In the existing provinces where cultural and ethnic minorities – the most vulnerable to change – were in numerical majority, even if their presence was little felt in day-to-day life, special measures were taken to protect them, from too rapid an evolution and from any possible pressure from those who were as alien to them as the Americans were to the Filipino Christians.

In this manner, the new administration, once it had decided to stay, moved vigorously and with a liberal foresight which remains admirable to students seventy years later. Where violence was offered, as it sometimes was in both the Christian and Moslem areas, it was met by force, often of a harsh and unswerving nature. But the pacification of the country continued, a strong American presence was maintained, and with it came simple educational facilities linked with instruction in hygiene and citizenship. A basis was laid down for democratic rule in an ultimately independent state. The second Commission's executive reinforcement of the military régime established a civil service, a national police force, and a number of technical bodies to direct public works in both the towns and rural areas.

After the defeat of the Spaniards it took almost fifty more years for the Filipinos to obtain their independence. As now, there was a wide difference between the articulate intelligentsia and the majority of the population, marginally literate but generally tied to a traditional life of husbandry or minor commerce. Some parts of the Archipelago exerted more social pressure than others: these were generally the areas where land tenure provided the least profit to the men who worked the soil. There was an anomaly here as well: many of the most vigorous of the nationalist politicians came from the Philippine-based landowning families – the *caciques*. Despite their undeniably liberal views, their personal independence was made possible by the funds obtained from land rental. Neither the Americans, nor today the Filipinos in their sovereign status, have been able to break the hold of this landowning class, but the Americans acted early in their rule to redistribute much of the friar lands which, although vulnerable to idealistic attack, were in practice more liberally managed than much of the other leased property. In addition, the priestly orders had already brought progress to their estates by providing irrigation systems which, with little modification, still operate today. After negotiations with the Vatican, the bulk of those lands owned by the religious orders was purchased by the state and redistributed to smallholders.

The agricultural policy of the new rulers was also vigorous and was linked with liberal trade regulations where exchanges with the

United States were involved. Officially, large funds were injected to restock and reorganize the war-devastated farms: unofficially, American business moved in to take a leading share in direct and indirect estate management. Free trade with the United States was established in 1913 and, as a result, there was soon a massive re-channeling of Philippine primary products towards America and European markets were almost abandoned. A real colonial economic policy followed and although Philippine imports into the ruling country were favoured, this new orientation was almost completely dominated by the commercial requirements of American commerce. Money was also provided for the development of mining and gold, silver, manganese, copper, and iron were successfully prospected and worked. It is indicative that no metallurgical finishing industry was established; these raw materials being shipped across the Pacific and, as with the other primary products, in United States vessels.

Before the outbreak of the Second World War, two further phases in Philippine political evolution took place. In 1913, the Philippine Commission, which served as the Upper House, was remustered, the Filipino members being given a majority by Governor-General Francis Burton Harrison – five out of nine seats. The Jones Law, enacted by the United States Congress in 1916, confirmed an American intention to grant complete independence as soon as conditions were appropriate and provided for a new interim administration by an American Governor-General and two elected Houses. The Commission was replaced by a 24-member Senate, in which all but two were elected. (These two were appointed by the Governor-General to represent the non-Christian areas.) The cabinet, with one exception, was constituted according to a normal parliamentary procedure. The Governor-General, sometimes in the name of the United States President, sometimes in his own right, had powers of veto and there were certain closed subjects. These powers were used only by Leonard Wood, who replaced Harrison in 1921 and who took hardly any notice of the Philippine legislature. The second stage towards independence was the establishment of the Commonwealth in 1935. After considerable Philippine lobbying in Washington, the Tydings-McDuffie Act was passed in 1934. This provided for a transition period of ten years before complete independence and the creation of a Commonwealth during this time. Under a special constitution, drafted by convention during 1934 and 1935 and approved soon afterwards, new elections took place and an all-Philippine administration, with a President (Manuel Quezon), a Vice President (Sergio Osmeña), and a Congress of two Houses was elected. The judiciary became all-Filipino and was quite independent. Residual United States powers, generally the prerogative of the American President, but in practice in the hands of a High Commissioner, included authority to suspend laws and decrees, the right to approve matters concerning currency, overseas trade, and immigration, and the management of the Philippines' external affairs. Although the Philippine judiciary was independent and to all intents and purposes sovereign, the United States Supreme Court retained powers of review.

The first President and Vice President of the Philippines had already had long and distinguished careers as politicians before their election to supreme office. President Quezon[5] had been a resident commissioner in Washington from 1909 to 1916, an early member of the Nacionalista Party, and an emphatic supporter, over the years, of Philippine demands for immediate independence. He became President of the first Philippine Senate and for many years was either a member or leader of lobby groups striving for his party's aims. As Senate President, he was the highest-ranking Filipino politician and his transition to national President was logical and popular. Sergio Osmeña had had as distinguished a career, also as a Nacionalista, although in the first all-Filipino legislature in 1916, he remained in the Lower House as Speaker. Both men were of the intelligentsia, trained in law, and tempered by a long and honourable opposition to American control. For a time they had split their party as the result of a difference of opinion on the terms of an earlier American project for quasi-autonomy,[6] but they came together again to fight the pre-Commonwealth election.

The Commonwealth was a success. The enlightened American tutorship over the years had produced an efficient apparatus of government and administration. It had assisted the Filipino leaders in their ultimate task of ruling and the economic situation was propitious for a change-over to an all-Philippine administration. In 1941, in the second election of this new régime, Quezon and Osmeña were returned and their party given a large majority. It was a major tragedy when the Japanese forces invaded Luzon on 10 December 1941, a month after the people had renewed their previous government's mandate.

[1] The reasons for the explosion have never been thoroughly explained, but it did give America the opportunity to act against Spain. As nearly 300 Americans were killed on board, it could hardly have been engineered.

[2] The Spaniards after surrender were generally facing Filipino revolutionaries who did not accept United States sovereignty as ceded in the Treaty of Paris.

[3] Members of the second Commission were William H. Taft (chairman), Luke E. Wright, Henry C. Ide, Bernard Moses, and Dean C. Worcester.

[4] The first civilian Governors-General were: William H. Taft (1901–04); Luke E. Wright (1904–06); Henry C. Ide (1906); James F. Smith (1906–09); W. Cameron Forbes (1909–13).

[5] A Filipino *mestizo*, born on 19 August 1878 in the little port town of Baler on the Pacific coast of Luzon, overlooked by the spiny Sierra Madre, Quezon as a young man joined Emilio Aguinaldo, but his first move into party politics came when the United States withdrew her ban on the free operations of the Immediate Independence Party in 1906: both Quezon and Osmeña were members. In 1907, merger with the Progresistas produced the Nacionalista Party which was to become the major element in the new Philippine Assembly, elected on 30 July 1907. For nearly two years, he was his party's parliamentary leader until appointment as Philippine Resident Commissioner in Washington in 1909. He remained in the United States until 1916 when he returned to become President of the Senate within the new congressional organization provided for under the Jones Law.

In 1935, he was still Senate President but, with the creation of the Commonwealth, took supreme office on 15 November 1935. Chosen for a second term during the early days of the war, he was sworn in at the island fortress of Corregidor, to which the Commonwealth government, its American advisers, and the Governor-General had been evacuated a little before the entry of Japanese forces into Manila. Quezon left Corregidor by submarine in February 1942 with his inner cabinet, arriving in the United States in May. He continued as head of government in exile until his death on 1 August 1944 at Saranac Lake, New York state.

His country will always be indebted to him, as his own story seems to have complemented the political evolution of the Philippines during the whole of the tutelage period. Although a fervent patriot and outspoken nationalist, he was also a practical politician who realized the importance of campaigning and negotiation. His period as Resident Commissioner was of primary importance not only for the Philippines in his character of exponent of her aspirations, but also for himself, for he gained experience in the tough proving-ground of United States congressional life. His personal efforts here had much influence on the debates surrounding the Jones Bills, which became the Jones Law and which, in turn, provided for the first wholly elected Philippine Congress. From there, he assisted the Philippine evolution towards total independence by personally negotiating the bases of the Tydings–McDuffie Act of 1934 which provided both for the Commonwealth and complete sovereignty ten years later. In a society where moral equality has always been cherished and where Jack is as good as his neighbour, Quezon by his reputation and experience rose above his fellows in office. In addition, he showed himself endowed with powers of command and organization and therefore quite capable of taking over the responsibilities which, earlier, had been those of the tutor power. His emphasis on the structurization of a liberal education system, equality of rights for women, and the build-up of a national infrastructure showed great foresight, but this was equalled by his firmness of purpose in office, his vigorous dealings in day-to-day matters, and his continued grasp of party political currents. Even in exile, he maintained the pressure, identifying himself and his country with the United Nations Charter and sitting on the Pacific War Cabinet. The tragedy of Japanese occupation was compounded in that it was designed to destroy all that Quezon had successfully built up during his long years in office.

His wife, Aurora, who had been his faithful companion, both in power and in exile, was murdered in a Communist ambush on the tortuous Baler–Cabanatuan road in April 1948.

[6] The Hare-Hawes-Cutting Act or Philippine Independence Act of 1933. This law had been submitted when Sergio Osmeña, Congressman (then Speaker) Manuel Roxas, and Benigno Aquino were heading a mission to the United States. This mission came out in favour of the draft bill. Manuel Quezon as Senate President opposed it, on the grounds that Philippine sovereignty would be impaired by the provision of clauses defining the Governor-General's residual powers, the proposed trade relations between the Philippines and the United States, and the power of the United States to maintain armed forces with almost complete extra-territorial rights.

Chapter 13

War and Independence

THE PHILIPPINES ENTERED the 1940s a well and popularly governed country, Asian, but firmly Christian in culture and with a European–American outlook. The Filipino tended to look overseas: many of his compatriots had travelled extensively; numbers of them had emigrated to Hawaii or to the United States; foreign trade was the most vigorous part of the national economy. Tagalog, the central Luzon Malay-group dialect, had been selected as the eventual national language, but English was to remain in official use until 1946. The growth of educational facilities throughout the country had been continuous and, with the Commonwealth, this movement became a symbol for the future. Leaning considerably on American advice and methods, educational programmes had already been modified to fit in with the spirit and foreseen needs of the future sovereign state. The Americans had built up an evoluted national infrastructure of roads, railways, harbours, and airfields. The Commonwealth continued the good work. Police forces were maintained and, where these proved inadequate, the Philippine Constabulary was always available to operate. The presence of quite substantial United States and Philippine armed forces under a unified command gave an impression of national security.

This impression, in the event, was a false picture, for these forces were inadequate to defend the scattered Archipelago against an attack by a well-equipped force unless they were reinforced by maritime power from the United States. The Japanese attack on Pearl Harbor, which took place on 8 December 1941, dislocated American naval deployment and temporarily removed all hope of any supremacy which she could have secured in the Pacific. The Philippines was almost immediately at war. She was subjected to Japanese air attacks, particularly against the important airfield complex which had been laid out in central Luzon, and landings were soon made at different points on her long and ill-defended shoreline. On 10 December, the Japanese landed at Aparri on the Luzon Strait and at Vigan on the north-west coast. On 22 December, they secured a foothold in the Lingayan Gulf, adjacent to the United

States bases at Clark Field and Subic. In the Bicol Peninsula of southern Luzon, landings were made at Legaspi and further north on the same eastern coastline, at Mauban and Atimonan, both of which had easy road access westwards to Manila over the rump of the Sierra Madre range. Manila was declared an open city on 26 December and the United States and Philippine ground forces, commanded by General MacArthur, began a retreat which was to bring them to the Bataan Peninsula, whose southern and eastern shores lie on Manila Bay, adjacent to the fortress of Corregidor, an island standing at its entrance. The remainder of the battle took place in this area, as did the political events which led to the constitution of a Philippine government-in-exile.

Philippine and American forces resisted the Japanese in Bataan until 9 April 1942. For over three months these men fought with no air support[1] and no protection from attack from the sea, the local United States naval forces having moved to Indonesian waters in December. Nevertheless, despite these hardships, they held out longer than either the Dutch- or British-controlled colonies and, in the end, they stood alone in a Japanese-dominated area. The Commonwealth government had evacuated Manila on 24 December, taking up cramped quarters in the Corregidor fortress which was strongly held by an allied force of almost divisional strength. As the situation deteriorated, steps were taken to evacuate the key members of the civil and military hierarchy. President Quezon and members of his cabinet left by submarine on 20 February, the United States High Commissioner, Francis B. Sayre, following him a few days later. In early March, General MacArthur and some of his staff were evacuated in light surface craft. On 6 May, General Jonathan Mayhew Wainwright, to whom MacArthur had handed over command, surrendered Corregidor and its garrison. Soon afterwards, he gave orders for all Filipino and American troops in the islands to lay down their arms. The Japanese occupation of the Visayas and Mindanao was completed by mid-May.

Japanese ruled

An analysis of Japanese rule in the Philippines shows little or nothing advantageous to the inhabitants. The two cultures were so separate as to make any understanding between the parties difficult, almost impossible. Some Filipinos initially saw the invaders as liberators, for their islands had been subjected to white rule for nearly four hundred years. Some co-operation between the Japanese authorities and the Filipinos was attempted and, for the good of the people as a whole, day-to-day relations were often maintained on a polite level. But the number of Filipinos who welcomed the invaders lessened as they had more and more contact with them, in particular with the members of the Japanese armed forces and security police.

The Malay, even in a rural area where the comforts of life often pass him by, has a standard of hygiene and conduct which is uniformly acceptable and the American had already laboured some forty years to improve this. The Japanese lacked such standards and their conduct, as the masters of the land, was in direct contrast to the avuncular attitude of the Americans. Neither did the hybrid civilization of the Philippines please them and the democratic political climate of the islands was contrary to all their traditions.

But of all the tragedies of war, the saddest was the material and spiritual destruction of the Commonwealth. Materially, the infrastructure had already been damaged by the military operations at the end of 1941 and the beginning of 1942. The period of occupation brought with it neglect and a lack of technical means to maintain the quite complex equipments which had been installed. The activities of the guerrilla movements brought further depredations and the allied operations to expel the Japanese in 1944 and 1945 brought with them widespread destruction. Against individual attempts to keep the spirit of the Commonwealth alive, all Japanese propaganda effort was directed towards the foundation of a quite different type of régime and the bulk of the political forces of occupation was thrown into a battle against Western-type democracy. A single party, the *Kalibapi*,[2] was founded during the rule of the Japanese military administration with Jorge Vargas as its leader. Vargas had been left behind by President Quezon to maintain some sort of dialogue between the Filipinos and the Japanese, and in this capacity he was nominated as mayor of Greater Manila. It was an unenviable task, but he and his collaborators maintained some sort of independent rule in a body named the Philippine Executive Commission which administered the country under the military government. The *Kalibapi* was a tool of the Japanese, planned by them to constitute a nationwide cadre. It was organized on a territorial basis at town and then provincial levels with a national executive in Manila. In theory, it was to serve as a means to indoctrinate, oversee, and control the population. In practice, Japanese directions were not always followed and because of the typical Philippine sense of adjustment, the organization was never so venal as the Japanese would have liked it to be. But membership did reach the million-and-a-half level and in its ranks were people who worked conscientiously to complete the destruction of the traditions built up over four hundred years. On this Japanese-inspired single-party base, the second stage of the occupants' political programme was erected: the formation of a puppet Philippine republic, with a president and a national assembly whose members were nominated at *Kalibapi* meetings which took place all over the country. The republic was set up on 14 October

1943, but in a country still occupied by substantial Japanese forces and itself directed from Tokyo, there was little chance of it possessing a really independent character. Dr José Laurel became president. Resistance to the Japanese began in the earliest days and many escaped Filipino servicemen continued to fight until the invaders had surrendered. They were joined and often reinforced in political character by members of the intelligentsia, but people of all classes took part in the struggle and they were assisted by American servicemen and civilians who either found their way from the Japanese-dominated areas or who were sent in from the United States at a later date. Separate from these broadly based guerrilla organizations was the Communist-directed *Hukbalahap*[3] which operated generally in central Luzon, where a sad history involving agricultural grievances and land tenures had embittered the peasant people for many years and had appeared as a threat to peace during the Commonwealth. The Huks not only fought the Japanese fiercely, but they maintained a political intransigence which was sometimes detrimental to their resistance colleagues in the neighbourhood. They organized their areas on a militant Communist basis and maintained a separate administration which they hotly defended.

So the years of occupation passed. In much the same way as in other Japanese-conquered territories, administration was slipshod, neglect was widespread, and the cultural traditions of the country were eroded. In the disorganized countryside, often dominated by guerrillas, the Japanese soldiery moved and acted with little regard for their fellow Asians. Commerce was at a standstill, even exports towards Japan being endangered by a growing allied power in the Pacific. It was against this background that United States aircraft began to appear over Philippine territory in the late summer of 1944 and the destruction of military installations and the interdiction of all Japanese movement followed. On 20 October 1944 the Americans landed in Leyte and with them came General MacArthur and Sergio Osmeña, the latter having replaced President Quezon, who had died in the United States on 1 August. The Commonwealth was reconstituted at Tacloban in Leyte, which became its temporary capital. After the destruction of the Japanese fleet in the Philippine Sea and the Leyte Gulf, American forces landed in Luzon. On 23 February 1945, Manila was retaken after a battle in which the tragedy of the destruction of the Japanese-held Intramuros was matched by the barbarous conduct of their soldiery during their last days in the city. It was no wonder that the overwhelming majority of Filipinos welcomed their former masters back with enthusiasm and gratitude. The remainder of the Philippines was generally cleared of the Japanese by May, but General Yamashita, who had recently taken over as their commander, remained with his residual forces entrenched in the mountainous areas of north Luzon and did not surrender until the final Japanese capitulation in September 1945. José Laurel, with some members of the deposed régime, was flown to Japan before the Americans could capture Baguio, where their ill-fated government had its last residence.

With the country in ruins, Osmeña took over his duties in Manila and the first meeting of the Commonwealth Congress since the evacuation of Manila in December 1941 took place in June 1945. New elections were held in April 1946 and Manuel A. Roxas was selected as President of the Republic. This was the last step before complete independence, for the Commonwealth had, in theory, existed for its ten statutory years. The Philippines became a sovereign state on 4 July 1946. Roxas and his cabinet became its first administrators.

[1] The majority of the allied air forces in the Philippines had been destroyed on the ground during the first days.

[2] Kapisanam sa Paglilingkad sa Barong Pilipinas (Association for Service to the New Philippines).

[3] Hukbong Bayan Laban Sa Hapon (People's Liberation Army against Japan).

PART THREE

The Republic of the Philippines

Chapter 14

The Independent State

INDEPENDENCE COULD HARDLY have been postponed. It had been promised; any delay would have resulted in mass protest, probably in civil disobedience. It was also in American interests to grant it: goodwill in the future would be required to capitalize on the investments already made in the country and those now to be provided in the form of war damage compensation and other grants. Nevertheless, unlike the year 1935, when the Commonwealth was established, the time was anything but propitious: it was one of the worst moments for a country to be completely freed from the relatively benign yoke of a highly organized and industrialized imperialist power. Very little of its own simple industry could operate. Roads, railways, buildings, and telecommunications were in ruins and the people had had to put aside much of their civic sense in their war of wits with the Japanese. In these conditions, on 4 July 1946, power was handed over in a country which, in the main, was kept together by a dwindling military presence and the determination of Filipino politicians to go it alone.

Most peoples owe much to both their environment and to their history. The Filipino is no exception and he is most probably more of a slave to these factors than others. Sometimes this background has assisted the newly independent country, sometimes it has given little or no help. In a number of cases, twentieth-century life has been complicated and even impeded by this varied inheritance. Almost immediately sovereignty is investigated, this becomes apparent.

The territories which the Americans made independent were those ceded by Spain under the Treaty of Paris in 1898. The area was made up of land and water; the internal seas and the straits between the various smaller Philippine islands and the larger masses being considered territorial. In Republic Act number 3046, this is defined by a baseline joining seventy-nine points, generally rocks or features of small islands off the shores of the bulk of the Archipelago. All seas inside this baseline are 'considered inland or internal waters of the Philippines'. The effect of the instrument is far-reaching, for it is a claim to sovereignty over an enormous polygon set massively across more than eight hundred kilometres of West Pacific shoreline with its contrasting face on the South China Sea. Three major seaways between the two, the San Bernardino and Surigao Straits and the Sibutu Channel, are claimed as under the jurisdiction of the republic, but if maritime navigation can only be undertaken through feasible waters, where there is sufficient depth and leeway for a ship to move in safety, this is not the case with air overflight. While the Philippine instrument concerns practically a very restricted number of international sea passages, it claims competency over an enormous slice of airspace. In the event, the goodwill and the commonsense of successive Philippine administrations have resulted in a *modus vivendi*. Aircraft, in any case, are obliged by international regulations to clear themselves with the local air traffic control centre and ships, by courtesy, generally signal their presence. But the Philippines' claim to complete jurisdiction over these important seaways is contested.

The Philippine view is a very understandable one. To check illegal immigration, the movement of contraband, and infiltration into the country by politically undesirable elements, only a certain number of ports and airfields are open to foreign vessels or aircraft. To implement such a policy, legal grounds must be available to check and eventually to apprehend. Moreover, no one likes anybody else playing in his own backyard and the movement of foreign vessels between the myriad of islands of the Archipelago is tantamount to this. But an overriding weakness is manifest in the system. Electronic devices can and do produce warnings of air intrusion and interceptor aircraft can be taken off to identify and act in accordance with a government policy: this is not the case with shipping. Effectively to control and patrol the waters claimed as internal, a considerable naval effort in both shore-based equipment and vessels would be necessary: the cost of such an effort is prohibitive for a country which has many more urgent calls on its available funds. It is difficult to see how such a sovereignty could really be maintained except with massive foreign assistance or by common international consent. If free movement in the region ever becomes of vital world importance once again, expediency could well impose its own solution.

Geographically, the Philippines is divided into those four elements already defined in Chapter 1: Luzon, the Visayas, Mindanao, and the Sulu Archipelago. These names are in everyday use to describe both the islands and the seas around them, but they have no administrative meaning under the republic. For this purpose, the country is divided into sixty-four provinces, each with its governor and its other elected officials serving on a provincial board. In addition, there are three sub-provinces, but these possess little real autonomy. Certain administrative matters are handled on a regional basis: some government departments maintaining local delegations in the larger provincial cities, these covering the needs of a wide area. Provinces and sub-provinces are themselves divided into chartered cities, municipalities, and municipal districts. Chartered cities have a special political and administrative status: they are less dependent on the central government, both for everyday affairs and for fiscal purposes, than the municipalities and they are almost independent of the province. Municipalities are more than just towns; they are mixed urban and rural communities, the seat of local government being in the town (*poblacion*) itself. With the chartered cities and the municipal districts they make up the whole of the land mass of the Philippines. Municipal districts, of which there were only forty-seven at the 1960 census, are the remnants of those parts of the country where the electoral system still remains impracticable, either for reasons of security or because, so far, a large proportion of the inhabitants have not reached the requisite status considered necessary for this form of government. The last two elements of the chain are the *barrio* (village) and the *sitio* (hamlet). The *barrio* has an administrative identity with a captain and a council elected by the villagers; the *sitio*, as in most countries, is an emanation of the village and, for all purposes, forms part of the whole.

Even at the establishment of the Commonwealth, all adult male Filipinos, if not precluded for some judicial reason, were already voters and in 1937 the women, after a national female plebiscite, joined the men. Today all citizens of twenty-one and over form part of the electoral college and, under the terms of the 1935 Constitution, they selected a varied and numerous set of temporary rulers, some of whom, in their turn, had the power to retain or dispense with a series of appointed officials: these were very often replaced by men of the same political party as the majority. National elections took place every two years, but the President, the Vice President, and the members of the Lower House (the House of Representatives) were elected every four years and for a term of four years. The interim election was for one-third of the seats in the Upper House (the Senate) and for the provincial and local posts: this is where a degree of uncoordinated, personally directed political violence showed itself.

Under the same constitution the administration of the Philippines was composed of three main elements: the executive, the legislature, and the judiciary. To these were added two independent bodies, the Commission on Elections and the General Audit Office. The executive consisted of a President, with wide personal powers to initiate and to veto, a Vice President, who automatically replaced him at death or after a successful impeachment, and a cabinet. The legislature was made up of the two Houses of Congress: the Senate numbering twenty-four members elected for a six-year term, one-third being replaced bi-annually, and the House of Representatives having a legal membership of one hundred and twenty, each representative being chosen by an electoral district. The judiciary consisted of a Supreme Court, a Court of Appeals, Courts of First Instance, Municipal Courts, and local benches staffed by Justices of the Peace. The Commission on Elections had a chairman and two members, each appointed by the President for a nine-year term, but being replaced singly at three-year intervals. The General Audit Office was controlled by an Auditor-General who was assisted by a staff of officials deployed in territorial groups over the country.

The constitution which provided for all this was that drafted in 1934 and 1935 in preparation for the establishment of the Commonwealth. It provided for the interim régime and for a fully independent republic at the end of a statutory period of ten years. In spirit it drew much from the Constitution of the United States, but echoes of the old Malolos Constitution of 1899 and of liberal foreign statutes can also be found. In the more practical clauses defining the powers of the President and of the remainder of the administration, it followed the American document very closely. The President's wide powers of execution and veto, of making appointments, of command over the armed forces, and of dispensing with normal rule in time of emergency were features of this: the separation of power, broadly extending planning and execution to a wide range of government departments (or bureaus), and the inclusion of the two independent bodies at a high level were equally in accordance with American practice.

Two other points were of major importance: the power of impeachment and the duties of the Commission on Appointments. The first was of academic interest only, for no official has so far been dismissed by this procedure. Nevertheless, such power was formalized and any elected or appointed official from the President downwards could be tried by the Senate as a collegiate court. The Commission on Appointments, however, was an active body. Its field was wide, for the number of posts filled by straight appointment was considerable, covering a broad range of duties. Senior armed and civil service officers, ambassadors, members of the Commission on Elections, the Auditor-General, and the senior justices are some of those whose posts were confirmed by this method, although it was the President, with the Commission's consent, who personally held the actual power of appointment.

In all, the 1935 Constitution seemed to be a happy marriage of those well-tried democratic institutions, so deeply rooted in North America, and a certain eclecticism manifested by an essentially liberally directed Filipino intelligentsia. In the event, its requirement to be served by elements which obeyed a relatively tight code of public discipline led to its downfall and, as we shall see, it has latterly given place to a more hastily conceived, more summary statute which is no longer based on the checks and balances of a long-term political evolution.

President Marcos's 1972 proclamation of martial law and the subsequent replacement of the 1935 Constitution by a new charter is described below (pp. 189–94). Much has already been recorded as comment on this renunciation of the political institutions inherited from the tutelage period; but to understand the present evolution towards this more direct form of government, the essentials of the earlier party structure must be examined.

The political parties of the republic have rarely been more than two in number, although a third did appear from time to time to pioneer a more progressive policy and advocate action against corruption and coercion. When this was the case, the number of seats obtained by the third element was rarely large enough to create a threat to the majority and some sort of accommodation was generally arranged. It is a feature of the organization of suffrage and the two-party system that power almost always changed over after each major election, bringing with it a new President and cabinet. This was not so when Ferdinand Marcos was elected for a second term in 1969. He was the first President to have been re-elected and to serve for eight years, although, during the Commonwealth, President Quezon was chosen for a second term in 1941.

The two major political parties are the Nacionalistas and the Liberals. The Nacionalistas have had a long history in the various legislatures since the 1907 Assembly. The Liberals embody what is spiritually an opposition to the Nacionalistas, inheriting this standpoint from the Democrats. The party was formed by Manuel Roxas and Elpidio Quirino in 1946, after their split from the main Nacionalista group, of which they were important members. All three parties have had similar policies, manifestly conservative in character. The Democrats no longer have a separate identity, but survivors of the old group can be found in the two other parties.

In addition to these officially recognized groups, the Communist Party (KPP – Komunist Partido sa Pilipinas) has always had a following among a distinct minority of the intelligentsia of Greater Manila and the larger towns, and in the rural communities of a well-defined sector of central Luzon: this, with its centre around Tarlac and Pampanga provinces, stretches out into the neighbouring Nueva Ecija and some growth into Bulacan, Zambales, Pangasinan, and Isabela has taken place over the years. Philippine official policy towards this party has run from recognition, with the seating of a Communist in the Lower House in 1948, to an all-out shooting war. Overall, although much has been bungled in the fight against the now illegal organization, repressive policies have been successful. The Communist Party was formed in the Philippines between the two wars and is a direct result of the Soviet political policy of expansion, exemplified in the Comintern. Concentrated in Manila and the lowland areas to the north, its programme was linked to land reform; this among a rural population which, without doubt, had suffered there more than in most parts of the country. Unrest and violence accompanied the party's operations in the 1930s and neither has been absent for long since. As recorded earlier, the Communists set up their own resistance force (the Huks) in the struggle with the Japanese and followed a policy of exclusion, often showing themselves dangerously hostile to the more liberal-minded anti-Japanese groups around them. When the 1946 elections took place, they mounted a campaign of political coercion and won two seats. After a blow-hot, blow-cold period in the time of Presidents Roxas and Quirino, during which a Communist representative, Luis Taruc, was allowed to take his seat in 1948, the government decided to wage an all-out war against the party. Once again it was declared illegal and to the accompaniment of murders and atrocities on one side and military field operations on the other, a long-drawn-out struggle took place, not only in the traditional Communist areas, but in other parts of the country where infiltration had taken place.[1] After this trial of strength, the government security organization succeeded firstly in containing the Huks (as they are popularly referred to still[2]) and later in breaking up their groups. Political policies, including land reform and a resettlement scheme for those Communists who submitted, were introduced and the fighting soon dropped to the lower tempo at which it stands today. The Communists still control some part of their old areas, but they rarely come into the open to allow the government forces to strike at them. Today, with links to China and a considerably diluted practice of their earlier faith, they still manage to constitute a security menace and, at the time of elections, they throw their weight behind the highest bidder. They undoubtedly have a liaison with some Filipino politicians and from time to time conspiracies are unearthed. As a political weapon in itself, the party has today a diminished direct influence, but it does attempt to suborn and to infiltrate both the bourgeois left-wing and the workers' organizations (students, schoolteachers, artisans), who themselves still constitute pressure groups in a country where the major political parties had such similar policies and where political activity has considerably diminished.

The Filipino people numbered 27,087,685 in 1960 and may well be more than 40 million after the census of 1972. Those speaking a Christian Malay dialect as a mother tongue make up 90 per cent of this population and it can safely be said that the overwhelming majority is ethnically Malay, professing Christianity. The Moslem element in 1960 was recorded as 1,317,475 or just over 5½ per cent. The majority of the latter is ethnically Malay also. This leaves approximately 5 per cent who belong to an ethnic minority, but here the Chinese population must be considered, for 0.5 per cent of the whole population is recorded as speaking Chinese and must therefore be deducted from the really indigenous majority. To the 0.5 per cent who stated that they still used their own mother tongue must be added an unknown figure, possibly 100,000 or more, who are Chinese, but for one reason or another professed to speak a Malay Christian dialect at the time of the census-taking.

Education is of immense importance to the Filipino and a large network of primary schools exist. It is indicative that, when touring the dusty unsurfaced roads in the more remote municipalities, the easiest way of identifying a *barrio* – or even a *sitio* – is by the name proudly displayed over the local schoolhouse door. The priestly primary establishments which existed in earlier times have given way to the state-run 'public' schools, although some religious-controlled elementary teaching continues in the municipalities. Secondary education is generally centred on the municipality. Colleges and universities, both private and state-administered, are to be found in the larger regional centres, with by far the greatest concentration in Greater Manila itself. Primary education at the local *barrio* schools starts at the age of six and, with an extra intermediate grade inserted in some of the more favoured schools, goes on until the child is twelve or thirteen. The biggest fall-out is reached before Grade 7 (thirteen years of age) where the number of such classes, normally reserved for children who are not to attend high school, is small, mainly because of a lack of demand, as a child of that age often returns home to assist his parents in their everyday life with six years of primary education behind him.[3] Secondary education should last four years; the first two are a continuation of the teaching in the primaries; the third and fourth, in theory, produce two streams, those of technical and academic preparation. There are, however, separate vocational training schools at this level and, in these, technical courses of four years are designed to take young people from the primary stage to an entry point in trade or artisanship. The national language, Filipino[4] (the name given to Tagalog), is taught in the first grades of primary school, the mother tongue being retained at this stage as the medium of instruction. English is also introduced early and is already partly used as a medium of instruction in Grade 3 (age eight to nine). University or college courses last for variable periods, as will be seen below. Of the total population of over nine years of age in 1960 (17,945,872), 4,211,315 had never completed one year's formal schooling. The highest non-attendance rate was, understandably, among the twenty-five-year-olds and over (3,157,015).

Higher education is in the hands of both the state and private bodies. Apart from the five state universities, there are seven 'normal' colleges for teacher-training and a number of specialized institutions, including the Philippine Merchant Marine Academy. The private sector of higher education has a considerable stake in the formation of young men and women for technical, commercial, and professional careers. Under the broad control of the Bureau of Private Schools, these institutions can be either religious or lay. The religious establishments are generally those which functioned under Spain, although additions and extensions have been made. The Ateneo of Manila and the University of Santo Tomás have the longest traditions, but there has been a wide expansion in the vocational training system, with the Don Bosco colleges filling an important gap in technical instruction. All the non-religious colleges work on a commercial basis and many run courses round the clock, so that some students can earn a salary during the day and can then put in five or six hours at lectures or with tutors. Some are more commercial than others and, with branches in the provinces, can constitute 'diploma mills'. This is a grave danger in present-day society; the best graduates having little trouble in maintaining international standards where a relatively high proportion of students attain little but mediocrity and have difficulty in earning a living acceptable to a white-collar worker in their own country.

Two further points must now be mentioned. The first is the difficulty for the Filipino to absorb a higher education taught, in the main, in English, a medium which, although not basically a foreign tongue, is for most students a second language. The other point is the definition of literacy and the proportion of literates in the country. The language difficulty is a real one. Although with great foresight the authorities have insisted that much of a student's higher education must be carried out through the medium of a major world language, American-English, a really full understanding of this vehicle is rare at the start of a graduate course and may never be satisfactory, even at the end of three years' higher study. As American occupation becomes more remote and Philippine culture diversifies, American-English not only evolves in a Philippine *ambiance*, but also takes second place to the mother tongue of the student and often to

Filipino (Tagalog), which is taught from the first grade at the primary school. There is, of course, a mixed formula, the Tagalog aside to complement the English-language textbook, but the result is not uniformly a happy one. The second point, literacy in the Philippines, is an environmental adaptation and not an educational standard. Officially it is defined as the ability of a person to read and write a simple message in any one language or dialect. In the census, only citizens of ten and over were examined. Of these, 72 per cent were considered literate: a high standard for any Asian country but corresponding to tradition, for, even in Spanish times when schooling was anything but universal, children taught themselves to count, read and write the alphabet, and compose simple phrases, all for the fun of doing so.

Under the 1935 and 1973 constitutions, freedom of religious practice is guaranteed. As in most countries, there is a varied mixture of beliefs. They range from the pagan traditions still alive among the remoter tribes, including the more evolved codes of conduct which prevail in the Luzon Mountains, to much of the whole range of the world's major faiths. The overwhelming majority of the country at the 1960 census was Christian, the figures showing an inter-denominational total of 94 per cent. A little under 84 per cent of the whole population professed Roman Catholicism; the diminishing Aglipayan sect, a national Church whose religious practices are close to the Roman, accounted for 5.2 per cent; Protestants, generally of a North American persuasion, for 2.9 per cent; and the *Iglesia Ni Kristo* (the INK) for the remainder. The latter is growing in size and already constitutes a social phenomenon, claiming today a million or more adherents (though the number is not proven). As well as being a religious cult, it is a symbol of social solidarity and of a predominantly middle-class way of life. Well organized, with a good proportion of lay officials, who personally keep members aware of collective requirements, it appeals to its congregations both as a belief and as a communal venture. Islam, with a little over 1.5 million adherents, accounted for 5.6 per cent of the total. There were approximately 60,000 Buddhists and a little over half a million 'others', the majority of whom were the pagans of the ethnic minorities, living in their traditional areas and treated in their time by both the American and national governments with understanding and a sense of objectivity.

Culture comes from a variety of sources. In colonial times, only the pagan minorities lived in the unmolested, traditional way which their ancestors had maintained for centuries before, the Christian and Moslem populations being strongly influenced by the outsiders who had brought these two religions with them. Since the end of

Spanish rule a greater awareness of a Malay inheritance has been apparent, although, because of environment, the rural and fishing communities had never lost the folklore which tradition had passed down by the spoken word. During the Commonwealth, and latterly, under the republic, this common background has been fostered and a certain Pan-Malayanism encouraged, making common cause with the ways of life of the true indigenous population of Indonesia and Malaysia. This similarity is more apparent in the non-urban populations where superstition and popular lore have never been completely displaced, either by beliefs or by codes of conduct imported from outside. Although these older and wider under-currents should not be exaggerated, it is a feature of life in the Archipelago that, despite the continuous efforts made by Christian and Moslem missionaries over the centuries, the two worldwide faiths as practised here have been curiously tempered with a regionalism contributed by these adaptable people. But if the purity of such alien importations has been somewhat diluted, particularly in the less-developed areas, the ancient Philippine way of life has been considerably enriched by external influences. The two major religious communities have emerged from colonialism with an outlook which is attractively eclectic, the Christian drawing from the Iberian and, to a lesser degree, from the North American, world and the Moslem from Arabian, Indian, and East Indian sources. So far as the liberal arts are concerned, despite the exclusivity of Spanish colonial policy, there is little doubt that the Christian element, even in proportion to its size, has produced more than the Islamic, a by-product of the latter's abhorrence of certain graphic portrayals which has left a curious vacuum. Even Moslem religious buildings in the Philippines possess little which can be considered as more than the characteristics of a broad influence and of a certain strangeness in a land which is so overwhelmingly Christian. Nevertheless, because of a true love for these arts, both communities maintain and practise a wide repertoire of music and dancing. The garnering and telling of old histories have a real place in the lives of the rural people, particularly in the more remote Christian areas and among the tradition-steeped Moslem families. The pagans also have their music, their dances, and their stories, many of which are based on animist threads. A distinctive and harmonious craftsmanship has been well established in most communities over the ages.

But the Philippines is predominantly Roman Catholic and the Aglipayan element does not differ overmuch from its more numerous neighbour where culture is concerned. Although the bells and the gongs punctuate the music and the dances of the minorities, the graceful, melodious songs and accompaniments, which are the inheritance of an East Indian aptitude infiltrated by Spain, provide much of the enjoyment of a population which has few other distractions in its hard and often unremunerative life. Music and dancing are classless and the graceful formalities of these curiously Mediterranean patterns may be encountered all over those lowland areas which are not Moslem. And this part of Philippine life is in constant evolution, for twentieth-century music and dances, imported from America and Europe, constitute a logical step, where a majority has been exposed to the influences of Western religious and lay music for centuries. It is not strange, therefore, that famous foreign orchestras, theatrical touring companies, and popular groups find packed houses and enthusiastic audiences waiting for them in Manila. To maintain balance, however, cities around the Indian Ocean and the China Sea enthusiastically welcome the gifted Filipino musicians who provide some of the best modern dance music in the world and whose reputation eastwards across the Pacific is already high.

Although their popular base is narrow, painting and sculpture thrive, particularly in circles influenced by Spanish and American custom. Aptitude, except in the case of members of the gifted *mestizo* community, seems to stem from the widely distributed crafts in stone, plaster, and wood which, in the past, were fostered by the priests. In particular, woodwork is traditional, of a high standard, and often of great beauty. The indigenous fabrics made from palm and pineapple fabrics provide a vehicle for an attractive cottage industry, and metalwork, now carrying with it both Indian and Iberian influences, dates back to prehistoric days.

Both the religious and traditional interests described above are of very real importance under the republic. Together with constitutional practices, they make up the treasured heritage of the country. The first two are an amalgam of Malay custom and a centuries-old penetration from outside. The contrasting population elements, the majority, the forceful and vociferous Islamic minority, and the older communities, which, for better or for worse, retain much of their outdated manners, make up a country culturally distant from neighbouring China, Japan, and Korea, more in accord, perhaps, with the peoples of Thailand and the former Indo-Chinese states, and having strong blood links, without any close day-to-day affinity, with the other East Indian peoples. The strong emphasis on religion and culture, which has been officially fostered from the Commonwealth onwards, produces much of the solid conservatism of the Filipino and, although in some left-wing and underground Communist circles efforts are made to counter this mainstream, it shares a place in the grass roots of the country with the traditional husbandry and the awareness of the sea. Successive governments have attempted to draw closer to the republic's Asian and South-East Asian neighbours in a more independently aligned foreign policy, but the Filipino will continue to be sharply different in character from these surrounding countries because of the singularity of his inheritance and because of the continual emphasis which the Establishment places on it. This does not in any way make such a regional alignment impossible, but it does produce many problems of adjustment, the solutions to which could well be, in the future, lessons for many other governments.

Before the proclamation of martial law in 1972, the Press had a privileged position in the Philippines. In many ways it was pampered by the inherited free-for-all traditions introduced during American tutelage and these were later reinforced by the loose political rivalry of the post-war parties. To these elements was added the elemental Philippine desire to show disrespect for authority. Within the limits of the libel laws, criticism, either founded on fact or merely the result of conjecture, was strongly defended as a healthy reaction to the conservatism of the Establishment. The Press was outspoken in comment and convictions, and was also prolific. Four major English dailies with Tagalog counterparts were reinforced by evening papers and a strong contingent of weeklies. By the post-war period, the whole had become an integral part of urban and even rural life: foreign and some elements of national news were made up from agency reports, often used verbatim; a wide choice of gossip and comment, criticism, and suggestion, together with the smallness of an outside staff contribution, made up the character of these publications. Although real news was generally authenticated and editorial comment authoritative and reasonable, the main daily harvest was made up of columnists' contributions and social gossip. Columnists did tend to be partisan, sometimes extremely so and sometimes to the point of emotive fantasy. Little responsibility was accepted by editors for such comment and, although some sort of national awareness was aroused, it was sometimes of an ill-informed and destructive character. Pre-1973 publications were not entirely irresponsible, but it was sometimes difficult to identify a particular publication with the party which nominally controlled it or the individuals who had major interests in it.

In 1971, the Press had already come under considerable fire from the government, which resented its 'non-objectivity', accusing it of 'schizophrenia' and other social maladies. There is little doubt that much of its activities must have been infuriating to an elected administration which depended considerably on the dailies for a good image. If anything, the weeklies, remoter from current facts than their colleagues, tended to be stronger in their speech. In such conditions, with President Marcos well into his second term and becoming more and more sensitive to ill-founded criticism of himself, his family, and government, attempts were made to widen the activity of the official news service. The results were not as positive as was hoped. Despite the Press's maturity and tradition of free speech, it often contributed over-hysterically to delicate political situations. With martial law, censorship was imposed and neither political nor social battles appear at present on the daily stage. With this understandable deterioration in the public's morning entertainment, there have been enormous casualties and the number of papers shrank at one time to a single, meagre, government-controlled shadow of a former galaxy of free-for-all journalistic talent whose character was a joyous agglomerate of North American format and Philippine irreverence.

Despite a measure of acceptance of the necessity for rule by exception, the emasculation of the Press is unpopular, as it did form one of the essential structures of a normal and permanent political struggle in the Philippines. Moreover, it was entertaining, even when hysterical; it often contributed constructive criticism; and, as we have seen, served as a voice for pressure groups in a system where the more important planks of both political parties were almost identical. Its present state is regretted.

The armed forces form an important part of the country's structure and traditions. The Filipino makes an excellent soldier and is naturally a good sailor. In the air, he assimilates his art rapidly and is a remarkably versatile operator. The Americans who trained the pre-war Philippine forces and who fought alongside them during the Second World War, regard them with affection and esteem. Affection because of their loyalty and their progress during the period of apprenticeship and esteem because of their bravery and aptitude. The President is the Commander-in-Chief and he controls the republic's forces indirectly through his Chief of Staff, with the permanent assistance of a Secretary for Defence. There are four elements in the forces: army, constabulary, air force, and navy. All four are well officered and adequately equipped for non-nuclear warfare. Training, discipline, and morale are good, and the organizations are vigorous, sensibly run, and administratively economical. The army, air force, and navy perform the initial tasks of training for war, exercising their possible emergency postures, and assisting in internal security operations, including measures to combat subversion, smuggling, and piracy. The Constabulary, which is the largest of the four, is a mobile gendarmerie with a peace and war role of keeping order and stamping out illegality where local police forces are found to be inadequate. All are loyal to their Commander-in-Chief and the administration of the day, but it would also be correct to say that they have also been loyal to the word and to the spirit of the 1935 Constitution,[5] even if the senior officers were sometimes appointed in circumstances and under conditions which underline the political nature of the system. But if the Constabulary is adequate for its peacetime mission and with reinforcements could probably cope in wartime, the other three services are inadequate for their task. The army would be incapable on its own, even reinforced, of repulsing a determined invasion by a well-armed enemy: the air force is in much the same position, although it could give a good account of itself, as it would probably have the first-line and base support of the United States forces already in the country. The navy is a light patrol force designed for peace and not for war, and it is not of a strength wholly to cover those waters which the Republic Act 3046 declares internal. All this should not detract from the value of the units which exist and which serve their country so well. The problem is not political, but financial. With all the calls made on the budget for schools, social services, the building-up of a public works infrastructure, and a state-directed economy, and where much of the defence budget (about 14 per cent of the whole) goes to the Constabulary, there is little money left to pay more men to do the job and so strengths are insufficient for any important military venture. But the Philippines is a member of SEATO and has a mutual defence pact with the United States which maintains large naval and air force bases in central Luzon.

[1] Particularly in the remote Sierra Madre Mountains east of Manila and in the north-east part of central Panay.

[2] The official title is *Hukbong Mapagalaya Ng Bayan* (the Liberation Army of the People).

[3] Of the 15,275,134 persons who had ever attended school in 1960, only 263,200 had attended Grade 7, but 679,470 had gone on from primary to some sort of secondary education.

[4] The name is sometimes written Pilipino, as in the seventeen-letter alphabet the F's and P's have the same identification.

[5] The proclamation of martial law in September 1972 was well covered by the terms of the 1935 Constitution and the circumstances in which the armed forces accepted such a necessity are examined below, pp. 192–3.

Chapter 15

The Economy

The Economic Tradition

BEFORE THE ANNEXATION of the Philippines by the United States, her economy was essentially colonial and, despite worldwide trade expansion of the last half of the nineteenth century, comparatively sluggish. Based on the production of domestically consumed foodstuffs and a restricted number of marketable items, the whole did little more than cover the needs of the country's own population, and as Spain drained more and more of the convertible proceeds away, there were minimal local reserves available to supplement indigenously produced foodstuffs in times of natural disaster. The Galleon trade, consistently entrepôt in character, continued to function during the first years of the century. Faced with this, Governors-General from Basco's time onwards had encountered great difficulties in replanning the country's fortunes. Certain of their ventures into a broader economy (raw silk and indigo, for example), as we have already seen, were unsuccessful. Of the remainder, sugar-cane, tobacco, abaca, hemp, coconut products, and minerals were produced on a growing scale and these form the bulk of what can now be considered as today's export range.

During most of the American period, free trade between the Philippines and the United States was practised. This favoured position provided incentives. Even before the end of the ten-year period of Spanish privilege[1], American business interests were investing considerable sums in the country. The sugar industry gained by their experience in Puerto Rico and Cuba, mining machinery and engineers were brought in, rope factories were modernized, and the tobacco factors were able to tap a more advantageous market for cigars, leaf, and fillers. Nevertheless, with almost no exception, the economy continued to be based on the same streams; semi-finished or raw materials still being channelled to the mother country, the United States having replaced Spain as the Philippines' major trade partner. However, with the new régime, the nature of commerce was profoundly modified; a vigorous capitalism was introduced and a considerable selective expansion took place; the overall pattern following the normal trend where a highly organized country exploits an underdeveloped one politically subservient to it. This is not to say that the United States consciously practised policies designed to retard a more balanced growth: she followed the same path as the other imperialist nations of the day, providing a competitive market for the world's primary products, her private sector investing large sums both to improve output and to gain control; government policy tending to design regulations to favour communal trade between the countries in its own national sphere of influence. With a large element of the world dominated by Britain, France, and the United States, this system, with subtle modifications injected by the sovereign power in the mid-twentieth century, brought a community of ex-colonial, non-European nations to their independence; their economies still orientated towards those of their former masters, who continued to provide the readiest markets for their primary products, the minimum of processing industries having been established locally. The Philippines, a comparatively recent recruit to this world of dynamic capitalism, with a fair degree of political stability and easy access to the American West Coast ports, attracted a large flow of funds which rapidly made her a perfect example of the system. Despite the period of political transition under the Commonwealth, the economy, although invigorated and streamlined, was already showing an imbalance by the end of the 1930s, a sophisticated and growing middle class demanding the local expenditure of an increasing share of the proceeds available from foreign trade. The destruction and neglect of nearly four years of war and Japanese occupation massively eroded the infrastructure and during the immediate post-war years a continual subservience to American interest maintained the traditional pattern in the major sectors of the economy. Although successive Philippine governments have struggled to set up heavier industrial undertakings, the bulk of exported produce continues to be shipped in an unfinished or semi-finished form.

When the Japanese surrendered in 1945, the country was largely in ruins. The transportation system, with its roads, bridges, and ferries, its railways, inter-island vessels, and harbours, had all been partially or completely destroyed. Sugar-mills were derelict, their light railways and embarkation facilities unusable. Mining equipment was largely inoperative and the systems formerly used to transport the raw material or the partially treated ore to points of shipment were almost completely lacking or had been summarily patched up and were fairly ineffective. The few light industries set up during the Commonwealth were equally undermined. Electricity supply was quite insufficient for more than restricted domestic purposes and public transport almost non-existent. As time went by, Japanese reparations and United States War Damage compensation and grants in aid were received in the Philippines and these slowly became available to re-equip the country. At first, short-term measures were adopted to patch up, so as to get both the infrastructure and the production facilities back into some sort of operation. Then, with the importing of specialized machinery and plant, rebuilding started. Transportation and electricity supply took a major slice, but the sugar-mills and the mines were not forgotten. Nevertheless, in those first years of independence, with the Trade Act and the Laurel-Langley Agreement coming into force, little movement from the pre-war pattern was encouraged and, although the light consumer industry quickly recovered, expanded, and prospered, the bulk of the Philippines' sugar continued to be exported to the United States in a centrifugal condition[2], minerals were shipped in the same state as before, and, with the exception of a small range of manufactured goods, such as cigars and cordage, the other items were sent overseas to service the industries of the world's developed countries.

The Trade Act and the Laurel-Langley Agreement, entered into mutually by the Philippines and the United States, are of major interest in any analysis of the post-war economy. The Trade Act, ratified in 1946, extended the earlier practice of free exchange between the two countries into the first years of Philippine independence. The Laurel-Langley Agreement, negotiated in 1954, formalized the pattern of commercial relations for the period from 1 January 1956 until mid-1974. A generous sugar import quota was granted by the United States and this carried with it purchase at premium prices. Since those days, free-trade conditions have slowly been whittled down by the provisions of the latter treaty, modifications being phased into the end of each three-year period of its existence with an increase of import duties for each partner's goods entering the other's territory. The increases are expressed as a percentage of total duty normally levied: 5 per cent was charged for the first period from 1 January 1956, 10 per cent for the next three-year cycle, 20 per cent and 40 per cent respectively for the third and fourth periods, until 80 per cent was reached on 1 January 1971. On 1 January 1974 a hundred per cent tariff will come into force and the trade agreement will lapse in mid-1974, unless it is renewed in some way by future negotiation. Americans also enjoy certain privileges in these packet deals, the most important being the right to own land and property, exploit natural resources, and to take part in retail trade, all of which are closed to other foreign nationals resident in the Philippines. Moreover, American-owned capital in

Philippines-based companies is at present classified as indigenous. This and the fact that such companies must contain a 60 per cent indigenous equity produce an almost unreal situation at a time when the life period of the Agreement is approaching fulfilment.

There is little doubt that the two trade treaties have done much to assist post-war recovery. An advantageous commercial climate was established early and the maintenance of a large and often favourable seller's market, which remained singularly preferential until the end of 1967, has been of immense value in the development of the country's embryo industries, not only producing a buoyancy, but giving both overseas and domestic investors opportunities in the traditional range of production. Nevertheless, although coconut products, timber, and minerals may well continue to sell advantageously on a wide market, the sugar-cane industry will be extremely vulnerable if the benefits of the Laurel-Langley Agreement are not continued in some measure or other after 1974. World prices would result in certain bankruptcy if the low production rates and the high costs of operations in the Philippines continue to be maintained. Here and in the broad lines of the economy, still in large part based on the production of staple foodstuffs and a restricted range of export items, the treaties have tended to assist the continuance of an outdated way of life which the Garcia, Macapagal, and Marcos governments have energetically planned to disturb.

Food Staples

Only highly organized, industrial countries can allow themselves the luxury of importing a large element of their foodstuffs from outside, exploiting favourable conditions overseas to purchase a wide and interesting range of dietary items. In less developed countries, this is not normally possible unless the financial proceeds of some exceptional activity, such as oil production or the mining of precious metals and stones, can support a relatively small population. The Philippines falls into neither of these categories and, moreover, she has a rapidly expanding population to feed. The imperative is to produce as much of her staple foodstuffs as possible and to devote any surplus currency to other sections of the economy, especially the undercapitalized ones in the transportation and manufacturing range. It is in these conditions that the two main food staples, rice and maize, are produced, and where these are not immediately consumed by the grower, they are purchased, distributed, and retailed to the population at controlled prices. In addition to rice and maize, fish and root vegetables are also most important in this context.

Rice is grown over more than $3\frac{1}{3}$ million of the country's $7\frac{1}{2}$ million hectares of used farmland and nearly 80 per cent of the

1 The Santo Niño, a Christ-child figurine believed to have been brought to the Philippines by Magellan. After his death, it was probably accepted by the people of Cebu as a rain god. Since Legaspi's capture of the city, it has been venerated there in the church of Santo Niño

2 Fort Santiago Gate, Intramuros, Manila

3 The University of Santo Tomás, founded by the Dominicans in 1611
4 Miag-Ao church, Iloilo. Its design is a mixture of Philippine and Spanish Baroque. The façade shows a native St Christopher under a papaya tree

5 Emilio Aguinaldo (1869–1964)

6 Luis Manuel Quezon (1878–1944)

7 Manuel Roxas (1892–1948)

8 Elpidio Quirino (1890–1956)

9 President Ramon Magsaysay (1907–57; *fourth from left, front*) at an academic ceremony with his wife (*fourth from right*) and Mgr Rufino J. Santos (*third from left*), archbishop of Manila
10 Emilio Aguinaldo joining hands with President Diosdado Macapagal (b. 1910) at the new Independence Day celebrations on 12 June 1962

11 Mrs Imelda Marcos arriving at London airport in September 1970 with her son Ferdinand jr

12 Philippine war veterans marching on Independence Day 1972
13 The mayor of Makati (*facing microphone*), Rizal province, presiding at a *barangay* in January 1973 to approve President Marcos's new constitution

14 President Ferdinand Marcos (b. 1917) signing the final draft of the new constitution at the Malacañang Palace, Manila, on 17 January 1973

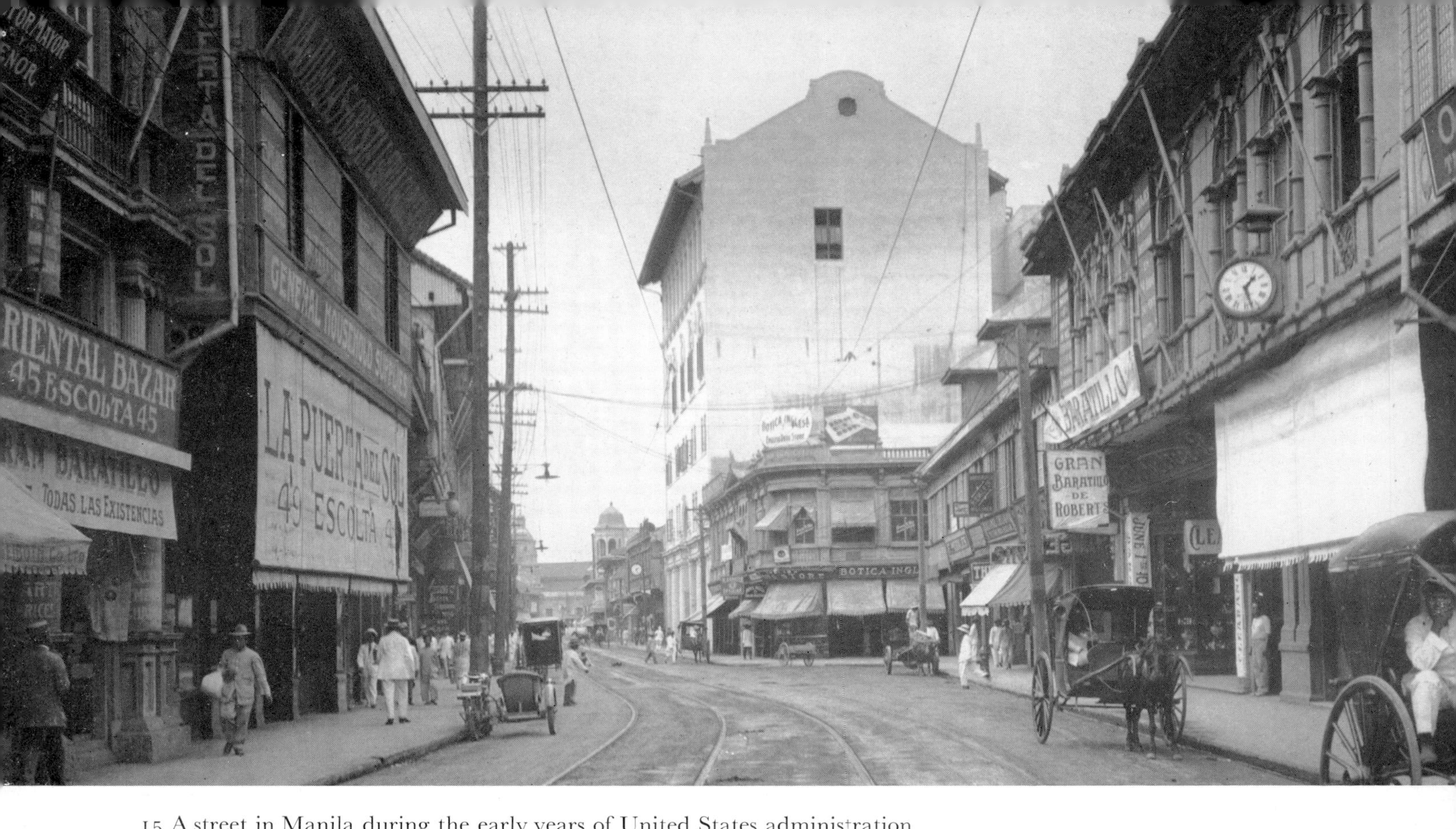

15 A street in Manila during the early years of United States administration

16 Roxas Boulevard on Manila Bay

17 Ayala Avenue, Makati, the new business and commercial centre close to Manila

18 The monument to José Rizal in Rizal Park, Manila

19 Rice terraces in the mountains of north Luzon

20 Refugees from the eruption of Taal volcano, Luzon, in September 1965

21 The so-called Chocolate Hills, Bohol

22 Talutasangay mosque, near Zamboanga
23 Houses on the island of Siasi, Sulu, built out over the sea through lack of space in the town. They belong to the Badjaos, sea nomads of Sulu and Mindanao, who are animists and excellent pearl-divers

24 Badjao children of Sanga Sanga, Sulu
25 Women, wearing the *malong*, at a Moslem wedding in the south

26 The Mayon volcano and the town of Legaspi, Albay province

population consumes this cereal as its preferred staple. It is grown as a lowland (wet) or upland (dry) crop, although irrigation can change this arbitrary division. Nevertheless, the existing availability of water for agricultural purposes is limited and less than 10 per cent of the total farmland in use at the 1960 Census was reported as irrigated. It is a time-consuming husbandry, the young shoots being planted by hand and the cultivation of most of the rice-lands being carried out with hand tools and the *carabao*- (water buffalo) drawn plough. Despite the efforts of the Rockefeller Institute at Los Banos, a few kilometres south of Manila, the Philippines has dragged her feet for many years, the lessons taught in this international establishment being heeded more in Thailand, Formosa, and Indonesia than in the host country. Yields in the 1950s were at an average of 1.21 metric tons per hectare against 2.84 in Formosa and 2.19 in Malaya. The import of rice to feed the rapidly growing population of the Philippines had to be undertaken during most of the post-war period, at least 10 per cent of the annual consumption being obtained from elsewhere at a cost of nearly £2 million annually. The use of fertilizers to increase production in these overworked lands was rare, but even the cost of this added refinement and of the various insecticides necessary to produce a higher yield was generally prohibitive to the farmer who had little or no capital to allow for the improvement of his methods of husbandry. The low annual yields of upland rice, the lack of irrigation and of technical facilities, and the fragmentation caused by the land-tenure system kept down the overall production figures in this poorly capitalized section of the national economy and output in a rapidly increasing community tended to lag behind the demands of consumption. This gloomy picture was altered in 1969: the cultivation of the various strains of high-productivity rice, developed at Los Banos, was at last popularized and, with the help of an increased use of fertilizers, self-sufficiency was once again reached and a modest export surplus obtained. Despite the damage caused to standing rice and maize during the typhoons of 1970, the 1970–71 crop also produced self-sufficiency and even a marginal surplus. Nevertheless, at present there is very limited flexibility here: although there has been a small increase in the overall area under paddy and improved seed is being used more and more, the majority of the rice-fields rely on the rain brought into the Philippines by monsoons and tropical depressions. Irrigation is still only practised over a very limited area and the use of balanced fertilizers is equally restricted. The advantages of the newly evolved seed and its subsequent generations can only at present reach an optimum where irrigation and fertilizers are used; so much of the land remains cultivated in a fairly inefficient fashion. This would not necessarily result in any grave problem in itself, but the massive population explosion in the Philippines at an increase rate of about one million annually, will almost certainly negate the favourable production : consumption ratio in a country where only small amounts of additional capital have found their way usefully into this important sector of the nation's life.

Maize (corn as it is called both indigenously and in the United States) is consumed as a main staple by a little more than 20 per cent of the population. On much of the 2 million hectares of land used for its production, two crops a year can be obtained from the benefits of a normal rainfall incidence in the growing areas. Maize is fractionally more advantageous as a dietetic product and retails more cheaply than rice. Because of its adaptability, lands which can only be considered as marginal often support family crops and, since the 1940–45 War, the area planted with this cereal has almost doubled. Nevertheless, low productivity dogs the industry and much has to be done to increase efficiency. Incentive is not so strong here as in the rice sector, for the overall increase in maize consumption is far less than in the former. Moreover, as social conditions improve, rice often becomes the daily staple for families coming from the maize-consuming areas. Government agencies tasked to improve cultivation oversee conditions in both the rice and maize sectors and have tended to operate in the larger cereal-producing areas. Maize is very often the crop of the small holding and of the domestic plot, and, although improved seed has been evolved, is available, and advice on better cultivation methods can be obtained, all these often pass the smaller farmer by. Nevertheless, in good years, surpluses have been produced and, without prejudice to the principle of self-sufficiency, quite a substantial tonnage goes to factories manufacturing starch, oil, glucose, and gluten, thus relieving the economy of the need to import large quantities of these finished commodities.

Sweet potatoes, cassava, taro, and yams are consumed by almost 2 per cent of the population as a food staple and are grown on approximately 4 per cent of the land under cultivation. As the growing areas are generally those where these vegetables are consumed, packaging and transportation are simplified: small local surpluses go to urban areas where they are used to broaden an essentially simple family diet.

The last element of domestic food production is fishing. Deep-sea fishing is poorly covered and here there are very few Philippine vessels operating. The majority of the overall catch is made up of anchovies, sardines, croakers, grunts, and other tropical fish found in the coastal waters around the shores of the island groups. But an important part of the nation's diet is made up from inshore and pond catches: the inshore activities are very generalized, fishing from beaches being an occupation and a pastime for many families living within easy reach of the sea, and in the Philippines, this constitutes a good proportion of the population. Pond cultivation is much more specialized and is a rapidly growing commerce. Fishponds have been constructed immediately adjacent to the coastline and are entirely dependent on the entry of salt or brackish water for the enclosed cultivation of milk fish (bangas), shrimps, crabs, small eels, and mullet. About 150,000 hectares of land have already been taken over and this has increased the overall coastal catch, which is still comparatively small on account of the narrow land shelves all over the area and the great depths encountered immediately off the Pacific and Mindanao shorelines. Traditionally a fish-eater, the Filipino has always made great use of marine products to diversify his diet, but the country can no longer maintain itself with domestic catches. So great is this habit that large quantities of tinned and processed fish are imported regularly, much being obtained from such politically undesirable sources as the Republic of South Africa. From £2 million to £3 million of valuable foreign currency are expended annually on such overseas purchases, normally made on a government agency basis. Despite this seeming extravagance, supplies of domestically produced and imported fish items contribute a relatively cheap protein addition to the diet of all classes, and in conditions where meat and poultry are rarely eaten by the poorer families, small quantities of fish are used quite frequently.

The Export Group

Coconut products normally lead all other exportable commodities (though in 1972 they were outstripped by forest products; see table, below, p. 228) and, with their growing worldwide industrial use, will probably continue to figure as a major Philippine earner of foreign currency for many years to come, although from time to time natural calamities and disease reduce the output for a period of one or two years. The coconut palm is ubiquitous in the Archipelago and, even where the destruction of rain forest through indiscriminate felling has caused erosion, as in the island of Cebu in the Visayas, the palm flourishes. An estimated 1½ million hectares were covered with this tree at the time of the 1960 Census, and there were some 200 million counted. These figures are given as an indication, as their accuracy is suspect for many reasons. Moreover, land planted with the palm is often used for extensive interline cultivation in season. Nevertheless, the coconut is an ideal subject for many parts of the country. There is often adequate moisture for continuous cropping, enough sun to dry the copra naturally,[3] and the tree can be planted on land where gradients preclude other types of vegetation. The coconut palm is reared as a seedling and takes some fifteen years to reach maturity, although production starts at between six and eight years of age. In these conditions, replanting programmes are easily managed. In addition, little real infrastructure is required to support the industry. Dried copra is bought by a local merchant, often a Chinese who services the farmer with loans. It is transported on trucks to local warehouses from where it is either shipped directly overseas or sent to a larger point of concentration for shipping or for fuller processing into oil or shred. By far the largest proportion (over 90 per cent until 1967) goes for shipment as raw copra, but the number of mills and processing factories is increasing in the Philippines and a percentage of the output is exported in the form of coconut oil, dessicated coconut, and copra cake or meal.

Normal markets for Philippine coconut products have been the United States, Japan, and western Europe, particularly Holland, Britain, and West Germany. Because of growing competition from Ceylon, Indonesia, and South Africa, who, if anything, produce a better-processed commodity (much of it sun dried), the Philippine government is at present looking outside its traditional markets and in 1969, for the first time, a shipment was authorized to a Communist country when 500 tons of coconut oil were released to Bulgaria. This is an example of the present government's policy of broadening trade relations to replace the structure which has resulted from American pre-war investment and the framework of the Trade Act and the Laurel-Langley Agreement. At present, little is gained in this sector from the terms of the preferential tariffs contained in the Laurel-Langley Agreement.

Forest products are of immense value and, with sugar-cane derivatives and minerals, make up the bulk of Philippine exports. The vast rain forests of the Sierra Madre in east Luzon and of the mountain areas of the island of Mindanao produce some of the world's most beautiful wood and a good proportion of the lower grades of hardwood used in the construction industry. The United States and Japan take the bulk of this commodity, in the form either of logs or veneer. The major part of concessions granted by the government have been to local contractors or to larger undertakings controlled by American capital. Many of the former are Chinese operated. Saw-mills are set up adjacent to points of shipment and timber is brought down, often to be concentrated in a log pond inshore and then loaded on to freighters moored as near as possible. Some mills have veneer factories adjacent and shipments are made directly to overseas countries. Philippine wood is generally processed into plank form in the receiving countries, but much of the better lengths are turned into veneer after export, especially in Japan. The exploitation of timber concessions brings in an important percentage of foreign earnings, but there are already some inbuilt evils within the industry. Where primary forests have been cleared, replanting with seedlings and saplings can guarantee a permanency for the industry and protect the area and the countryside around from erosion and from detrimental changes in micro-climate. But there are two major enemies to this fairly simple system of *roulement*. The first is the unscrupulous entrepreneur who fells, extracts, and abandons; the second is the farmer who follows in the wake of the logger and who burns, plants, reaps for two or three years and then, in his turn, abandons the area. In many cases, where the larger logging companies have carried out reforestation, the primitive farmer arrives to destroy the vegetation cover required by the tree in its first years and he often burns the young trees themselves. Although the Philippines still contains enormous tracts of unexploited primary forest, considerable damage has already been done and will continue to be done as the abandoned areas turn into secondary jungle. As the logging concessions are extremely remote, control is difficult, almost impossible, reliance being placed on the felling entrepreneur. In such conditions, the current rate of production cannot be maintained indefinitely and the continuance of the industry during the next century relies totally on the success of reforestation today. In 1970, forest products came second in the list of exports; in 1972 they were first; and there seems to be no limit to the market for high-grade wood. Nor at present does there seem to be a drop in demand for the cheap hardwoods used in industry. It would be a great tragedy if this most important element of the Philippine economy died out because of a lack of scruple and control, but despite government attempts to hold down felling at a constant rather than increased rate, an annual renewal of licences tempts holders to extract as much as possible within the period so as to provide against a possible withdrawal of concessions.

The sugar industry forms a homogeneous group, producing centrifugal and refined sugar, molasses, and alcohol. The industry is predominantly of a colonial tradition, the present Centrals,[4] with few exceptions, being the direct descendants of those set up in Spanish and American times. The number of centrals tended to diminish over the years, only the most viable making sufficient profit to pay their way in a climate where salaries and infrastructure and transportation costs have been mounting rapidly. The sugar-producing areas of the Philippines are grouped traditionally, central Luzon and the Visayas being the major concentrations. Sugar-cane is harvested over much of the year and the centrals normally have long-term agreements with the farmers which include financial aid, collection details, and seasonal planting dates so that the mill can spread operations fairly equitably over the whole of its production period. Thus the central manager must be an agricultural co-ordinator and a mill overseer at the same time. Mills produce centrifugal sugar and molasses for export and alcohol for the domestic and foreign markets. In rare cases, such as Victorias on Negros, refined sugar is produced for domestic consumption. Sugar-mills are expensive projects with little or no flexibility, and the ancillary shipping facilities are almost as costly to set up and operate in this island nation. Light railways have been laid down in the majority of cases and these bring cane in from the collecting points to which it has been brought by truck or buffalo-drawn cart and evacuate centrifugal sugar, molasses, and alcohol to shipment points on the nearby coastline. In some centrals, those generally set up or refurbished in later years, trucks replace light railways. In central Luzon and on Panay, broad-gauge railways, operated by the government, carry centrifugal sugar and the liquid derivatives to major ports. Shipment overseas is made from bulk terminals with deep-water wharves and modern handling plant. Guimaras Island in the Iloilo Strait handles much of Negros's sugar and all of Panay's, also accepting consignments from the more distant islands of Leyte and Cebu. All is brought by lighter from trans-shipment points; in the case of Panay, from the broad-gauge railway siding at Iloilo port and in that of the others from small sugar-wharves, normally served by the light railways adjacent to the centrals themselves. Other bulk terminals exist, at Palupandan on Negros and on Manila Bay itself, but there is little difference between their operations and those at Guimaras. Normally, all centrifugal sugar for export goes to the United States, but some of the molasses is despatched to Japan. The United States continues to pay a support price well above world market rates for Philippine raw sugar which is generally refined on her West Coast. This is a major factor in the Philippine economy and, as we have seen, contains the germs of a major adjustment when the Laurel-Langley Agreement terminates in 1974. The present sugar industry not only lives on such advantageous terms – the same enjoyed by United States domestic production – but for very practical reasons, lacks any inbuilt incentive to expand, as the United States quota allocated to the Philippines is passed down to individual mills and, with few exceptions, remains much the same from year to year, although the exclusion of Cuba in 1961 did bring in a bonus. Sugar producers and their associates, the stevedoring companies which take a large share of global turnover by operating the bulk terminals and the tug and lighter trade, have relied massively on this exceptional sellers' market and would normally only be persuaded to expand their costly infrastructures if world prices increased or if some sort of subvention was offered. Although the domestic market is covered by government allocations which, in turn, are added to the quotas of individual centrals, any planned increases so far executed have been generally designed to cover deficits in the annual availability used to fill the quota and domestic requirements. Nevertheless, some expansion outside these restricted lines is now taking place and new centrals have been constructed, their utility being at present marginal. Politically they can be used to counter the stagnation caused by the almost complete reliance of the Philippine sugar industry on United States interests in the country and the quota allocated at premium rates. In good years, a small surplus of centrifugal sugar could be produced and in mediocre times the sugar industry obtains sales for all its production in a milieu enjoying above the world market prices. Cane derivatives bring in substantial sums of foreign currency, but in both good and mediocre years net earnings have remained favourable: in such conditions any major shift from supported prices would bring with it upheaval. With its present quota system, its fixed and costly infrastructure, and its long-term farmers' agreements, manoeuvre is difficult. Much of the sugar land lends itself to the cultivation of rice paddy, but change would bring with it concrete problems: farmers' agreements run out piecemeal and a fragmentation of land usage would follow in the short term if change was to take place; rice surpluses are growing in South-East Asia and with each country's arrival at a degree of self-sufficiency, markets shrink. In these conditions, returns from rice sales are now no longer always favourable and, in these changing circumstances, it must be seen whether sugar or rice is the most advantageous crop to sell on the world markets. With the run-out of United States tariff agreements before 1974, all these factors will come into the foreground, although with the conservative character of Philippine farming traditions and the capital sunk into an inflexible part of the economy, a considerable dislocation could well ensue.

Mining is anything but homogeneous, but it does possess a number of constant factors. Equipment is costly, engineering personnel are often expatriates or national expatriates, most of the raw ore, pig, or concentrates are shipped overseas, and prices are governed by world demand. Nevertheless, the widespread range of these commodities does bring with it self-compensation, for the Philippines produces copper, iron, manganese, chromite, silver, zinc, and quicksilver as well as some gold, either mined as a primary product or, with silver, refined out as a by-product of the copper plants. In the last few years, deposits of ferrous aluminium bearing laterite have been prospected and full-scale exploitation could commence fairly soon. Nickel is also present in the same areas and studies continue with the more industrialized countries to find common ground for a well-balanced exploitation.[5] Of the non-metallic commodities, pyrites are generally the by-products of the copper-mines. Other valuable deposits exist, particularly sulphur and silicate, but little is exploited because of a lack of capital and the present depressed state of world markets. Coal is found in the Bicol, on Cebu, and in south-west Mindanao, but only those deposits on Cebu, adjacent to cement factories, are now being worked economically. All is of a fairly soft quality.

The industry as a whole faces a situation where little finishing is undertaken domestically. Processing to an economically transportable form is carried out in some cases, but much is shipped as raw ore and only the higher-grade deposits are at present exploited. Additional plant could only be located in areas where adequate power facilities and resources in semi-trained manpower were available. Moreover, a considerable investment programme would be required. Power in the form of hydro- and thermally-produced electricity is available in central Luzon and adjacent to the Maria Christina complex on the Agus River, a few miles from Iligan on the north coast of Mindanao. Manpower is available in central Luzon, but often has to be brought in at Iligan. Official and private-sector capital has proved inadequate to allow rapid development in either area, although melting and rolling plants manufacture iron products in central Luzon, and a start on a steel factory has been made in Iligan. Neither area has adjacent mineral deposits and all raw materials have to be brought in. Capital for finishing is difficult to obtain, for the introduction of installations to process steel, copper, nickel, aluminium, and the more complex alloys would produce a threat to the Australian, Japanese, and United States industries in an already competitive market. Nevertheless, with the present advances in electric-power generation, the production of these items, including high-grade steel, is a possibility and only a lack of capital and the drive to set up finishing industries stand in the way of a domestic processing of more of the minerals already produced in the country.

Copper concentrates, with the derivatives from processing, gold, silver, lead, zinc, and pyrites, lead the mining field. At present exploited in the mountain areas of north Luzon, on Marinduque and Cebu Islands, and on the Zamboanga Peninsula of south-west Mindanao, these deposits are worked and processed for a market in which Japan is the most important partner. Other external deposits exist, especially in Surigao (north-east Mindanao), where laterites containing ferrous aluminium and nickel are currently being studied. The growing production of copper and its derivatives may well be a significant item in a future Philippine economy, and the future planning to extend these exploitations is described below (pp. 203–6).

Iron ore is found and exploited in the Bicol, Marinduque Island, and in south-west Mindanao. Deposits are also immediately available in the Sierra Madre range of central Luzon and in Surigao. Elsewhere prospecting has shown additional sites, but those listed above would be adequate to serve any indigenous finishing industry for many years. At present, the bulk of all ore is exported in a raw or pellatized form to Japan.

The production of chromite and of manganese is concentrated in the Zambales area of central Luzon, although some deposits are worked in south-west Mindanao and larger reserves of the former have been prospected in Surigao. As with the quicksilver exploited on Palawan, the products are exported to Japan and the United States. Goldmining as the production of a primary product is subsidized and is used to reinforce the currency.

Other major exportable items come within a group of textiles, of which abaca, hemp, and sisal are the major items. The demand for abaca has fallen and the famous Manila rope, one of the few exports which were despatched in a finished state, has been threatened by the introduction of stronger man-made fibres. Adjustment here has been proceeding for many years and, whereas abaca earned nearly $42 million in 1960, the sum reported for 1970 was only a little over $15 million.

Tobacco, mainly in the form of leaf and fillers and of finished Manila cigars, continues to earn fringe currency, but a large percentage goes to the domestic market.

A further and important export item is the pineapple. Produced in Mindanao on plantations owned or manipulated by the American Del Monte and Dol companies, canned fruit is despatched from adjacent ports for both the overseas and domestic markets. This is a welcome diversification in the economy, although it is not too popular for idealistic reasons, as the impetus, capital, and control are vested in two powerful foreign companies whose operations elsewhere have been criticized freely. With the Philippine sense of adjustment, however, the situation in Mindanao would seem to be much more advantageous than in other parts of the world and, although highly disciplined cropping operations have been introduced, no real evidence has been given that the projects are not managed benignly. In any case, they earn an important sum in foreign currency for undertakings which occupy quite a restricted space and living conditions around the plantations are generally better than in other rural areas.

Philippine exports rely greatly on the coconut palm, the sugar-cane, forests, and metallic mineral deposits. All remain confined to a quasi-colonial pattern, although production of coconut derivatives, timber, and metallic minerals has increased considerably since independence and a diversified market for these is being sought. All four items contain germs of instability in modern conditions. Foreign competition may well check the expansion of the ideally adapted coconut palm industry. (The palm is not indigenous, but it does flourish.) Modification to trade agreements between the Philippines and the United States could well unbalance the sugar-cane industry, already severely inhibited by a lack of competition during the years of privileged operation. Forest products will probably continue to earn increasing sums of foreign currency in the foreseeable future; but the fate of this part of the Philippine economy seems to rest solidly on the close control of effective replanting. Its top export position cannot be maintained. The 1971–74 Plan emphasizes export of finished and semi-finished goods, and reduced felling to conserve forest areas. The mining industry remains a servant of the United States and Japan, and diversification within the structure of world markets can only be obtained by the sale of strategic materials to Communist countries or by the establishment, little by little, of a domestic heavy industry. Outside this export quadrilateral are the smaller contributions to the balance of payments: the abaca-hemp group, traditional but declining in importance; the tobacco leaf products, also traditional, but whose run-down to present level took place in the earlier years of the century. Other agricultural surpluses do provide welcome additions: the pineapple has been established, a temporary self-sufficiency in rice has been followed by a small export capacity, although with continuing population growth and surpluses established by other South-East Asian countries, it is difficult to see how a regular export growth can be maintained. The Philippine government is well aware of these factors, seeks to diversify further, and has been very successful in the promotion of exports and invisible exports from the cottage industry section, from the re-exporting of petroleum products, and from the foreign currency spent by tourists visiting the islands. Nevertheless, the total of these earnings would be insufficient if all consumer goods had to be imported and, in a country with so significant a population increase and where a growing middle class enjoys an increasingly higher standard of living, export growth-rate would be inadequate to meet the foreign exchange bill. Thus the domestic sector is a major factor in the economy and the savings obtained by the local assembling of vehicles, the production of glass, cement, beverages, and foodstuffs, even of hydroelectric power, are of an overwhelming importance.

Trends in Self-Sufficiency

There are a number of very real blanks in indigenous output. One is endemic to sub-tropical and tropical countries – dairy farm produce. Another, as far as can be seen at present, is a freak of geological make-up; there are no known sources of commercially exploitable mineral oil in the whole of the Archipelago. This may well vary in the future; prospecting has taken place and small reserves have been located, but these are in no way viable, especially where crude can so easily be brought in to the four national refineries on Luzon from Indonesia, Brunei, and even the Middle East. Dairy farm products in the form of milk furnish a significant proportion of the protein in the poorer man's diet. Milk is brought in direct from overseas in a tinned or powdered form, or it is imported for processing with certain local additives and for sale as a highly fortified substitute. Although there is little flexibility in the day-to-day range of the working-class family's diet, a growing proportion of this imported milk or of the locally confected milk substitute finds its way to young children whose traditional protein intake was formally based on items which contained a large element of carbohydrate. Butter and cheese consumed in the Philippines is almost entirely imported: these latter foodstuffs generally form part of the diet of better-off families,[6] but, with the expansion of the middle class and of its prosperity, an increase in demand is registered annually.

The other widely used import commodity, mineral oil and its derivatives, has a very broad consumer range, running from the fuels used in passenger-carrying vehicles to such major users as electric power-stations and industrial plant. There are other blanks, but these are of a much less generalized impact. Of the dietary items, flour is probably the most important: used in the manufacture of bread, confectionery, and noodles, the whole of the country's requirements in the refined white-flour category are imported, either as a finished product or as wheat delivered to the deep-sea wharves of the eight flour mills[7] which have been strategically located over the Archipelago. Flour is also a semi-luxury, but one which is becoming popular, even among the less privileged.

In the category of imports used to supplement, we have already seen that fish from outside the country constitutes an important element for all classes. Quantities of cheap cotton textiles are produced locally and these fill a gap in the daily needs of a large proportion of the population. But better cottons, all silks, brocades and satins,[8] and much of the man-made fibres used, are still brought in from Japan, the United States, and western Europe.

Apart from these items of current consumption, almost a hundred per cent of the heavier industrial goods, broadly described as 'capital', have to be introduced from the more developed parts of the world. Some heavier consumer goods, which cannot at present be manufactured locally because of lack of investment and the generally underdeveloped conditions of the country, are assembled in the Manila area. These cover a fairly broad range: vehicles, refrigeration equipment, radio electric and electrical items, the majority of which are destined for middle-class consumption or use in the business community. The heavier range, which has to be specially ordered from outside, includes power-producing plant, earth-moving equipment, precision instruments, ships, and armaments. Here the practice of successive Philippine governments has been to fit requirements into the programmes provided by Japanese Reparations, United States War Damage compensation, and general or specific grants and loans. The majority of the weapons and the warlike equipment used by the armed forces is provided under the terms of a mutual defence treaty with the United States.

Nevertheless, there is a sector of the economy which covers much of the country's requirements: this is within the range of rapid domestic turnover. Cement, plate glass, paper, leather, rubber products, simple fertilizers, certain petro-chemicals, fresh and manufactured foodstuffs, tobacco, and beverages are provided in near self-sufficiency in many cases and are of good quality. Unfortunately, for one reason or another, the home output has to be occasionally supplemented by importation. There are a number of cement factories in the country, but in times when a rate of development in both the public and private sectors brings with it exceptional demands for the construction of roads and urban and industrial building, the output can become insufficient, although in present conditions, capacity has outstripped consumption rates. Locally manufactured paper, plate glass, and footwear cover much of the day-to-day current consumption and here only a marginal amount is brought in to cater for individual tastes. The rubber plantations which have been established in south Mindanao[9] by the tyre industry are now supplying the manufacturing side of the industry with much of its raw material and, providing there is adequate capital for investment, there is no reason why self-sufficiency in latex should not be reached, although any surplus production would be hard to dispose of in a region where Indonesian and Malayan plantations have long furnished much of the export capacity and where intensive cultivation on a large scale results in highly competitive offers. Except for dairy produce and fish, most of the country's raw food is indigenous. Rice and maize have already been covered. Poultry, pork, and much of the other meat is also home produced, although the supply of beef is insufficient for urban consumption and all mutton must be brought from temperate-zone countries. Consumption of most of the latter imports is restricted to the better-off classes. Adequate tropical and semi-tropical fruits and vegetables are farmed, but because of the latitudinal stretch of the Archipelago, growing seasons differ and transportation inadequacies often cause a lack of choice. Temperate-zone fruit and vegetables can be grown on the higher ground, particularly in the mountain areas of north Luzon, Cebu, and Mindanao, but to maintain a continued supply of luxury and semi-luxury items, small amounts are imported from Formosa, the United States, and Australia. Manufactured foodstuffs are essentially traditional, although a sophisticated delicatessen trade has recently grown out of the conditioning of pork products, a market where South-East Asian taste, local supply, and Spanish influence have now crystallized in the contrasting manufacture by the same factories of cheap luncheon meats and very high-quality hams and sausages. To cover the demands of the supermarket trade – a manifestation in itself of the purchasing power of the better-off element of the population – the normal range of Western-type produce is carried. In the current consumer range, although there could be more than adequate supplies of home-grown tobacco for the needs of the smoking public, taste, as in foodstuffs, plays a great part and here it joins with a prestige value in a demand for imported cigarettes. Soft drinks, beer, and rum are all manufactured locally, are of excellent quality, and are adequate in quantity for the country's needs. Once again, the more affluent require imported spirits and wine, and much foreign currency is used on these items.

The bill for these imports in foreign exchange is considerable and controls are not necessarily the solution to the problem, as smuggling can bypass normal commercial procedures and restrictions are harmful to the status of the peso. Over the past twenty years, Philippine governments have co-operated with local and foreign capitalist bodies in a wide range of local undertakings to diminish the drain in foreign currency. In the foodstuffs group, the flour-milling industry, although often uncompetitive, does save a proportion of the total cost of the finished product: the use of certain local additives in the make-up of milk substitutes is also important and domestic pork-meat canning contributes considerably. The assembly and light manufacturing industries also save large amounts of convertible funds, and even where there could be a complete drain, as in the mineral-oil sector, surplus refinery capacity is used for the provision of bunkering fuel and certain grades of hydrocarbon fuels for despatch to neighbouring South-East Asian centres. Heavy capital goods, as in all other essentially non-industrial countries, constitute a major problem, particularly where the broadening of the infrastructural and industrial base is accompanied by a requirement to refurbish where war damage still throws its shadow and where tropical conditions and indifferent day-to-day maintenance standards bring a high usage rate. Here control is very marked. The introduction of such goods, for institutional reasons, generally requires funding from sources which are outside the country, although, in either the public or private sector, this may well be in some way or another under Philippine control. These items normally fit into a national development plan or some subsidiary maintenance scheme. Even if private funds are available for smaller projects, the amount of foreign currency necessary to cover such items brings them within public control. The major element, however, is fitted into the Japanese Reparation allocations, grants from friendly governments, or is serviced by officially negotiated loans which are made for specific purposes.

In a country where official adherence to non-Communist principles has been a maxim since the Korean War and where strong links exist with the United States, Japan, and western Europe, it is not surprising to find that a considerable share in the nation's economic fortunes is contributed by capitalist-type operations. Ideally, the Philippine economy would be a partnership of state direction and institutions, and the complementing participation of private enterprise in both essential and fringe activities. Unfortunately, this has not always been the case, and, as in many countries whose budgets are limited and where electoral promises seem to mean so much before the polls, a certain flexibility, in both principle and practice, creeps in. There have often been anomalies, but, considering the heritage of a markedly colonial economy and much war damage, achievements have been considerable. This is due to the adherence of successive governments to fairly similar programmes of economic and infrastructural planning, and, although timetables have rarely been kept to, the bulk of the goals are accepted by either party in power and, when the whole is reviewed, it is amazing how much has been done by the efforts of the long-range planners, by the cajoling of ministerial and provincial officials, and by the 'do it yourself' type of operation which has benefited so many of the country's rural inhabitants. Unfortunately, attempts have been made to operate and maintain too sophisticated equipment in order to broaden the economic base, and a number of local projects have been realized which come directly into competition with similar enterprises in more highly industrialized countries. In a permeable community like the Philippines this often leads to the import of cheaper goods to the detriment of the indigenous operation.

[1] Under the Treaty of Paris of 1898, Spain enjoyed preferential trade tariffs for a ten-year period. These were on the same basis as those levied on the Philippines–United States exchanges.

[2] Centrifugal sugar is refined to a point where about 2 per cent molasses remains in the product. In the Philippines this is normally shipped for final processing to white sugar in the United States.

[3] The majority, however, still has to be dried in open kilns.

[4] A central is a milling complex to which the sugar-cane producing area around it is more or less tied for its livelihood.

[5] These are already bearing fruit in the Surigao project described below (p. 204).

[6] Tinned processed cheese has a much wider market. Imported under the terms of the National Marketing franchise, this product finds its way into the general stores of many village communities.

[7] Because of a small throughput, milling charges are high and imported flour is often cheaper than the locally processed commodity.

[8] Brocades and satins are used in the formal dressmaking trade, but locally *piña*, a fine cloth made from the pineapple, and poplin also figure in the more expensive items of dress for both sexes.

[9] All are local companies set up by the major United States producers.

Chapter 16

Filipino Life

BEFORE EXAMINING recent trends in everyday practices and in the economy, it is useful to fit together once again the jigsaw which now forms the base of Philippine society. In the early 1970s, the evolution of recent years is readily discernible and it is evident that life is still strongly rooted in its past traditions, although occupation by the United States and the spirit of the independence movement have brought with them a widespread liberal current which continues, despite political change, to run through its whole strata. This in itself was not necessarily absent from the spirit of much of former colonial life, for unless a man was given specific powers by the foreign administration or by the Church, he was always considered as essentially on the same level as his fellows – a tradition which was and still is fostered by the 'Greater Family' system. With independence, few exceptions to this belief now remain, although priests are still considered apart because of a general respect which ordination continues to carry with it. Conversely, a lack of respect for the origins of almost all other beings is widespread and is only tempered with a somewhat grudgingly bestowed acceptance of an individual's position in society, derived from some particular circumstances, be it wealth, administrative or political ability, or learning. These conditions are viewed in much the same light as bad luck, illness, and physical impediment. The former are the assets from which the whole of society can eventually profit, while the latter are the scourges whose effects must either be overcome or be supported with patience. Thus, although position and power are to be admired in themselves and individual attributes can be considered worthy or despicable, the reaction of the Filipino to such matters follows from either envy at not having been allowed the same opportunities or 'but for the Grace of God go I'.

The sea and the land are the most important elements which serve to colour the basic weave, and with them goes climate, which can bring both wealth and disaster, not only to non-industrial society but also to the populations which cling around the urbanized centres, for even these live a semi-rural life. The land and the sea, in a country where techniques are meagre and population increase is rapid and frightening, cannot be over-generous and semi-poverty is the order of things. The Church continues to impose a way of life which is Christian in its broader social application and this provides admirable stability. But stability is not lacking in other fields, for semi-poverty in tropical conditions, where local society provides assistance spontaneously, engenders neither widespread revolt nor constructional dynamism from inside. Movements with such a character can only come from outside; from religious organizations and from political groups or the administrative entities of the nation which seek to change so as to produce a new pattern, thought advantageous to the country and its people.

If such a society constitutes the level ground, there are elements which emerge from the plains and which are in contrast to the majority life. Urban organization has to some extent modified the Philippine way of life, but, even here, the village and hamlet are not distant, for, although there may be buildings in concrete and stone, some sanitation, running water, and cinemas, the bulk of town-dwelling families continue to occupy nipa and palm huts and are grouped together in much the same way as elsewhere; with their church, their local *plaza*, and the administrative buildings around it. Only the brittle nature of these people's economy gives them a different character, for here it is not the crops grown and the fish caught which produce the bedrock, but it is the wages earned and the prices to be paid on the market place which govern family life. Population pressure, employment, wage structures, and the cost of living are the essentials and where poverty and overcrowding go together with a certain tropical squalor, some modification to the general way of life takes place. Radical politics can emerge, but despite a seemingly appropriate breeding-ground for political unrest, a placid acceptance of conditions continues to exist and, surprisingly, much of political radicalism, as we have seen earlier, stems from an exploitation of land-tenure grievances by Communist elements in the rural areas.

This land-tenure system and the grievances surrounding it constitute a continuing source of unrest, which, although firmly entrenched in the tradition of the country, produces a second social minority. We saw above that, on the colonization of the Philippines by the Spaniards, land, which before had been owned freely by individuals or families, was expropriated and formed into large estates. Fringe lands of lesser economic value were often left to their original owners, but the richest passed under the control of either the *haciendas* or the Church and were worked or rented out according to the system practised. Unrest stemming from land problems has existed since then and the purchase by the American Insular government of the friar lands did not go very far in the event, as the basic poverty of the new owners, coupled with continuous profligacy and a lack of good seed and fertilizers, often ended in indebtedness and ultimate repurchase by members of a latter-day landowner class. The Communists began to exploit this state of misery in the early 'thirties and, by 1940, had obtained a hold over much of central Luzon. The 1940–45 War served much to consolidate this position as their own resistance movement against the Japanese, fanning out to southern Luzon and the Visayas, took with it political indoctrination. Land reform has been a major economic and political problem since independence and successive governments have made their attempts to grapple with it. The sensitive area remains the rice- and sugar-growing provinces to the north and north-east of Manila, and here the Communists still exploit a situation where political tradition and economic inequality join hands to foster revolt both in that area and among the more radical elements of Greater Manila itself (intellectual groups, including teachers and students, and left-wing elements of industrial trade unions). By its ruthless methods, designed to destroy society, the Communist agrarian movement – in association with the urban elements – has always hoped to break down the well-entrenched Filipino way of life. At present, Communist attempts to dislocate and to induce political and social fragmentation continue and for years to come will constitute an unharmonious, although not necessarily foreign, element in Philippine society.

The cultural and religious minorities continue to flourish and, again, are in contrast to the general current of Philippine life. Cultural minority groups – those communities which may well be of an earlier immigration – still live in isolated areas, although some tribes have been successfully assimilated and now have the same Malay Christian way of life as their neighbours (as is the case in the fringe areas of the Cagayan Valley). Nevertheless, the bulk of the 350,000 or so people of this category who do not fall within the majority, live their almost Stone Age lives in the remoter areas. As we have seen earlier, except for the mountain peoples of northern Luzon, they are grouped in small scattered elements of a tribal nature and here no spontaneous cultural minority movement exists. Any pressure-group and any political organization among these peoples have derived from the work done by the Bureau of Non-Christian Tribes during American tutelage and the enlightened treatment of minority problems since independence, resulting in a slow, unhurried formation of leaders and professional people, and the continuing gradual absorption of the varied elements into the national political and administrative structure.

Although the cultural minorities differ from the bulk of the population in their religious beliefs and are overwhelmingly pagan, the expression 'religious minority' is applied generally to the Moslem community, which is massively Malay in ethnic origin. Despite a lower population growth-rate in earlier times (sporadically compensated for by increases through kidnapping into slavery), these peoples are now enjoying much the same relative freedom from disease and infant mortality as their Christian neighbours, and the birth-rate among them is often higher than in the Christian areas. This community, which in 1972 probably amounted to nearly 1½ million, constitutes the fourth exception to the majority way of life. Today the Moslem community is still highly stimulated by Pan-East Indianism and a sensitivity to Middle East currents, and, although it has elected its congressmen from among candidates belonging to one or another of the major parties, life is seriously influenced by politico-religious practices. Political questions which touch on relations between the Philippines and Moslem countries, both in the region and elsewhere, are also of considerable importance, and for any government to ignore this would be disastrous. Although now economically near to their Christian neighbours in so far as agriculture and fishing are concerned, certain elements of the community continue to live by less peaceful methods and piracy in southern waters, and banditry and smuggling continue to lend colour to what otherwise would be a tropical agrarian society.

At this stage, further description of the wealthier elements of the community might seem to be fastidious. While the middle classes have their easily traceable roots in the majority culture, a well-defined element of the wealthier strata is much more isolated and here some particularization is evident. Foreign to the general way of life, being composed of families of pure or of mixed blood, predominantly of European or American descent with some Malay and Chinese interbreeding, it nevertheless enjoys Philippine citizenship. Small in numbers, this community has disproportionate economic and political power, controlling important parts of industry, developing inherited landholdings,[1] and, in association with foreign and Philippine banking houses, takes a leading part in the development of real estate and the lighter consumer industries. Despite a history which in the recent past has, on occasions, inclined to the sinister because of an ability to influence political processes, this group now constitutes a favourable stabilizing force, reasonably benign in character and attracting, by its image, valuable foreign capital into the country. By the 1970s, this socially monolithic group had become a valuable partner to successive governments in their attempts to reorientate the economy.

In any examination of Philippine society, a reconsideration of two of its most important assets is valuable. These assets are of particular significance in the struggle for the political and economic independence of a comparatively underdeveloped Asian country. The first is the inherent capacity of the Filipino to absorb education and training, and the second is the practical and worldly nature of the Filipina who, although essentially modest and shy in outward appearance, can bring strong practical influence to day-to-day transactions, be they slight or important in character.

In the capacity of her citizens to absorb learning, the Philippines is rich in her reserves. The Filipino, a hybrid creature, possesses an excellent adaptability to mind process and is always capable of original thought. Although rapid population growth has made education difficult to liberalize and a certain adhesion to North American systems has brought with it a levelling-out and a penchant to parrot-wise assimilation, these often disappear at the highest formative levels or with the experience of years. But such criticisms are not definitive, especially where natural ability contributed by mixed blood and the stability of an almost monolithic culture form the threshold to intellectual capacity. The relatively high ratio of professional people in the Philippines bears witness to inborn standards and, although the more liberal disciplines are still overfavoured and result in a marked imbalance, the Filipino technician, be he graduate or artisan, is of an undoubtedly high level, especially where more disciplined methods have been fully absorbed by the individual and pride is taken in an adherence to them. In any independent country, where an expatriate continues to be a challenge to the indigenous professional system and where his cost of maintenance is high, replacement by a native is both politically and economically desirable. Nevertheless, it is also unfortunately true that only the existence of really suitable locally born candidates will make for continued efficiency. It is salutary therefore that, in the Philippines, a country which exports certain types of graduates, a respect for technical efficiency, a certain tolerance based on the native ideals relating to equality of man, and the presence of a comparatively well-qualified labour pool go hand in hand to bring about the current situation where expatriate and indigenous labour complement each other and where, in the very near future, Filipino nationals will be able to operate everything but the latest-introduced systems. In such circumstances, at least some part of the economic dialogue is made easy and a respect for the most recent technical innovations to assist in the transformation of the economy is genuine and brings with it greater mutual understanding and tolerance, so often absent in less mature societies.

Lastly, to the female element of the population and its influence on daily cultural and economic life. In the pagan communities, the overwhelming majority follows the traditional life of such societies, a life, however, somewhat tempered by the respect which women enjoy in most Malay and Proto-Malay populations. Here there has been little or no great movement from domesticity, although, in tribal consultations, the woman has generally had her place. In the Moslem community, essentially that of the Sunni sect, a woman's life is comparatively liberal in comparison with that of the more enclosed and stricter conditions of the Middle East. In recent years, many girls have attended both Moslem and Christian schools, and a welcome emancipation has spread, particularly in the more monied classes where day-to-day contacts are maintained with Christian families. But, among the Christian lowlander element, the majority of the population, the woman is an equal and accepted partner, often as well or better educated than her menfolk and generally more practical and less inclined to irresponsibility, her current contribution of enormous positive value. Not only does she bring stability to family life, but she also forms part of the workforce, in positions which run from the factory floor to executive posts in industry and political appointments. Despite the continuing practice of rearing large families, the Filipina has played her part in giving her country the Westernized structure and outlook which it now possesses.

Ideals and Acts

Against this almost permanent background of Philippine life exists a 'grey' area composed of elements which place ideals and practice in sharp contrast. Although the political changes of 1972–73 have been partially directed to narrow the gap between these two poles, the measures which have already been taken are too recent to be judged objectively and, even if the various factors involved were only destined to be stored away in history to be heeded as a warning for the future, they are worthy of study. They could well be national and even cultural manifestations which might remain quite as constant as those already described above.

Before the appearance of martial law in 1972 and the setting-aside of normal party politics, enormous sums of money were spent on election campaigns, both for the organization of normal political activities and in the wooing of individual voters and groups of voters to a candidate's or party's point of view. Within these global amounts were items of public expenditure: the costs of countrywide tours by the President and his close associates which, at least for the last nine months of his office, could be considered as having a significant bearing on the major elections to come. In addition, quite legally, parts of the last annual budget of the outgoing administration were normally retained for use during the final assault period and transfers from one departmental allocation to another were manipulated. Supplementary sums were voted and generally a degree of inflation resulted. Much of these sums were devoted to public works of a fragmentary nature. The concreting of a dusty national road within the territory of a *barrio* or municipal *poblacion*, the building of a bridge, or the construction of a town hall or welfare centre. Where there would be so little change in the main lines of national policy if the opposition had captured power, why did such feverish activities take place and why were such lavish sums spent both to invigorate the party machine and to encourage the electors with cash rewards and with what is termed the 'pork barrel'?[2] Office in the administration is always coveted. Again there has always been a conviction among politicians holding important positions that the personal emphasis they can bring to their jobs might help to improve their country's fortunes. Moreover, official salaries are relatively generous and further account has always to be taken of politicians' expenses, which can be great. Nevertheless, all things considered, an impartial assessor might think a more urgent current must have been behind such periodical upheavals. If he looked further – only as far as the front page of one of the Manila daily newspapers – he would have obtained a lead to the real state of affairs. Office in the Philippines has generally brought personal gratification.

In the Philippines itself, accusations and counter-accusations have seriously involved the reputations of individuals bringing charges of irregularity and those accused of such practices. Political bodies and splinter-groups are permanently embroiled and press columnists have added their own personal brand of written comment, varying from discreet musings to outright and vituperative accusations. When such matters come to the attention of foreign reporters and are carried by the news agencies, they become world news. If, as in the United Kingdom, the Philippines is practically unknown to the general public, the bulk of references to that country in the national dailies is based on this sensationalist material.

The written constitution of the Philippines has always provided exemplary safeguards against the abuse of national institutions and of personal power. The laws are as good as any democracy would wish. The judiciary is well organized and staffed by lawyers holding the highest qualifications; the executive organizations and the elected apparatus are well adapted to basic, traditional needs and all normally functions smoothly. Even when momentary disruption takes place, emergency or extraordinary measures are taken to patch up and replace. The Filipino is an experienced improviser and community assistance is both generous and kindly. In contrast, however, there is a time-honoured practice of simplifying procedures, legally, or illegally, for personal or collective aims or for moral or immoral ends. The individual, family, or collectivity which is to gain from this kind of transaction rarely worries about the damage it could cause a third-party individual, family, or collectivity. Spanish colonial rule was manifestly corrupt: certain practices inherent in the democratic way of life of the United States, which has been enthusiastically adopted in the Philippines, could not be judged as outstandingly moral and many Filipinos had waged an unceasing, skilful, if contemptuous war against the detested Japanese, where the most effective weapons were wits, sharp practice, and a gentle but almost constant disregard of the occupants' needs. A degree of corruption continues to flourish, although generally, where public opinion has been roused and official agencies are poised to administer a salutary blow, the operators retire gracefully: much to everybody's relief, because past involvement can be considerable and it is rare for a real story to be revealed, consent and complacency having been widespread. In the most favourable conditions, the system of appointment to office[3] is a good example of what possibilities rest with officials of the faction in power. Actions are not necessarily prompted by corruption: the reward for political support, personal or financial, is often office: from the highest not normally reserved for career public servants to a job in the police in a remote municipality. Family ties also have some bearing, although it is rare to see kinsmen who support an opposing political faction appointed to the highest positions.

On a lower idealistic scale, reward for complacency or the correct and prompt channelling of papers through official or unofficial hierarchies is often offered, often solicited. The Philippines is not the only country where such practices occur. Nor is the Philippines alone where graft is offered to change the course of justice or the impartial handling of other matters *sub judice*.[4] Again, coercion, either imposed by blackmail or by a threat of violence, is widespread throughout the democratic world: smuggling takes place everywhere and piracy still rears its ugly head from time to time: murder and violence are well-known human failings. All these practices are reported from the Philippines and to some extent find a favourable climate in which to operate.

An awareness of the degree to which irregularity has become common has become reasonably widespread in the republic and, as liberal education gains a greater hold and the real tenets of Christianity are understood (rather than the outward trappings of the faith), more and more individuals react positively against the evil and a discernible trend to diminish rather than eradicate has already borne some fruit. In the immediate post-war days the situation was much worse. Now the two most important factors, a realization of the basic evil, with its far-reaching social effects, and the removal of at least some of the causes of corruption, have reached the middle classes and latterly spearhead political movements geared to change. It is salutary to see that glaring excesses were often revealed by the Press and soliciting for small rewards was more and more resisted. Nevertheless, the closer-knit, well-organized, quasi- or totally criminal circles continue to be a grave problem to the government and at least some of their power is inextricably mixed up with the past funding of political campaigns. It was not only the barons of criminal groups who assisted candidates; the illegal Communist Party had also been known to supply votes against cash. In the case of the criminal organizations, the reward generally accepted was official complacency towards their operations. Threats, violence, and even murder may well pass unpunished, even after complaint. Smuggling continues unchecked, unless it becomes too blatant or if the government is waging one of its periodical campaigns to suppress it. Piracy, always endemic in the southern Philippines and even practised in Manila Bay itself, gets much the same treatment.

So deep-rooted are these irregularities and so widespread are the operations of professional criminals that the government is quite unable to cope with all at the same time. Nor has it adequate or ideally adapted forces at its disposal to counter certain moves. Much of the petty graft and small-time smuggling is condoned by the population as commonplace. In these circumstances, information is difficult to obtain and the local police, who in any case have often been involved, make little headway in its suppression. But corruption in high quarters, smuggling on a large scale, and piracy by armed bands are damaging to the country's image, morally reprehensible, and economically harmful. There have been frequent reports of embezzlement and misappropriation in official quarters; an estimated £10 million is thought to be lost to the revenue annually through the smuggling of cigarettes and luxury consumer goods from Hong Kong and Borneo. Over-the-side pilfering and full-scale piracy have put up insurance rates, given the port of Manila a dubious name, and have caused considerable loss to the passengers and the owners of smaller inter-island craft. Although it has been said that much of the smuggling and armed attacks at sea are traditionally the work of the Moslem populations of Sulu and the Moro Gulf area, operations up to 1972 in Manila Bay and the north and north-west coast of Luzon were the work of Christians resident in north and central Luzon.

With urban police forces, raised and trained locally, generally inadequate to suppress such acts, two nationwide bodies are of considerable value. The first, the National Bureau of Investigation (NBI), serves as a co-ordinating agency, but in the case of major crime has a role of both investigation and arrest. It is a dedicated organization, fairly well set up with radio links and criminal investigation equipment, and it manages to score successes where the local police forces are unable to progress. The second is the Philippine Constabulary, the oldest and most numerous element of the armed forces. Organized like the army into four territorial zones and a central headquarters possessing technical sections (Traffic Control, Criminal Detection, Firearms, and Ballistics, etc.), it is a national military police force of a gendarmerie character. It has an excellent reputation and is often called in to counter law infringement on a larger scale: anti-state conspiracy; insurgency (the Huks); the land side of piracy; and smuggling and major crime committed outside the larger urban areas.[5] Further, where a town's police force is deemed inefficient, the Constabulary can be ordered in to take over. In nationwide operations, its excellent radio systems and mobile potential are used to block communications and to search. Since martial law, and the waving-aside of local political practices which fostered a fragmentation of judicial authority, the value of the force has been readily admitted. A third peace enforcement element is constituted by the Philippine Navy, whose patrol craft keep surveillance of inter-island waters and the Manila Bay area itself. Once again, assisted from time to time by reconnaissance elements of the Philippine Air Force, they form together a well-organized and dedicated force.

Planned threats of violence (*estafada*) practised by groups, often end in their consummation, for the Filipino is proud if hot-headed and can respond to threat positively. In much the same way, pride and anger has led to assault, wounding, and death in normal daily life. It is most probable that the wholesale carriage of offensive weapons is an important contributory factor in these cases. Knives and *bolos* (a type of machete) are carried throughout the rural areas and are often found in the towns as well. These weapons are lethal, but unlike the Moslem's *kriss*, they are generally used for mundane tasks of husbandry and primitive construction. The carriage of firearms has, however, escalated since the troubled days at the turn of the century, almost reaching a tradition with the guerrilla activities of the Second World War. In theory, firearms must be licensed and a good character and some simple reason must be available to obtain this franchise. In practice, too many licences have been issued and a far greater number of illegally held weapons existed until 1973 (200,000–

300,000?). If a weapon is carried, it is generally loaded: ready for immediate use. Where violence can erupt and weapons are available, wounding and death are the logical consequences.

In any assessment of law and order, the best evidence available must serve as data. We have not been assisted here by crime reporters or by the statistics of the local authorities who have often been quite deeply involved: the former have tended to be sensationalist and the latter bland to a degree. What seems to be evident is that certain simple irregularities, petty graft and minor smuggling, are generally condoned and this provides a solid threshold for irregularity. Escalation to individual crime is not difficult to envisage and, in such conditions, group criminality jumps off from a higher point than in countries where basic manifestations are condemned. Surveillance is another important factor. The suppression of crime relies heavily on the receipt of information and the efficient deployment of local police at the earliest moment. In the Philippines, this vital link can be missing in both the urban and rural areas. The patrolman is rarely in the right place at the right time, the town police forces are not able to operate a constant and satisfactory watch, and the rural areas are hardly surveyed at all. A further factor is the deterrent. When a criminal is apprehended, the executive authorities have had considerable difficulty in obtaining a conviction. Bail is easily obtained and legal loopholes are numerous, especially where local police are poorly trained in judicial procedures. Corruption based on personal, pecuniary, or political motives can halt initial proceedings and, even when a case is brought to conviction, appeal and legal argument can quash the sentence and in many serious cases urgency and meaning can be lost in long-drawn-out legal argument.[6] The most important check to the growth of lawlessness is the efficiency and nationwide co-ordinating activities of both the National Bureau of Investigation and the Philippine Constabulary. Despite a poorly covered local sector, they also take on the investigation of individual criminal acts from the base. If the training and application to duty of the local police[7] could be improved and this was accompanied by a secure climate in which citizens could give information, much of the difficulties now encountered might well be removed.

Piracy is a traditional sport in southern waters and its extension to Luzon dates from the earliest days of Moslem expansionism. Smuggling is natural, for tariff barriers are manifestly unnatural and the Philippine coastline is longer than that of the United States. Small craft used for these illegal occupations are well adapted, generally being long country-made outriggers, riding low in the water, light in construction, and with powerful outboard engines. The low silhouette and the speed obtained by this combination makes them ideal in attack as well as in withdrawal and they can be used for both smuggling and piracy, for their profile escapes radar and their speed allows for rapid operation, surprise, and either diplomatic or fighting withdrawal. In the event, the occupants, who carry a powerful armoury, will fight it out with the forces of law and order. Although piracy is a traditional occupation which could well be diminished by the availability of an alternative trade, smuggling is based on a constant and profitable consumer market, the major element being the imported cigarette, for a few better-off citizens will not smoke the indigenous product, American brands constituting an important status symbol. Foreign-made cigarettes attract a considerable duty, and this is the basis of the trade, which also broadens out to other luxury consumer goods brought in to make weight. Hong Kong and North Borneo (Sabah) are the main buying markets, but once shipped aboard the smuggling craft, either in a foreign port or by transfer from ships in the South China Sea, the operators will land their freight at any place over the long coastline. Local inhabitants tend to be terrorized and evidence is fragmentary. Hence the continued success of the smuggler. His market is constant and lucrative, his equipment ideal, and despite government propaganda little has been done morally to erode his profession's status. The only cloud on the horizon is the growing efficiency of the NBI and Constabulary, and here counter-measures have to be studied continuously in order to maintain profitability.

This catalogue of irregularity and lawlessness may well seem repellent to those who have never visited the Philippines. To place such matters into a proper perspective, therefore, it is necessary to examine briefly their effects. There is little doubt that all are damaging to the national image, given the willingness to buy smuggled goods and toleration of petty lawlessness. Again, all cause moral harm, for complacency encourages escalation. In their more malignant forms, they can produce coercion and an important loss of private and public funds. All are facets, are generally inseparable, and the present Philippine administration knows well the evil of the whole. Luckily, it is much less a slave of its environment than earlier governments, for political morals have improved. Rule by exception has provided both a legal and executive striking force and suppression campaigns are now real ones instead of a mere lip-service to ideals.[8]

In daily life the situation is well understood and both the urban and rural populations have learnt to live with it – which might seem incompatible to the Westerner. There are parts of Manila and other cities which are extremely dangerous during the hours of darkness and some rural areas are also unsafe because of endemic banditry.

Violence, kidnapping, and threat can take place if simple precautions are not followed. Crime can still pay quite well, but the official struggle against it continues and less complaint is now made of the government's complacency and of the population's reluctance to assist. Some basic training of the younger elements in local police forces is undertaken by the Constabulary. Certain of their officers, especially those appointed in the larger urban concentrations, are dedicated men and in time may become less baffled. The efficiency of the deterrent remains difficult to assess, but this can often be bypassed (and is), for armed criminals may well stay to fight it out: in these circumstances judicial proceedings are limited to an autopsy and summary police enquiries.

A possible solution is to remove the major cause of gross irregularity and leave the minor ones to the police. Here a departure from the reliance of politicians on funds from questionable sources, the abolition or minimization of entry duties on tobacco, and the raising of the salaries of the more subordinate officials could do much. Nevertheless, a large number of people continue to live by crime, although the majority of this element have some consideration for their fellow-citizens and act without necessarily disturbing the placidity of the everyday, conformist law-abiding life of most Filipinos.

[1] The *cacique* tradition, despite some sociological refinement, remains very strong, although diversion of family funds to industry has occurred, and a mixed-type investment practice is rapidly evolving.

[2] A term used for vote-catching items of public expenditure and rewards of the same nature allocated to loyal constituencies.

[3] Appointment to office for political reasons is not, of course, restricted to the Philippines and the system is often attacked on moral grounds.

[4] Even in socialist eastern Europe reports lamenting the lack of ideological integrity are sometimes published. And in Britain cases of police corruption and abuse of office in financial and contract matters often come to light.

[5] There is a qualification here: the Constabulary, although it possesses initiative, is generally tasked by the government which sometimes purposely turns a blind eye to some cases of organized crime.

[6] I note a case where the ambush of a political convoy in Ilocos province in 1965 resulted in nine deaths. Only in May 1971 was confirmation obtained of the sentences of seventeen of the accused found guilty.

[7] The local police are often impeded by the activities of paid security guards whose only loyalties are towards their hirers or towards themselves. Moreover, their initial training is cursory, with no continuing supervision. Tradition too still expects a corrupt cop.

[8] On 8 August 1973 the Philippine government reported that it had disbanded 145 private armies and reduced major crimes by nearly 75 per cent in 10 months of martial law. The 'armed apparatus of the Communist party' was almost completely dismantled. (*Daily Telegraph*, London, 9 August 1973)

Chapter 17

The Republic Since Independence
Roxas to Magsaysay

MANUEL ROXAS, elected as the last Commonwealth of the Philippines President on 23 April 1946, a little before his country's independence was proclaimed on 4 July 1946, became its first Head of State on that day. Although past elections in the Philippines had often been coloured by campaigns where all the armoury of lawful political manoeuvre was reinforced by a leavening of illegality, the 1946 struggle was already a notable epic in all respects. Manuel Quezon's successor, Sergio Osmeña, had returned with General MacArthur over the beaches of Leyte and for a year and a half had assisted the Americans in their attempts to put the Philippines back on a running basis. Latterly, he did more than assist; judging the time opportune, he slowly assumed the full responsibilities of his office.

Osmeña was a courageous man who, with Manuel Quezon, had been reared as a politician in the first years of American rule. Leaning heavily on those democratic traditions which the Americans were attempting to transplant in the country, both he and Quezon had progressed during a period of vital political evolution, a process which, although expressly fostered from 1908 onwards by the new rulers, was in no way unadapted to the spirit of the islands. On the contrary, the Filipinos readily took to political activity and to its practical application to Philippine needs in particular. Practical application closely followed the mechanics of the art as set up in the United States. Quezon the *mestizo* and Osmeña, a scion of a rich Visayan family, teamed up to head the Nacionalista Party and to rule during the Commonwealth tutelage period. Quezon's contribution was enormous. His powers of leadership and insistence on social justice, and affection, respect, and national pride in his exceptional qualities, ensure continued reverence for his memory and, although outshone by his colleague, Sergio Osmeña shared much of the genuine admiration of the Filipinos for their first native executives. Nevertheless, this was not enough to produce Osmeña's automatic election in 1946. Then the Commonwealth was a memory and Japanese occupation, with the violence and chicanery which accompanied it, was more vivid in the minds of the men who were to take leading parts in bringing the country to independence so soon after its liberation. Their conduct was symptomatic of this new current and among them were Roxas and Elpidio Quirino, who, breaking away, took with them an element of Osmeña's following. They attracted the majority of the opposition, forming in this latter-day period the Liberal Party. Manuel Roxas and Elpidio Quirino became Presidential and Vice Presidential candidates. This might well seem to have been an almost spontaneous reaction, based on an antipathy to the political traditions which had been current during the Commonwealth. In the event, it was probably nothing of the sort. Personal ambition, the fascination of politics, and the desires of at least some of the more powerful landowning families and industrial coteries were three of the factors which produced the apparently unpredicted opposition to Osmeña. Opposition was more complex than this, however, and the complexity is still half shadowed by the reluctance of the major participants in the 1945–46 events to state their full involvement. The United States government seemed to welcome the election of Roxas, a man reputed capable of firmness and determination, and behind him stood a large proportion of the richest and most powerful elements of society. Today, there are few Filipino statesmen or politicians who could look back to the 1946 election with overmuch pride, although those violent events for once and all seemed to confirm a spontaneous desire for a two-party-type political structure which, until the early 1970s, functioned fairly well, although it might well be argued that both American tutelage and the Philippine character were really at the root of its success.

Violence, graft, and political chicanery of almost every type must have been present in June 1946. It was as though a major desire for change was being reinforced by lessons so easily learned during Japanese rule. Despite the emergence of a relatively strong government, so much desired by the Americans to rule a country where their own commercial and defence interests were so important, the memories of this upheaval have proved difficult to erase and throughout the Philippines they remain to this day. The 1946 election was no revolution, but it had many of the elements which normally exist in such a situation, the most striking being conspiracy and violence, although the comparative political maturity of the leading participants avoided more than a passing and minimal phase of bloodiness.[1]

President Manuel Roxas must have been well informed of the responsibilities which he was to accept as first President of the

Republic. In the event, not only was he capable of taking hard decisions based on a need to steer his country along a path which closely followed that of capitalistic rehabilitation, but also, from what we can now see from the records of his speeches and memoranda, was well able to appreciate the extent of the devastation all over the islands as well as his own people's aspirations during these difficult years. Like so many of his colleagues, he was himself a man who tacitly respected expediency. In the circumstances, he was a near slave to the elements which had contributed to his translation. In these first years, United States political domination of South-East Asia was manifest, particularly where it involved a country in which government institutions were so similar to her own. The larger and more well-disposed groups which had helped to bring Roxas to power not only continued to assist him, but also expected government policy to give them priority for re-equipment, satisfactory legislation, and a suitable social climate in which to operate. The lower, more debased, elements which had directed and fought the violent election battles in the streets and in the hamlets demanded their own cut, and development plans and Philippine management of money and equipment which were now arriving to rehabilitate the country were not untouched by a broader debt which the Liberal Party had to bear as a gage for its success.

Despite all this, assisted by the inherent willingness and optimism of the people, some reorganization and re-equipment did take place and, with only the Huks and a few intellectuals to harass him, Roxas progressed, despite the time-honoured political attacks he continually received from the columnists and his professional opponents. He died suddenly in April 1948, to be succeeded by Elpidio Quirino who, in 1949, was re-elected on a straight Liberal ticket. Quirino was defeated in the 1953 elections by his former Defence Minister, Ramon Magsaysay, who, with a number of the Liberal Party cadre, formed a third element, the Democratic Party, which during pre-election manoeuvrings joined the opposing Nacionalista Party. Magsaysay thus obtained a Presidential nomination. He was killed in an air crash in Cebu on 17 March 1957. His death confirmed the end of an era in which, despite continuing administrative inefficiency, political corruption, and endemic lawlessness, the Philippines had become a fairly stable non-Communist Asian power.

At the time of Manuel Roxas's death in 1948 rehabilitation was the key to all national politics outside the Communist-controlled countries, for ideological ascendancy and defence build-up had priority in the latter and the Russian-dominated states were slowly being enclosed by the Iron Curtain. In China and Indo-China armed struggle for political supremacy was bitter and drawn-out, already showing signs of Communist ascendancy. In Indonesia, the Philippines' nearest southern neighbour, the result of a decolonization movement fostered by indigenous left-wing nationalistic elements confronting the Dutch régime was already a foregone conclusion. Malaya was threatened by a Communist Chinese-dominated anti-colonial revolt and, in the Philippines the Huks, as we have already seen, had never ceased to harass the authorities in their attempts at complete political disruption. In Europe, the tragedy of Prague, which symbolically closed the Iron Curtain, brought about a strong political reaction among the West European powers with whom the United States firmly associated herself. Thus, with Indonesian independence a certainty, the Communist rebellion in the Philippines contributed to the anxieties which the United States, Australia, and New Zealand felt not only for the world, but also for the stability of a neighbouring continent, already menaced by the Communist war-machine in China, Korea, and Indo-China. Although the struggle for idealistic supremacy in Asia is still only in its infancy, during those early days the initial stages of political change had international importance. The defeat of the corrupt and externally supported régime in China by the Communists and the corresponding development of an artificial 'little China' in Formosa and its surrounding islands took place at much the same time as the security situation in Malaya and the Philippines was at its worst. As an antithesis, however, invasion of South Korea by the Communists in June 1950 brought a swift reaction to what was legally flagrant aggression. Covered by a symbolic United Nations character, the non-Communist nations rapidly formed a strong force to fight an all-out conventional war within the confines of Korea itself, assisted in the event by military, but non-operational, elements from certain of the unaligned countries. South Korea held firm and, in time, her own forces were massively reinforced to become one of the largest of the world's armies. The 'Nationalist' Chinese became firmly entrenched in the Formosan group and their industrial evolution commenced. By the late 1950s the British Commonwealth forces in Malaya had won the battle against the Communist Chinese revolutionaries and Malayan independence became possible. The Indo-Chinese empire split up on French evacuation, crystallizing into four widely divergent states, at least one of which, South Vietnam, was rapidly becoming an American satellite. And, in September 1954, a regional mutual defence grouping, the South East Asia Treaty Organization, was set up to resist aggression against the area from outside. By the time of Magsaysay's death, all this had already occurred and the Philippines had fallen into place as a loyal and politically aware member of a non-Communist grouping. Although underdeveloped and quite poor, she contributed generously where she could.

These years were not without political difficulty for the Philippines, but a country which had wholeheartedly adopted a Western-type democratic system, which was overwhelmingly Christian in both its religious practices and its majority way of life, and which had already suffered from a foretaste of an Asian brand of totalitarianism could hardly be over-sympathetic to communism. Philippine antipathy to an undemocratic way of life was reinforced as the communism which sought to infiltrate the region was evolving towards an undoubted Chinese type and in these islands the memory of a former Chinese expansionism, with its claims to sovereignty in the Middle Ages and the Parian revolts of the sixteenth and seventeenth centuries, had never been effaced. Moreover, the current activities of the resident Chinese merchant class were viewed with hostility – a hostility to the seeming ease with which this foreign element (although often of Philippine birth) could obtain control of land, business, and industry, often by the judicious practice of usury. This reaction to any threat of Chinese political ascendancy, particularly of an atheist Communist nature, was understandably positive. The overwhelming majority of the electorate was therefore behind the government in its support of military and political policies fostered in the region by the United States and the European and Australasian non-Communist powers. In such circumstances, political decolonization was in practice hampered by a large-scale non-Asian intervention in regional affairs.

The defence treaties established between the United States and the Philippines legally bind the latter to continue to be host to large American bases on Luzon. It is clear that, during this earlier period, there was never any question of resentment and units of the Philippine armed forces fought successfully in Korea. At the same time, the native Philippine Communist threat was reduced. Today it is an endemic, armed political opposition, using illegal methods, but assimilated into the grassroots of a comparatively small area, now traditionally dissident. These Philippine contributions to the overall anti-Communist campaign in South and South-East Asia were made at a time when the economic fabric was still mainly unrepaired and often when funds and skilled effort had to be drained away from such a rehabilitation. The United States did give massive financial assistance, not only in return for the establishment of a friendly climate, but also for aid in military manpower and for the prestige value of being accompanied into the struggle by a theoretically free Asian nation. Despite these material considerations, it must be accepted that successive Philippine governments, generally with popular agreement, not only contributed generously to regional stability, but did so after democratic consultation. There is also little doubt that the exigencies of this period contributed markedly to the conservation of a near-colonial-type economy. Thus in the political and economic fields, the maintenance of a now traditional way of life by an adherence to a counter-revolutionary movement, supported from outside Asia, slowed down real independence. This phenomenon was probably beneficial in character, as it served further to adapt the young nation to the political system which it had chosen in 1946.[2] This is one of the most important reasons for the republic's relative political maturity.

Within this framework Roxas, Quirino, and Magsaysay led their republican administrations. Magsaysay's term as President is often now confused with his period as Quirino's Secretary for Defence, for even then his dynamic personality overshadowed his other colleagues in power.

The short tenure of Manuel Roxas was one of intensive effort to ratify and bring into execution the instruments of independence. It is clear now why the United States was so satisfied with Roxas. Independence was negotiated as a package deal. Both the Mutual Defence Treaties and the Philippine Trade Act (known as the Bell Act) of 1946 were conceived to perpetuate a neo-colonial system, although both gave the young republic solid economic privileges perpetuated later in the Laurel-Langley Agreement. With the Bell Act came the Philippine Rehabilitation Act which provided war-compensation payments and grants to re-establish the economy.[3] Roxas's presidency was dominated by his successful political campaign to obtain ratification of this deal; he had little or no time to free himself from the influence of the more powerful *cacique* formations, who had, among others, helped him to power;[4] and his tenure was shadowed by his inability to deal with many facets of political dishonesty: particularly graft, nepotism, and maladministration of office. The Huks continued to prosper in this period when government control of the rural areas was anything but effective and where memories of the war were still fresh. By Roxas's death, a start had been made at economic renewal and American money and aid in kind were continuing to flow in. For all this, however, internal peace was still a long way away. The politicians were often the worst offenders. They became accustomed to use violence to achieve their own ends within a creaking democratic framework. There was worse to come.

Quirino was a different man. Where Roxas had been the brilliant younger politician, with firm ideas on the economic future and popular because of his military record (he was a wartime brigadier-general), Quirino was a typical middle-class politician. He lacked the flexibility of Roxas, although he had personal charm and was an excellent negotiator. What was less satisfactory was his automatic assumption of power (he was Vice President) at a time when the Liberal Party's retention of office relied upon all the armament of unrestrained political expediency. Quirino's Presidency is now remembered as a peak of corruption and violence, and the 1949 elections, which confirmed him in office for four more years, were marred by murder, coercion, and blatant illegality at the polling booths. This trend continued until it was partially checked in 1951, but these conditions have not yet been forgotten outside the Philippines. Today's poor Press in Europe stems from those convulsions, which Quirino himself was quite unable to control, as his own position was maintained by a scarcely concealed reliance on such violence. Nevertheless, outwardly, he was popular and successfully exploited modern public relations methods. He also instituted machinery to help improve social conditions: management-labour advisory bodies and government credit organizations in the agricultural sector. During his tenure the traditional industries began to recover, but there was still the burden of deep-rooted problems of land tenure and the dangerously unbalanced distribution of wealth. These, along with political corruption, did much to push Ramon Magsaysay into the ranks of the Nacionalista party. But the international and regional ideological struggle was mainly in favour of Western democracy, assisted by the traditionalist yet strong-arm policies of Formosa and South Korea. The Philippines had much in common with the former and continued to assist the United States in her anti-Communist Asian policies. Security became an important aspect of the Mutual Defence Agreements, which allowed her to maintain her precious naval and air bases on Philippine soil.

The Quirino period lacked positive dynamism. Most of the surplus effort available at that time was channelled into coercion. When Magsaysay won the Presidency in 1953, his success was due not only to his making common cause with the majority of Filipinos who had become sickened by the Liberal Party's conduct, but it also stemmed from his own appreciation of two basic factors. First, since his appointment as Defence Secretary in September 1950, he had led the country's only real dynamic movement – the Anti-Huk campaign. He saw that this was already succeeding through his use of a democratic combination of civic and military action. Secondly, the 1951 mid-term election (for the Senate and local appointments) had produced an overwhelming Nacionalista victory. If he himself continued to stay with Quirino for the 1953 Presidential elections, his political future would be more than uncertain.

Magsaysay became President when the country demanded democratic progress, but without the accompaniment of an unacceptable degree of illegality. With his Malay profile, face, and almost ugly attractiveness, and with a native rather than a Spanish family name, he was born in 1907 and came from relatively modest roots in Zambales, that part of central Luzon which projects into the South China Sea, with its eroded mountains, its rugged coastline, its *negrito* tribes, its expanses of poor land, and its Huk problems. Magsaysay studied law and, as an attorney, easily turned to politics and became a congressman for his native province. He returned to the way of the law, reinforcing it with administrative reforms at the lowest level to start with. Rural development accompanied his measures to lessen the Communist hold on isolated communities and both were assisted by practical land reform. His decision to act first in the *sitios* and *barrios* provided at last a social balance, for both Roxas and Quirino had relied on a more traditional approach – the reinforcement of the capitalist element by the channelling of war-damage compensation and development funds into already well-established sectors of the economy.[5] Magsaysay's hand was also strengthened by the final agreement on the form of Japanese war reparations. Although little advantage could be observed during his lifetime, the Agreement was signed at the Presidential Palace on 9 May 1956.

After Magsaysay

At his death, President Magsaysay was already convinced that the major part of his struggle against Philippine communism had borne fruit and that clear lines of policy for the future had been laid down to pacify and reconcile much of the dissident element. The glory of those days is now over, but much of the spirit of his policies remains. In the resettled areas of Mindanao, ex-Huks live normal agrarian lives with newly settled ex-servicemen as their neighbours. The social policies which Magsaysay instituted carry on, as does his general military policy of replacing the armed forces in dissident areas as soon as possible by the para-military Constabulary, so echoing Napoleon's views on the development of a gendarmerie deployed all over the countryside. The enthusiastic and courageous Magsaysay was closely confined by Philippine reliance on the United States and by sheer force of character had already obtained a degree of political independence, foreshadowing Presidents Macapagal and Marcos. He died at the zenith of his popularity and his reputation remains scarcely unchallenged.

President Carlos Garcia, who as Vice President assumed full powers on Magsaysay's death, was re-elected for a full term in 1957. He was replaced in 1961 by Diosdado Macapagal, a Liberal. The

Nacionalistas returned to office in 1965, when Ferdinand Marcos was elected. In 1957, Carlos Garcia signed into law a bill outlawing the Communist Party, but although this had been done before (under Roxas) and revoked in attempts to bring the dissidents into legalized politics, the measure was merely designed to straighten the books and give the police, armed forces, and magistracy adequate formal powers to cope with the insurgents. In the circumstances such a measure was logical. President Magsaysay had succeeded in pacifying all but the hard cores, deployed in traditional areas. Numbers of dissidents and fellow-travellers, with their families, had been resettled in new lands. There remained the seriously disaffected and these had no intention of entering legal politics. They were mediocre enough Communists at the best of times and except for a small leavening of intellectuals, some of whom furnished a political direction, saw that their best means of success were in the traditional rural movement where mass involvement hid the flaws in their own political reasoning and personal conduct.

But the Communists' poor quality did not make their basic complaints against the administration less weighty, especially on questions of pure principle. Here the Communists, *inter alia*, have continued to accuse successive governments of resorting to and condoning bribery, corruption, and nepotism, and failing to obtain a proper redistribution of land titles, which results in nationwide land-poverty. There is more than a germ of truth here and both the Nacionalista and Liberal parties have been conscious of their past failures to cure these two main social evils.[6] Land tenure presents a problem which, without revolution, cannot be solved overnight.

When the American administration purchased the 'friar lands', it struck at both a cause of former dissidence and the result of deteriorating social conditions, particularly where smaller landowners were being forced to sell out for economic purposes and, having no alternative livelihood, continued to stay on the land under quasi-serf-like conditions. As the years went by, despite this earlier attempt at redistribution, tenancy agreements increased and, in 1948, over 37 per cent of all farms in the Philippines were held under lease.[7] The situation further deteriorated in the period 1948–53 and, even if Magsaysay found a reasonable solution when he resettled ex-Huks on a sufficiently exploitable land surface in Mindanao, he did so at that specific moment to remove the less virulent Communists from the troubled areas rather than to pioneer a policy of overall land reform.[8] If he had lived and had obtained a second mandate from the people who so admired him, he would probably have gone some way further, despite the then current inborn reluctance of the Nacionalistas to break down the pattern of ownership. It had to be left, therefore, to Diosdado Macapagal, a Liberal and also of modest origins, to bring the problem of land reform before Congress and to take the first steps to set up some of the complex machinery designed not only to buy selected areas for resale to tenants, but to keep the new owners on the land through government-sponsored bank loans. Unfortunately, funds to translate words into acts were meagre and it is only under Marcos that the improved rice and maize seeds have become available to make husbandry more profitable. A solution to the landownership problem may have been studied in the past and some mechanism set up for an implementation of policy, but we still have to look to the future for really concrete results. The two Four-Year Plans, both described below (pp. 199ff.), show how much the present administration is involved in this vital social issue.

Under Macapagal the Philippine government, largely on the President's own instigation, became more concerned with South-East Asian affairs.[9] At the same time, a marginal withdrawal from the spirit of the agreements imposed on the Philippines by the United States at independence was noted. The aid, trade, and defence pacts had all assisted the country between 1946 and 1961, but, as will be seen, the terms of the trade agreement were becoming successively less advantageous and everywhere areas producing raw materials were less fortunate in the struggle against worldwide inflation. The new period (after 1961) also brought with it a comparative peace in the region despite the American involvement in Vietnam and, where the Communist giants seemed to be less of a threat than before, the political disadvantages of remaining host to foreign troops became a little more onerous. The occasional SEATO exercise and short exchange visits of servicemen did not seem to hold any great political danger, especially where the Philippines approved of the anti-Viet Cong operations in Vietnam and, latterly, contributed fighting troops to these. It is interesting that there was practically no opposition in Congress to the idea of contributing this contingent, the size of an engineer battalion, to the United States dominated anti-Communist struggle in Vietnam. Most Filipinos who are politically aware are also generally convinced that they are already in the second line of the front against Chinese political expansionism which supports both the North Vietnam and North Korean party apparatuses, has had considerable influence in Burma, and maintained alien pressure in Indonesia during Sukarno's later period. The Philippines was quite strongly behind such United States military policies and maintained her unit in Vietnam for over five years, not only assisting the military effort but giving a moral boost to the Americans. These policies were also popular with the soldiers who are good fighters first and were never averse to earning the little more pay which became available in such conditions. Although obviously unacceptable to the small numbers of left-wing socialists and Huk fellow-travellers, opposition to such involvement was minimal and continued to be so to the end. Withdrawal took place in 1971 and was mainly influenced by the general American policy of leaving the fighting more or less to the Vietnamese. Nevertheless, the growing wish of Filipinos to be more independent of the United States probably contributed as strongly to the final decision to evacuate.

What was irksome was the continuing presence of large United States military concentrations, adapted to offensive warfare, both in the Philippines and in the South China Sea, and also the means, firmly planted on Philippine soil, to maintain them. Nevertheless, except for a little whittling-down of earlier American extra-territorial privilege and the announcement in November 1970 that the United States naval base at Cavite (Sangley Point) was to be returned to the Philippines, little change has been negotiated and successive Philippine governments have stood by these agreements.

But the years from 1962 onwards saw a number of changes in South-East Asia. The Philippines challenged British sovereignty over a part of North Borneo (the Sabah Claim). Malaya, already independent, became Malaysia in September 1963, with (at the time) Singapore and the North Kalimantan states of Sabah and Sarawak as integral parts. Indonesia, increasingly militant, attempted to challenge first Britain and then Malaysia; the Vietnamese War became bloodier, with the United States attempting to draw in the aid of her allies. Against this background, a number of essentially regional dialogue groups were set up, the Association of South-East Asian States and Maphilindo being the first (1961 and 1963). The Philippines, as the 1960s passed by, became more and more an East Indian state with regional interests than a former colony and a sure base for United States political and defence interests.

Maphilindo came and went. President Macapagal had probably conceived it as a vital forum for useful dialogue planned to reduce tension between his two neighbours, Indonesia and Malaysia. At the same time, many Filipinos hoped that, in its broader application, the organization might serve to bridge the gap between the three East Indian nations which, ethnically, had so much in common. Even before the appalling Indonesian reaction to the Communist-inspired massacre of their senior generals – late in 1966 thousands of left-wing adherents and Chinese residents were slaughtered – Maphilindo was a lame duck and obviously a dying one. It was originally intended as a forum for the discussion of East Indian common objectives; but at the time individual objectives were difficult to reconcile, especially where one member country, Indonesia, was so ethnically akin to the rest, but so set aside in her efforts to obtain political ascendancy, coupled with the promotion of a vague type of neutralism whose character was quite alien to Malaysian and Philippine ideals for national evolution. But the years of Confrontation (Konfrontasei – the Indonesian expression for positive hostility towards Malaysia during 1963–66, which only fell short of declared war) with the neighbourly interest which the Philippines took in the political events brought out a number of points which had not been necessarily accepted before. First, the three countries possessed divergent interests and cultures, resulting from their colonial development, their different religions, and their political systems, which had grown up quite separately. Secondly, despite the militant expansionism of the Sukarno days, the Indonesians were a fairly easygoing people whose problems were not all that different from those of the Filipinos, although the more liberal American colonial system and the physical hybridization of the Filipino had resulted in his higher technical achievement. Thirdly, the Malaysians were a more difficult community to understand, and generally not so genial as the Indonesians, showing mistrust for the Philippine way of life and basing their own on a multiracial, multi-religious society where corruption was the greatest of all possible sins. With the help of Britain, Australia, and New Zealand, they had weathered the storm of nearly four years of armed confrontation by a nation of over a hundred million. Fourthly, President Sukarno's personal magnetism made a favourable impression during the first months of confrontation and, at least initially, he was greatly admired, but his later association with leading Filipinos was marred by his many marriages and relations with still other women; his frightening aggressiveness and illogicality; and his expressed opinion that Indonesia should have the predominant place in any regional grouping. Although Tunku Abdul Rahman might be intransigent, his way of life was respected and Malaysia's politics, although suspect, were not expansionist. Maphilindo died because there was no reason for its continuance, but it was, for thinking Filipinos, a useful, if somewhat frustrating, exercise. It was also the first formal indigenously initiated probe into East Indian co-operation.

Although the election events of the late 1940s may well be considered to have been a catalyst, a quiet evolutionary progress to a state of real independence has continued ever since, although some slowing down during the 1950s was evident. Many North Americans and Europeans living in the Philippines through this slow evolution have scarcely realized the deep-rooted wish of the Filipino to free himself from foreign domination, and have been irritated by some of its manifestations, particularly where regional politics tend to take on a South-East Asian character rather than a frankly Western one or where internal measures to adapt the country to an eventually self-reliant, non-colonial economic policy are pursued. As a regional forum, ASEAN[10] is now of considerable importance and the Philippines has much to contribute to it. The character of the Philippine participation here is interesting to analyse. With little or no reliance on a really ancient Asian civilization, as is the case with Thailand, and predominantly polyglot rather than positively nationalistic, her contribution is that of a geographically assimilated entity with an almost non-Asian viewpoint. A hybridization of character is mixed with an awareness of and sensitivity to world politics. The uniqueness of the Philippines' latter development makes her not only an evolved partner, in so far as national administration and fiscal organization are concerned, but a reserve of skilled and semi-skilled labour which could be readily adapted to regional advantage.[11] Although positively aligned to Western-type democratic principles, for her neighbours the Philippines is becoming a more flexible partner to deal with, despite her still solidly capitalistic character. This new and enlightened independence and Manila's excellent international radio and radio-telephone links were some of the reasons leading to the establishment in 1966 of the seat of the Asian Development Bank in the Philippine capital.

The quasi-satellite period of the 1950s gradually gave way in the early 1960s to a regional outlook in Philippine policies. Any real independence which exists today in Philippine external affairs is as complete as is possible in a world where there are only three superpowers and where positive action by all others is still commensurate with a country's cultural, geographical, and economic importance. Within this framework, often completely overshadowed by power politics, the Philippines has come a long way down the road of nationalism in its purest sense. Those North American and European elements already referred to have witnessed the growing reluctance in official Philippine quarters to accept a *status quo*. The last overt attempt of an outside power to influence East Indian politics was the British Commonwealth support of Malaysia against Indonesian expansionism. Earlier, the mission headed by the American diplomat Ellsworth Bunker which mediated in the dispute between Indonesia and the Netherlands over West Irian in 1962, and which resulted in Indonesian absorption of the territory, was a mere facet of a policy of expediency which advocated decolonization at the periphery, while solidly maintaining, for strategic reasons, an externally supported, almost foreign military régime in Formosa.

Thus a full participation in regional affairs, albeit in a local situation still greatly influenced by United States Asian policies, has been the desire and the practice of successive Philippine governments since the early 1960s. In its individual stages, there was nothing spectacular in Philippine decolonization. In particular, under Macapagal, it had been the assumption of practical responsibilities as and when thought expedient, leading to a current situation where only defence still cannot be debated without due reference to the goodwill of the United States – but here, the Philippines is not alone in the non-Communist world. There still remains a requirement to adapt the economy to a more liberal system, particularly where an almost complete reliance on the sale of raw materials is not only an impediment to progress, but a source of weakness in a world belaboured by inflation. This movement is made more difficult by past investments of a neo-colonial character and, for the future, the government will have to show caution in its approach to the capitalist money market in any attempt to change the direction of the economy. Nevertheless, in the wider field, the gradual assumption of full sovereign powers, without overmuch friction or irritation, has been an object lesson in restraint and commonsense.

The Marcos Old and New Eras

If a gradual and growing participation in regional affairs and the seeming confirmation of a two-party parliamentary system can be recorded, the outside world, never static, has recently brought problems to the Philippines which, although often purely internal problems, are much influenced by external factors. The Communist-inspired dissident movement, reinforced by Maoist infiltration, still exists. The urban student reaction to authority is present in the larger cities and is both part of a worldwide attack on a social system which has relied on bumbling adjustment to obtain progress and a willingness to destroy extensively in order to rebuild once again. With all the outward signs of a more opulent society all around them, the peasant farmers and their social equals are now becoming more sensitive to the hardships which a benign capitalistic society continues to see as their destiny. Rapid population increase makes no contribution to material improvement and often nullifies any progress obtained from long years of technical research, followed by the conscientious application of such newly proven methods.

In the later 1960s and early 1970s, dissidence, which in the Philippines means an unconstitutional movement often assisted by banditry, evolved rapidly, for with the arrival of Maoism, the methods used to change a political course took on an even more positive destructive character; and with this new influence attempting to gain ascendancy, the former loosely grouped Communist organs split and a translated element, the self-named Mao Tse-tung Thought Party (with its military wing, the New People's Army, slowly replacing the Huks), was thrown up effectively to oppose the KPP which, itself formed in 1930, had absorbed much of the Philippine Socialist Party in 1938. Although the KPP has no tradition of legality, nor of any use of democratic methods, the new party may well be able better to exploit the country's simmering violence, so forcing the KPP to enter legal politics (should government prove conciliatory) once again. Openly Chinese influenced, the new party may have some success among the student body and within the intelligentsia, but its rural activities already encounter both the antipathy with which anything with a Chinese trademark is welcomed and a national policy which has resulted in the armed forces ultimately meeting any increased violence with an adequately gauged measure of increased armed intervention.

The student movements in the Philippines are, of necessity, centred around the most important urban areas and these contain less than 2 per cent of the adult population. Although Filipino parents are indulgent with their children, family ties are still very strong and those students who have their parents or their relations living near their colleges tend not only to lodge with them, but if housed elsewhere, visit them frequently. Others are often maintained with the support of an influential neighbour, possibly a politician who, originating from the same area, directly or indirectly looks after the sons and even the daughters of his constituents, often providing some form of board and lodging during term time. There is, therefore, a continuing confrontation of ideas in the home, but, as elsewhere among young people, there is a silent majority which returns home after lectures and a vociferous minority which, in recent years, has met outside the family circle to advocate political extremism in a country where such politics seem almost unreal. Those who have absorbed and accepted Maoism veer further away from the majority than before. In the Philippines, they have reinforced the extreme left wing, surpassing the radical nationalist[12] currents of the 1960s which also gained support from the student body and teaching intelligentsia. The latter, although not without foreign influence, did little more than preach mild sedition and anti-Americanism. They even had their democratic *raison d'être* in a country where majority politics were firmly conservative, adding a justified and marginally useful presence to the more stratified pressure groups which already existed.

It is sad to record that, despite the steadying nature of its moral teaching and continuing missionary activities, often vigorous and positive, the Roman Catholic Church, now an almost indigenous manifestation,[13] has contributed to the furtherance of a system which might well become a potential threat to both social progress and economic stability. Population increase in the Philippines is not unique in the world and there are other countries which have yet to reconcile unrestricted births, accepted by all but a tiny minority, with a productive land area which is being rapidly filled with additions to an essentially rural population. In the Philippines, the main reason for a continuing ignorance of the danger of producing too many people is undoubtedly the reluctance, if not the opposition, of the Church to anything more than a restricted dialogue on the subject within the country itself. As in other largely Roman Catholic countries, there is a percentage of society which not only takes a personal decision on this subject, but also openly advocates some positive measure to limit population increase. The majority, however, must remain in full or partial ignorance, either because birth control appliances are outlawed by government policy or because (and this is more general) propaganda for population control is actively discouraged by administrative action or moral pressure. The latter is the case in the Philippines and despite the fact that the Church is quasi-indigenous, it is part of a predominantly European-based society whose influence comes from outside the country. Thus population stabilization in the Philippines is actively hindered by an international force.

In any study of population control in a developing country, the denial of the right to wage an effective and all-out campaign in favour of limitation is tantamount to the acceptance of a measure of demographic increase. Where, as in the Philippines, a degree of administrative efficiency and medical skill diminishes the mortality rate throughout the age spectrum, such a demographic increase can only be accentuated. Without infringing on either moral or sectarian beliefs, it is essential to examine how such a society can evolve without harm, not only to the material wellbeing of its people, but also to political stability. The basis of existing religious resistance to population limitation is both moral and practical. Morally, the use of mechanical devices or of chemical product prevents life. Practically, reorganization of the world's economy and the production of better types of currently used foodstuffs, together with the confection of newly discovered ones, must result in added means with which to support a much larger global population. Moreover, within a short span, some acceptable way of limitation will be discovered by the ever-searching intelligence of man. These are of course theories, even dogmas. They are not universally accepted by a partially non-Catholic and strikingly materialistic world, and they produce no true reconciliation between a build-up of population and a build-up of technical achievement.

Therefore the Philippines could well find herself alongside a number of other countries whose economies are based on raw materials and where population increase might well outstrip the availability of foodstuffs.

The obvious questions are how long will it take for a serious deterioration of living conditions to appear and, for practical purposes, how long can this brinkmanship situation last? With 40-odd million inhabitants in the early 1970s and a population increase rate which adds over 50 per cent to the community between each twelve-year census, we can look forward to over 60 million Filipinos in 1984 and to a little under one hundred million in 1996, if the present rate is maintained. Various estimates of the country's capacity to provide for its inhabitants have been made and figures from 60 to 90 million have been suggested. It will need all the planning and execution of a properly balanced economy to arrive at an acceptable level to maintain the children who are being born in the 1970s and it will require not only a continuing, almost superhuman, effort to arrive at an overall production to maintain the additional millions in later years, but favourable world conditions and an international acceptance of the measures to be taken by the Philippines to maintain such an increased population. This is particularly the case where many other countries are planning positively to forego such a luxury. Brinkmanship can go on for as long as there is a capacity to produce suitable living conditions both for an existing population and for those unborn children already conceived, but it is almost impossible to give a time-scale for this in years as there are many imponderables. What is certain, however, is that with each year's population additions, a proportion of the basic flexibility to improve disappears and, as the years go by, even the means to prevent deterioration could well vanish.

By the end of 1970, President Marcos, midway through his second term, had clearly become preoccupied by his own and the Philippines' political future. That he was the first President to have been re-elected for a second term was already a break with tradition. In such circumstances his personal popularity must have made him believe that his own experience of leadership (with his distinguished war record as a guerrilla fighter) might well fit him to reshape the republic's longer-term fortunes. An alternative to winning a third term, impossible under the 1935 Constitution, was the selection of his wife, Imelda, as the Nacionalista Party's candidate. Such a formula must have been tempting, especially as Imelda Marcos more than shared her husband's popularity.[14] If he and his party had seriously considered this possibility, it is at present difficult to say when it was put aside. As before, it is necessary to examine the conditions which led up to the President's declaration of martial law on 22 September 1972.

Student unrest had intensified and had not been helped by extra-Philippine influences. The new Maoist-type Communists had shown themselves more idealistic and more vigorous than their predecessors. Marcos's opponents were understandably, after nearly seven years of personalized political ascendancy, becoming increasingly restive and looked to the 1972 elections as a supreme trial of strength, with all stops pulled out. In such conditions a political upheaval was inevitable and could be profoundly disrupting. Inflation, which had forced the floating of the peso in 1969, might well ensue. In South-East Asia there were signs of fundamental change. Although Indonesia, a previous challenge to East Indian stability, was now ruled by a nationalistic military junta whose anti-Communist policies were encouraging and non-expansionist character reassuring, Malaysia continued to be suspect. Developments in mainland Asia showed that the Philippines was bound to be submitted to increased regional political pressure. The American decision to withdraw from the former Indo-Chinese states was easily foreseeable and had probably been communicated by diplomatic channels, as a political flotation of Formosa would have been. Polarization around Japan in concert with Thailand must also have seemed inevitable. The ability of a traditionally elected Philippine government to deal with these conditions so soon after an inauguration in early 1973, especially where untrammelled party politics would have tended to nurture lawlessness, could only have seemed reduced. Such circumstances and consideration of certain violent internal manifestations – in November 1970 Pope Paul VI was attacked at Manila airport by a crazed Bolivian; on 21 August 1971 a Liberal Party rally in Manila was attacked with hand grenades, with over a hundred killed or wounded (President Marcos claimed this to be the work of 'Marxist–Leninist–Maoist' elements supported by a 'foreign power' and suspended *habeas corpus*); a brutal attack on Mrs Marcos at a beautification contest on 7 December 1972 – probably confirmed the necessity for a reinforcement of the powers of government rather than a relapse into such free-for-all conditions normally attendant on a general election. Although President Marcos's personal ambition must never be discounted, the desire of the United States to reinsure her new lines in Asia should also be considered. Nor, in such circumstances, could Japan and Indonesia be disinterested: Japan as the Philippines' major trading partner and Indonesia as a sister Malay nation with strong anti-Communist policies.

Impatient of opposition sniping, reinforced by those elements who desired the downfall of authority; unsure of the results of a general election where Mrs Marcos might or might not have been the party's candidate, the President once and for all dissociated himself from much of the political caucus around him and severed the easy relations which had hitherto been possible with the opposition, in turn selecting a limited number of powerful technocrats as his closer collaborators. The next step was a take-over of the Commission on Constitutional Reform. Programmed by the legislature, this body had been sitting since the beginning of 1971 under the chairmanship of the former President, Diosdado Macapagal. In mid-1972 its deliberations were incomplete and rumours were already circulating that attempts were being made to subvert it, the name of the President's wife being cited as one of those who had become involved in the subversion. From then on, things began to move. The Commission was enlivened by the drafting of new members and a concrete project was agreed. Martial law was proclaimed on 22 November 1972 and a new draft statute published on 1 December.

The new constitution was simpler than the old, more compatible with the problems which conditions in the Philippines now raised. Two courses of action were envisaged: first the setting-up of an interim national assembly, consisting of all willing, previously elected Senators and congressmen, together with all those members of the Commission who had voted for the final draft; this was to be followed by a national referendum to ratify the new permanent constitutional structure which provided for a single chamber, elected for six years, which was to choose a President (Head of State) and a Prime Minister. The President was to be a figurehead with no legal responsibilities, but the Prime Minister was to have wide executive powers. A cabinet would be appointed, the majority of its members coming from the Assembly.

There is little doubt that, by such methods, constitutional democracy could be safeguarded, although certain short cuts had been taken which, in the event, seemed logical and expedient. The process of deliberation and referendum seemed to accord with evolutionary political processes which, nevertheless, remained well within the limits of democratic change. The election of an Assembly for a six-year period not only confirmed the sovereignty of the majority of the electorate, but also sought to eradicate the evils which had attended the two- and four-year elections, with all the frightening political and economic upheaval which seemed inevitably to follow. The designation of the President as a figurehead, leaving the single-chamber Assembly to choose the administration, would remove the often tedious upper- and lower-house infighting and the tendency of many to enter politics for gain or for a game of political dialectics. A more direct and more intimate parliamentary process had been proposed and could well be the answer to nepotism, corruption, and coercion.

Arguments against the project stemmed initially from the frightening depth of the change envisaged in a well-tried and locally cherished political way of life and these reactions were echoed by foreign observers inside and outside the Philippines. Moreover, the Filipino had from infancy been taught to revere the constitution and although it might well have been one which by its liberality and its dependent law processes had invited political malpractice, the projected sharp departure from many of its tenets came as a considerable shock to an unprepared electorate. This in itself seemed to produce a natural brake to the evolution Marcos so desired. Furthermore, the checks and balances contained in the new charter seemed to be so much less satisfactory than those which had been painstakingly prepared for the 1935 Constitution. Consultations were perhaps too loosely arranged to allow effective power to be retained by a real nationwide majority and the possibility of a number of non-elected technocrats in the cabinet could be considered a further threat. (Although non-elected ministers had always been nominated, their presence in an absolutist state could be disturbing.) The proposed new electoral and legislative processes promised to be unpopular, not only with the professional politicians whose interests and livelihood depended on political intrigue, but also with the party organizations, the Press, the administrative hierarchy, and even with the local policeman who owed his job to an elected official. In addition, there were the local party managers and their strong-arm followers who revelled in the nine-month battle which had preceded every bi-annual election in the past.

With the proclamation of martial law and the proposed substitution of this new charter for the 1935 Constitution, if agreed in plebiscite, there seemed to have been nothing distasteful in President Marcos's actions. It is now evident, however, that he had covered himself by obtaining confirmation of support from the armed forces, themselves loyally tied to legal process, as defined under the constitution of 1935, and again in 1946. Once assured of their loyalty and the generals' agreement, he could go ahead with his proclamation of martial law and announce the intended referendum.

Such a proclamation had been fully covered in the 1935 Constitution. Presidential power was thereby strengthened. The *a priori* support of the generals was a necessity in such conditions and they had to be convinced that the internal security situation really merited such emergency measures. With external, Pan-Asian pressures well defined and a recrudescence of Communist rebellion (the result of the influence of Maoism), urban and rural lawlessness would have to be reassessed. To these would have been added a further factor: firm reports on the activities of a new separatist movement among the Moslems of Mindanao. The armed forces could not remain indifferent to such threats and the proclamation went forward.

It is too early to sum up the political and practical results of the proclamation of martial law. Nor is it possible to state other than probable reasons for the proclamation. Nevertheless, three main points are apparent. First, Marcos's authority was increased and the armed forces, albeit somewhat purged of 'non-reliable' elements, assumed a major role in urban and rural peace-keeping and in the overall surveillance of the country's essential industries. Secondly, the maintenance of both law and order and the management of public concerns improved. The security situation in the large towns also changed immensely for the better and both this and the restrained conduct of the military brought public support for the state of exception. Thirdly, firm control of information media was obtained through censorship and normal political activity almost immediately ceased. Attempts by individual politicians and journalists to break out of this restraint entailed arrest, limitation of personal liberty, and even summary detention.

But, if this solution to many current problems was already in draft form, time was against President Marcos, for the traditions of 1946 remained strong, even after the introduction of martial law. Against this seeming dislike for political change was the practical effect of the generally reasonable application of the state of exception: criminal activities lessened and so did political coercion and corruption. The carriage of illegal firearms, outside the Communist-dominated and the traditional Moslem areas, became a less important problem for the security forces.[15] A curfew was imposed from 1130 to 0400 hours, almost puritan influences began to erode the hitherto gross night-life of Manila, and the Constabulary replaced the more corrupt elements of the urban police forces. In such conditions, playing the cards of social progress and personal popularity which followed on from improved living conditions, President Marcos finally saw his way to cutting the knot which bound him to the past.

As a result of the declarations of 1 December 1972, a countrywide referendum was to be held by 15 January 1973 to ratify the new constitution. The normal machinery, supervised by the Commission on Elections, would be used to organize such a procedure and to promulgate the results. By the end of December, it must have become quite evident that, to obtain a mandate for the new charter, a much longer preparation period would be necessary if the people were to be fully informed of the practical advantages of such a decisive step. In the circumstances, either the referendum would have to be postponed, so as to get a general propaganda programme under way, or some more summary form of affirmation arranged for. Playing his two trump cards, President Marcos announced that, because there was not sufficient national understanding, a system of nationwide soundings in the form of citizens' assemblies, held at *barrio* level, would be taken and if by 15 January 1973 a favourable overall opinion was obtained, the new constitution would be considered ratified. Two interesting points follow from this. First, if the new constitution was ratified, the existing House of Representatives and Senate would be automatically dissolved. Secondly, the nationwide sounding would be made in a plebiscital college of 39,000-odd *barrios*, where assemblies of all citizens of over fifteen years of age would be convened.

The President called a *Katipunan* at the Malacañang Palace on 17 January. This was attended by a gathering of governors, mayors, local officials, and *barrio* captains. At this assembly it was announced that the citizens' assemblies had endorsed the new constitution, which was to be considered ratified. It was also announced that they had declared a new legislative assembly unnecessary at present; that no elections should be programmed for a period of seven years; that martial law should be continued; and that President Marcos should remain in office. There was, therefore, no question of calling a provisional assembly and the old Congress was automatically dissolved. At the same time, it was stated that the citizens' assemblies would be reconvened in January 1974. As a rider, it was announced that a certain consensus of opinion within these assemblies had demanded that the President should call on a revolutionary government to take over power. Marcos replied that he had turned down this suggestion as being undemocratic in spirit.

These are the basic facts of the present Philippine situation. It is certain that evolution will take place as the newly authorized régime takes on a more permanent character. President Marcos, with a handful of so-called 'technocrats', rules with the aid of a Supreme Court, which has remained in office (although the President can dismiss judges), a framework of provincial governors, municipal and city mayors, and *barrio* captains. He has won the support of the armed forces and the civil service has been suitably purged, its senior officials being appointed by the President. At the same time, it seems that the electoral procedure outlined in the draft statute of 1 December has been temporarily set aside and that the country's sounding-board will, for the time being, be the citizens' assemblies and occasional referenda.

[1] The two ensuing elections were accompanied by an even greater materialization of illegality and, together, marked the peak of a destructive movement, without bringing overmuch social advantage.

[2] In Malaysia, something of the same kind of evolution occurred at the same time, but here independence had to be postponed until after the Emergency was over.

[3] American aid to the Philippines exceeded $2 billion during the first five years of independence, including war damage claims and veterans' back pay. The Rehabilitation Act, pegged to the Bell Trade Act, demanded an eight-year extension of free trade and of parity in exploitation of natural resources. The latter demand required an amendment to the 1935 Constitution. It barely got the three-quarters majority it needed in the Congress, and 60 per cent of the people abstained from voting in the 1947 plebiscite that followed.

In 1950 Quirino invited a United States economic mission to survey the Philippines. An initial grant of $250 million in aid was released shortly after the reforms which the mission had recommended were enacted.

[4] It is not certain that he even wished to do so in these first post-war days.

[5] This was difficult to avoid as these sectors had lost the most during the Second World War. Nevertheless, the resulting imbalance caused social grievances.

[6] The Philippine Communist organizations are essentially dissident and they themselves actively contribute to corruption, nepotism, and coercion. If these particular social grievances were phased out, new ones would be found to replace them as a platform. The ultimate aim of the Communists is the breakdown of Philippine society as it is now known.

[7] As opposed to the free-holding of land through a purchase agreement.

[8] A 'Land for the Landless' campaign accompanied this and some solid anti-dissident propaganda was achieved.

[9] There had been earlier manifestations of both regional grouping and a desire to follow a more independent path. During President Quirino's term, the Baguio Conference of seven Asian nations took place (May 1950) and the Philippines was ably represented at the famous Bandung Conference of 1955 by President Magsaysay.

[10] ASEAN, Association of South-East Asian Nations, a grouping of Indonesia, Malaysia, the Philippines, Singapore, and Thailand, created in August 1967, to promote economic co-operation.

[11] Already in the early 1960s, the Philippine-sponsored, non-official 'Operation Brotherhood' scheme was providing aid in skilled manpower to neighbouring states.

[12] Earlier manifestations tended to be centred on anti-American, even anti-foreign, influence in both the Philippines and the region, although their views might often have been in direct opposition to those of either of the two major parties.

[13] Despite the presence of a large number of foreign priests who continue to be necessary where parishes grow in size and where Filipinos still seem reluctant to enter the priesthood.

[14] Imelda Marcos is undoubtedly a competent political operator, an excellent wife and mother in the classic Philippine mould. Coming from a not too well-off family, she seems eager to demonstrate an unpretentious way of life. President Marcos's long period of office has brought her more and more into the limelight, although she has generally become involved in the less contentious side of Presidential life: the development of cultural institutions and the fostering of social works on a national scale. Here, and in her more informal contacts, always possible in the Philippines, she excels, with her quiet charm, her intelligence, and her unflamboyant beauty.

[15] As the result of a proclamation which included a form of amnesty for possession of illegally carried firearms, a large number of these weapons were surrendered in the Christian areas.

Chapter 18

The Material Future

The Factors Involved

IN ASIA, the Philippines has a unique place. Underdeveloped as she still is, she shares with peninsular Malaysia many characteristics which give her a sure material advantage for the future. Although hybridized in culture and by ethnic origin, she is unified as only an island nation can be and her population is politicially conscious to a far greater degree than those of her neighbours. She possesses a substantial pool of semi-skilled labour, a fairly sizeable endowment in medium- and high-grade artisan skills,[1] and a steadily growing number of specialized technicians and engineers. In addition, the practical formation of this more sophisticated stratum has now entered into its third generation and is a welcome supplement to a modern educational system which not only has traditions reaching back to the beginning of the century, but already has shown itself capable of accepting the larger part of the post-war generation in its primary establishments and has, more recently, provided some sort of a secondary education for about 25 per cent of them, using a world language, American-English, as the medium for both academic and technical instruction.

An inventory of the advantages which the Philippines enjoys in the materialistic society of the late twentieth century is reassuring. To be added to the relative political stability of the country and the inherent adaptability of its people, there exists a cultivable land surface which will probably be adequate to feed its population for at least one and perhaps two generations to come, as well as providing the area necessary to maintain a substantial production of exportable items: coconut products, sugar-cane, and a small number of subsidiary crops such as tobacco, abaca, hemp, etc. A climate and rainfall pattern which, despite occasional natural disaster, is benign and adaptable to a multi-cropping programme also contributes positively. To these must be joined the more particularized resources of the country: its forests, its mineral deposits, and its hydro-electric power potential. The physical position of these islands and their natural harbour facilities on the west coasts have also been of considerable advantage in the establishment of transformation industries designed to contribute to the national economy by a local processing of both Philippine and imported raw materials, either for local or for regional consumption. Further, there exist the beginnings of a quite sophisticated natural infrastructure, albeit fragmented at the present time.

There are, however, a number of internal factors which tend to militate against the efficient operation of even that traditional economy which has resulted from the former colonial system and the later pressures mentioned above (pp. 141—2). First, the island patterns are essentially broken in physical character, with interrupted coastal plain areas and a striking dearth of navigable rivers. Because of this, transportation is manifestly inefficient by nature and comparatively costly, resulting in a favouring of the relatively advantageous conditions existing in the Manila area and a continuing lagging-behind of development in other parts of the Philippines.[2] A complete lack of workable mineral oil deposits and the poor quality of the small coal reserves which exist in the country are also negative factors, and, if the beneficial elements of the Philippine political scene and the level of efficiency of Philippine labour have already been calculated among her assets, the sensitivity of elected governments to what must be considered as illogical pressures and the conditions resulting from corruption and illegality should be counted in any appreciation of impediments to progress.

The Programmes

Nevertheless, it must already be apparent that the material future of the Philippines will be more influenced by world conditions than by those internal questions which have been mentioned above. A completely rationalized utilization of the material advantages of the country may never be really possible if the monopoly of the already fully industrialized nations is maintained and, here, such a monopoly would seem to have been recently strengthened rather than weakened; the position of non-industrialized countries having been made more sensitive to worldwide inflationary currents. But, in such conditions, it is only a small shift from the present marketing profile which would bring benefits and it is here, in a slow planned change of course, that the Philippines may well be able to absorb at least some part of a rapidly growing population into her own economy. Such a programme, however, not only requires sophisticated planning, but fiscal efficiency, sound administrative methods, capital investment, and a widespread maintenance of existing objectives.

Within the Philippines' economy, there are both those general problems caused by underdevelopment and the inherent shortcomings resulting from earlier practice. Past American aid not only contributed to the improvement of infrastructure conditions, but also tended to ensure the continuity of the existing character of the economy. The reinforcement of an infrastructure useful to the country's new requirements and the planning and execution of programmes to produce that marginal change of course referred to earlier have been the preoccupation of successive Philippine governments, in consultation with experts, regional partners, and, to some extent, with the United States. To achieve such results, the first two four-year programmes were designed and it is interesting to refer to both of these in order to follow the thinking of the last three Philippine administrations on this subject.

Reliance on a primitive agricultural sector was one of the cornerstones of the original appreciation of the economic problems of the country. The functional inefficiency of this sector was recognized and here the requirement to improve was considered imperative for three reasons:

1. the need to produce more food for a growing population (where any increase in the land area used could only be marginal) without recourse to the importation of rice, maize, and tinned fish in ever-increasing quantity at the cost of foreign exchange;
2. a growing demand from other sections of the national economy for increased adult manpower in order to achieve an internal economic buoyancy so that demand for industrial consumer goods might increase;
3. an eventual need to increase industrial efficiency and lay down a suitable base for a consumer-goods production directed towards at least a regional market.

Population change and employment prospects are also complementary subjects. With a demographic growth of a little over 3 per cent per annum, sluggishness in the agricultural and industrial sectors has brought with it a substantial increase in unemployment and underemployment, resulting in an unused potential which amounts to an aggregate of between 10 and 15 per cent of the employable population. Adverse terms of world trade have also been a challenge to Philippine viability. Every proposed increase in prices demanded for raw material has not only been countered by a confirmed reluctance to pay more by the highly industrialized nations, but also by continuous attempts on their part to initiate competitive movements among producer countries to the advantage of the institutionalized buyers. This movement is in direct contrast to the structures and spirals now reluctantly accepted by the suppliers of more sophisticated industrial products, where a growing improvement in living standards in producer countries has been accompanied by a worldwide inflationary movement.

The shortcomings of the national infrastructure have been of considerable influence on the problem as a whole. The damage caused by the Second World War has still not been fully repaired and the greater demands, based on the Philippines' changing needs, have added to the capital works which are currently called for. An initial requirement to maintain the original infrastructure has been broadened by the necessity to service a far larger system constructed since the 1940–45 War. Roads, bridges, land irrigation, and electric-power production equipment are the most important components of this growing national asset.

By the time the second Four-Year Plan (1971–74) had been commenced, the mere fact of living with stated problems allowed the planners to see much further than before, although there was never any doubt that the basic appreciation of the earlier plan (1967–70) was valid in its conception. The Second Plan was more sophisticated, more inventive, and was a subtle mixture of expertise and a truly Philippine utilization of expediency. Thus the nationwide transportation system was examined by foreign experts and the basis of an overall network inserted into the plan, taking with it the rather reduced achievements of the first period. Investment funding, outside aid, and the growth-rate of the Gross National Product were examined and feasibility studies completed. A priority for the increase of home-produced foodstuffs was stipulated and this latter consideration was maintained, although improved rice and maize seed might well have seemed to solve much of the problem of current self-sufficiency in the preferred cereal range. Again, although the exploitation of mineral resources, the overhaul and addition to the transportation and irrigation systems, the increased production and milling of sugar-cane, and a step-up and diversification in the coconut industry were retained, a planned brake on forest commodity production was included so that some measures could be taken to slow down devastation to the watersheds. A surplus of imports over exports was purposely foreseen so as to obtain capital equipment with the plan's life, to build the foundations for the maintenance of the greatly increased population, which was bound to emerge as the result of the sustained birth-rate. A suitable school-building programme was carried over from the first plan to provide for the education of these new Filipinos.

The traditional economy has been discussed (pp. 75–6, 87–90, 141–2). The two Four-Year Plans have included elements designed to alter the economic course sufficiently to take more advantage of the material capacity of the country. Sufficiency or near-sufficiency in so far as a number of manufactured and processed items are concerned has almost been achieved in certain particularized sectors: cement manufacture, pulp and paper production, plate glass, footwear, and textiles being some of the most important. The production of mild steel and galvanized items from melted scrap also provides an effective contribution to the balance of payments, as does the growing output of certain chemicals and fertilizers.

Nevertheless, the priorities contained in both plans were conceived to provide a degree of self-sufficiency for this growing community, an increase of production in most of the well-tried industries, and a diversification in order to allow the Philippines to go a few steps forward in the heavier processing sector, so that the manufacture of more sophisticated items from indigenous primary products could satisfy some of the needs of a home market and, in due time and course, provide surpluses for export.

World and national conditions accompanying the two plans have brought their own impediments and it is obvious that the 1967–70 targets were generally unachieved, although it is still difficult to say where the exact shortfalls were. In particular, infrastructural objectives were poorly covered and there were very few cases where the industrial development programmes were properly adhered to, a notable failure being the planned exploitation of the Surigao laterite fields. The 1969 election campaign caused some extra-plan expenditure and, in many cases, the fragmentary application of a part of an item for purely political purposes. A national monetary crisis in 1970 caused dislocation, and the currency weakness of the United States has also brought with it perturbation and a requirement to rephase funding. In such circumstances it is difficult to see the second of the two economic programmes becoming an unqualified success, although some cumulative benefits from both of the two exercises may well serve to build a fairly advantageous threshold for a third.

Despite such pessimism, a short study of what the second Four-Year Plan hopes to achieve is generally of considerable interest as comparative figures for many of its facets exist. The plan sees an annual growth-rate of 5.5 per cent, rising to a Gross National Product of 306,308 billion pesos by 1974. The first Four-Year Plan saw an average growth of 6.3 per cent annually, but in practice the latter years were less productive than the earlier and there was some falling-off of impetus. Investment growth in the 1971–74 exercise is designed to reach 21 per cent annually. It is important to retain from these figures that, despite a certain buoyancy of the national economy, the institutionally preferred sectors are not necessarily those which were favoured by past growth. Investment in and the maintenance of the future Philippine population was undoubtedly the major consideration of both the programmes, not only in their provision for the immediate needs of the people, but also in the eventual evolution of the economy from its present quasi-colonial status. The average rural Filipino is needy but not starving and we have already seen that the society in which he lives does provide him with the bare essentials and even some cultural relaxation of a simple nature. The improvement of his material life and the provision for population growth are requisites which successive Philippine governments, never very remote from the masses, have attempted in their fashion to obtain. An increased supply of foodstuffs to feed this growing community is essential to the maintenance of even the existing low standard, but to this must be added the means to purchase more if these standards are to improve. In the same way, a reinforcement of educational facilities should not only cover the requirements of an increased population, but also add to the qualitative product. The strengthening of the infrastructure and the development of export potentials form part of a campaign not only to increase Philippine participation in world activities, but also to place some insurance for the future in the improvement of living conditions within the country itself. In a world ruled by purely materialistic demands, these aspirations are generally recognized, although outside assistance to provide for them is not always forthcoming.

Material Objectives of the Second Four Year Plan

An overall view of the character of the Philippine economy, the needs of the Philippine population, and the measures conceived to produce the change of course necessary to adapt the economy to the country's future have been given above (pp. 141ff.). So that present trends caused by the second Four-Year Plan can be understood fully, a brief examination of the individual sectors will serve to complete the economic picture. These are essentially broken down into agricultural production, mining and manufacturing, export production, and public sector investment.

As we have seen earlier, a stated priority has been placed on agricultural production, even to a point where an export surplus of home produced foodstuffs is obtained. The targets for popular staples (rice and maize) are an increase in production of 6.25 per cent annually and the latest plan now foresees the need for a thorough reorganization of this sector with the provision by government of grain storage, marketing, and co-operative facilities. The increase of irrigated areas to take advantage of the new paddy and maize seed is a further important consideration. A real breakthrough has already occurred in the production of foodstuffs and, with the introduction of the new seed strains, a surplus has been obtained, although this situation is still somewhat precarious and only a complete change-over to new seed wherever this is practicable[3] will allow a continued self-sufficiency in an expanding community.

Commercial cropping also figures in the plan and the targets here are to increase the annual production of coconuts and sugar-cane by 3·5 and 3·8 per cent respectively. As in the foodstuffs sector, this growth will be obtained by better husbandry – the introduction of improved seed and the gradual improvement of cultivation methods. In addition to these two giants of the agricultural field, a certain official interest is being taken in the improved cultivation of bananas, sorghum, and soya beans. Here, despite favourable climatic conditions, production has been quite irrational. In a country where the soya bean could be of considerable use, hardly any commercial planting has taken place post-war and even the ubiquitous soya sauce has to be imported. Locally grown bananas, although widely used as a dietary item all over the country, are of little use for export, as the types planted are not over-popular outside the domestic consumer area, where this fruit is normally eaten cooked. In addition to these three particularized items, a study of the possibility of increasing the area planted with oil palms is also being undertaken. The cultivation of the oil palm is at present restricted to certain areas of Mindanao (Davao and Basilan Island) and is essentially in the hands of a few owners of large estates. If this tree could be grown more generally and improved markets obtained overseas, a modest local processing industry could be set up and a welcome diversification might be introduced into the smallholding sector in Mindanao.

The development of the locally produced meat industry is also covered by the plan. In 1969, the indigenous output only covered 45 per cent of local requirements and animals from as far away as Australia were imported on the hoof. This is in direct contrast to the establishment in the mid-1960s of a highly organized and efficient processing and canning industry turning out high-quality foodstuffs which would do credit to any European country. The target here is to increase production from local beef herds, from piggeries, and from modern poultry batteries to cover at least 65 per cent of home requirements (corrected for population increase), during the lifetime of the plan. This should make supplies of cheaper meat available to the less privileged members of the community.

Meat of any kind will be a luxury for the majority of Filipinos for some time to come and, as a protein substitute, fish has been popular with the rural population since time immemorial. Deep-sea fishing is not a traditional occupation and any Philippine-based operations of this nature are generally in the hands of large organizations established in Manila, often manipulated by foreign capital. The bulk of the country's supplies come over the coastline from inshore operations or are taken from the coastal fishponds. The plan envisages the increase of supplies from the sea, so as to produce almost self-sufficiency by the end of the period. Here the three areas of improvement will be offshore operations, fishpond production, and industrial infrastructure. Offshore operations will be assisted by the provision of credit for and the construction of larger fishing vessels which will be based throughout the Archipelago. Credit for fishpond construction and the dissemination of the necessary expertise will also be provided. The construction of improved wharves, storage, and marketing facilities are also part of the plan. This is a practical move on the part of the Philippine government and one which mixes tradition with novelty. Offshore fishing requires capital and some infrastructure, and so has lagged behind in the past. The provision of equipment and shore facilities, including landing-points equipped with ice plants, etc., may well result in a real benefit, if properly maintained. The development of the fishpond industry, however, is reinforcing a well-tried success, albeit a fairly recent one and one which is as essentially untraditional as the deeper-water fishing operations. The intensive production of specially selected types of fish in the brackish waters of controlled coastal ponds does supply a good-quality product at fairly cheap prices. The extension of this modest industry is not over-difficult and for a small outlay and the provision of some fertilizer to improve the vegetation in the pond, an almost continuous harvest can be obtained.

In the mining sector, the future of the various segments of the industry are much more at the mercy of external factors, for there is practically no real domestic market for the product, which is predominantly a raw material or a semi-finished sophistication, concentrated for ease of transport and exportation. Such metal production is governed by world supply and demand, and the renewal of sources is always a delicate financial operation, for only major war can cause starvation and an ensuing spontaneous offer of funds to build up complex mining infrastructures. The expenditure on armaments during the Korean War was the last real threat to the stability of metal prices. Short military campaigns and the rise and fall of demand caused by worldwide capital projects can now normally be satisfied, so far as metals are concerned, from the finishing industry's stocks and current production. In addition, a second line of defence is held in the form of the large reserves of refined metals and material for processing built up under the control of the major industrialized countries. Nevertheless, in the non-ferrous group, some erosion of the consumers' position is already apparent and for the producer a certain welcome movement upwards in prices is generally forecast; here the Philippines, already a major supplier of copper, chromite, and manganese, will be the first to benefit. Although not totally depressed, the metal market is only barely at a level to encourage important reinvestment and the continuing search for new sources tends to be based on a need to discover long-term deposits in relatively stable political conditions.

Most of the modern mining infrastructure of the Philippines was built up at a time when the market going was good and there was an ample supply of rehabilitating grants and loans to cover the cost of expensive extractive and processing plant. Now things are not so favourable and if the government requires, for economic purposes, the extension of the country's mining operations, it must say so, give firm incentives, and provide means to maintain a social climate which would attract not only investment, but also managerial and executive personnel with highly specialized skills to man the new complexes. The Philippine government has taken the decision to expand the industry and it has said so definitely in its second Four-Year Plan, calling for an increase in the overall production of copper from the pre-plan tonnages of 63,000 in ore form and 350,000 in concentrates to 100,000 in ore form and 820,000 in concentrates. This foresees not only an overall increase in output, but an installation and operation of concentrators which are quite sophisticated plant. To the older-established mines in Mountain and Cebu are now added producer units in Marinduque, and a continuing search for fresh deposits goes on as copper is present in many areas. The second main prong of the non-ferrous metal drive is the government's target to bring into operation nickel-mining, with an eventual extension into refining, using the large reserves located in Surigao del Norte as a base for exploitation. There has been some delay in this sector as the French company which initially considered the project decided to withdraw at the commencement of the plan's life and some modifications of target dates then became necessary. The concession has now been accepted by a Philippine company, Marinduque Mining, with large-scale Canadian support, and some early production may well be shown by 1974, although any local refining is still a long way off. This exploitation, on Nonoc Island, which lies off the extreme north-east tip of Mindanao, may well become a major provider of foreign earnings, despite the considerable physical problems inherent in the maintenance of a sophisticated project in such an isolated area. The plan's level of production, valued at $100 million annually by 1976, could well be achieved although the market is still somewhat depressed by Japanese stockpiling. Some quite important foreign earnings might be apparent before 1976, but the current indication is that, before favourable marketing conditions return, adverse world prices could cause havoc in newly projected exploitations. The installation and maintenance of an important mining infrastructure in a newly developed area, far distant from any urban centre, will have already meant the introduction into the Philippines of costly, foreign-manufactured machinery and plant, and large quantities of ancillary equipment to build up all the trappings of a modern mining camp. Despite the importance of the ore body, which is reputed to be one of the largest in the world, such a project is not automatically a money-spinner, although the comparative nearness of the main consumer markets, Japan and Canada, makes early disposal of the product easier.[4] This consideration could have tipped the balance in the concessionaries' earlier planning, but large capital outgoings give the impression that all working reserves risk being swallowed up before any self-financing operation gets under way, and here a failure to obtain satisfactory prices may be crucial.

In the medium term, the mineral reserves of copper and nickel, and to a lesser degree of the chromite exploited in Zambales, are of considerable importance, although the life of the currently planned production must be relatively short.[5] Such metals provide a welcome supplement to the export earnings of the sections which may well continue to be the permanent riches of the country; sugar-cane, palm, and forest products. With the extra foreign exchange, earned during the last years of this century, ensuing administrations may be able to retain an economic flexibility and reinvest in future mineral exploitation or in more diverse sectors so as to provide the necessities of life for the increasing Philippine population of the future. In principle, with a certain advance in the prices obtained in the non-ferrous metal markets, there are grounds for a cautious optimism here, although the opening-up of the new mines and the establishment of the processing plants to assist in 'decolonizing' the economy bring with them a real necessity to change everyday life in the areas exploited. Not only must the government assist in providing a suitable social climate for the operating companies, but it must also attempt to eradicate corruption both among local officials and within the customs districts involved. Workers' union activities must also be guided and aimed at the improvement of overall conditions, and not at the translation of a small minority of its members to more powerful places. Rural and semi-rural life in such industrialized circumstances can only change. With increased revenues, new mining areas show a tendency towards profligacy: in the Philippines, personal expenditure is often marked by a real wish to assist others, generally those in the greater family, but it can also take on all the airs of showmanship and petty aggrandisement. Often, increased earnings are squandered, under-nutrition continues, and the wage-earner in the new society remains inapt physically for the continuous rigours of industrialized life, including the eight-hour shifts in the mine, the plant, or in the transport organization attached to the complex. In such a life, charity does really begin at home and with the present modest returns on expensive infrastructure, mining companies can no longer afford to lose money by the way of officially sponsored nepotism, corruption, or simple industrial inefficiency caused by the ineptitude of the workers employed by them.

An increase in iron-ore extraction is also envisaged during the life of the plan, with a shift from the production of ore to concentrates. Approximately 1.75 million tons of production for export to Japan is foreseen.

As in the metallurgical sectors, a changeover from the export of all raw products to a proportion of a semi-finished or finished item is foreseen generally by 1974. In the timber industry, the increased manufacture of veneer and plywoods will provide employment at home with less advantage to the present consumer countries; in the coconut-palm sector much has already been done to set up a Philippine-based industry to process oil, meal, cake, and desiccated coconut for shipment. An attempt to capture a large share of the United States centrifugal sugar market is also written in and a number of new centrals have been opened with government approval and institutional aids. Here, however, refining capacity remains almost unchanged as the semi-finished product is exported in great part to the United States refineries which pay prices well above the current world rate. For this reason, the Philippines is here a complacent captive and it is difficult to see her for some time to come being a major source of white sugar, although she has an enormous production potential.

If the economic policy of successive governments has been both the provision of sufficient home-grown foodstuffs for an increasing population and the decolonization and streamlining of export industries, planning for increased economic efficiency has not ceased there and, in particular, the social problem of land distribution and the eventual economic viability of these areas have not been ignored. In earlier chapters, problems related to communications, urban development, power supply, and the irrigation of farming lands have been discussed, as have the political and social facets of the past and present distribution of land. Echoes of all these are to be found in both economic programmes and the second Four-Year Plan establishes targets which have already been partially fulfilled, although, with the current modification to the expenditure slices and priorities, a further period will be necessary before a real advance towards completion is seen and even then there will be underprivileged sectors.

The functional inefficiency of existing communications has already been examined and the outstanding factor, the continued expansion of central Luzon to the detriment of the other parts of the Archipelago, recognized. To this must be added the practical difficulty of moving anything but bulk shipments of raw or semi-processed export commodities around or out of the islands. This has resulted in an enormous entrepôt port trade in Manila, where handling is anything but efficient and wharf-side factions practise some refined manipulations of illegality. As a direct outcome of the predominance of Manila, a decline in the importance of the larger secondary ports has been recorded since the 1940–45 War. This and the incomplete state of the island road network have had a stifling effect on the extension of a decentralized economy and have tended to increase the prices of consumer goods in many of the areas outside central Luzon. The improvements which are now being carried out to the secondary ports and to trunk-line and feeder airfields all over the country are of use, but the lack of an overall road transport network still causes double, triple, and often quadruple handling in journeys which do not exceed three hundred miles. The first Four-Year Plan foresaw the establishment of a Pan-Philippine Highway with a main north-south road axis supplemented by fast ferries from Luzon to Samar and sea bridges and ferries connecting the south-eastern Visayas to Mindanao (see map, pp. 236–7). The plan's life came to an end without overmuch progress being made, although the Manila complex and its northern and peripheral access roads were completed and a number of additions had been made to the Mindanao network. The Second Plan accepts the necessity for the highway but, as the result of the survey carried out by French consultants, integrates it with an overall road-network project which logically links much of the country together. This is a considerable step forward so far as planning is concerned, but if the real priority is lost sight of, the construction of a north-south axis with its costly ferry infrastructure and its sea bridges, very real temptations will exist to produce the ancillary equipment and the feeder and secondary laterals which would have some political influence in the lesser preferred areas, and could be used for vote-catching. Progress generally is still unspectacular and it may be many years before the Philippines has its planned road systems, and during that time, the inter-island shipping companies, which have maintained an illogical but required service, will continue to operate, prolonging a tradition and providing quite fair returns on the capital invested by a small number of influential families, many of which are Chinese by origin.

In the general world of communications, there is still much to be done and much to take up government-supplied funds. The official telephone and telegraphic network is insufficient to cover the country and licences have been awarded to private companies to operate part of the system. In particular, the PLDT (Philippines Long Distance Telephone Company) maintains a most efficient telephonic and radio telephonic network with microwave and VHF equipment linking most of the major cities with Manila and with overseas outlets. The preliminary aim of the Philippine government here[6] is to produce parallel services so as to improve links in and between Manila and all the provincial capitals based on an official microwave/VHF/UHF grid. Telegraph facilities will be included so as to service smaller population centres and the existing VHF/UHF network on the island of Mindanao will be added to and improved. Mindanao, as a more lately developed area of the Philippines, was poorly equipped with pre-war constructed overhead line. This and the rapid growth of quite recently implanted population centres brought an urgent requirement for the provision of new-type communications, for both administrative and social purposes. Quite solid advances have already been made here, especially with earlier aid from Japanese war reparations. The plan envisages the reinforcement of this regional network and its link-up with an improved national system, which is slowly being modified by the bringing into service of modern equipment to replace the earlier long-range HP circuits.

Modification and improvements to the ports' infrastructure continue and funds were allocated for this purpose in both Four-Year Plans. An additional pier has already been constructed in the international section of the port of Manila and improvements are being carried out in the domestic section which services over 70 per cent of the inter-island shipping tonnages. A fishing wharf is also being constructed at Navotas, north of the main port area. Considerable improvements have already been made to the domestic air trunk-line infrastructure and the majority of the essential airfields of this sector have been established and can accept medium-range jet aircraft. There is a real need, however, to rehabilitate some of the older airfields of the system and the Second Plan includes provision for some of this and the improvement of the facilities available at smaller fields. With the current slowness in the establishment of the integrated road network and the inherent impediments caused by the poor east coast harbour facilities, there is a continuing isolation of certain of the smaller major islands (the projected road system would do little to help here) and the natural physical barriers made by mountain and torrent river mean that the improvement and addition to existing airfield infrastructure is much more than an accommodation. Even with the eventual completion of the Pan-Philippine Highway, the need to service the remoter areas will continue. An efficient passenger and fast freight service flowing outwards from the air trunk-lines will complement newly constructed surface facilities as well as providing a momentary relief of pressure in the earlier years.

The supply of electrical power is the last of the infrastructural requirements which is based on almost purely economic need. As has been recorded earlier, there are at present no domestically exploitable sources of mineral oil and all supplies of crude have to come from overseas, although refined items are produced in excess and are released to export. The domestic coal production is small and of too poor a quality to use economically very far from the producing areas in Cebu and Mindanao. Coking grades have to be imported from the United States and Australia. In such circumstances the only really efficient means of generating power from indigenous sources is by the use of water and, where water does not exist or has to be supplemented, oil-burning stations must be established. The consumption of power for industrial and domestic use has increased considerably since the early 1960s, although it lags behind that recorded in Malaysia, Formosa, and Hong Kong. As in other groupings of the economy, the largest consumer area is Manila and its neighbouring towns to the north and south. Nevertheless, the larger of the country's provincial cities also consume electricity in some amounts for domestic, commercial, and semi-industrial purposes, and here the establishment of oil-burning, medium-size production units has taken place. In addition, the industrial complex in north Mindanao (Iligan, in Lanao del Norte) not only produces large quantities of power from the Maria Christina-Agus River complex, but is attracting a growing industrial consumer clientele because of the availability of cheap power in large quantities. A further element which is now well established is the requirement, in an age of improving living conditions and a spread of smaller commercial undertakings, for power and light in rural areas.

The cheapest source of power, the hydro-electric plant, can often be linked to an irrigation scheme, flood control measures, or even a domestic water supply and so here there is already the seed of a social service, which can be exploited, albeit in most cases in a somewhat fragmentary fashion. The projected Philippine government scheme for the use of the Magat River, a tributary of the Cagayan in northern Luzon, is a good example of a hydro-electric infrastructure which will probably produce an output of 100,000 Kw, irrigate some 75,000 hectares, and control flooding along both the lower Magat and the upper stretches of the Cagayan. Other existing projects are mainly conceived for flood control and irrigation purposes, providing small amounts of domestic electricity as a sideline (such as the M'lang River project which, as a by-product, will generate about 750 Kw for the town of Korandal) and sometimes power to operate an associated water-pumping system.

Production of electrical power is planned to increase substantially during the second Four-Year Plan and the provision of a wider-based transmission line infrastructure, linking the Zambales and Bicol areas to the main Luzon grid, is to be completed during that period. The commissioning of the first element (75 Mw) of the Bataan Thermal Complex will be followed by a second and a third element (150 Mw and 200 Mw respectively), although completion of these latter stations will not take place during the plan's life. To the already considerable hydro-electric organization on Luzon it is planned to link a new project, for which feasibility studies are being made during the Second Plan's life. This is the Caliraya scheme on the upper stretches of the Pampanga River, north of Manila, which will also provide extensive irrigation services. In Mindanao, the completion of the Maria Christina and Agus projects will bring into service a total capacity of 175 Mw. Outside these more favoured areas (Luzon, Iligan Bay, and the large populated centres) plans to provide smaller electrical-supply plant are being sponsored through the National Power Corporation. These are essentially government-aided mixed ventures, money being provided from national, municipal, and private sources to set up small electrification co-operatives with generating sets of a hundred Kw as a basis.

There are a number of other elements in the two economic plans which are of interest outside the purely social programme. Thus, the support of the home-based shipbuilding industry at Marivales, in the teeth of overwhelming competition from the highly industrialized countries offering attractive credit terms, is confirmed, as is that of smaller projects to set up lighter industrial complexes, including one in Bataan which will give to foreign companies customs privileges for the manufacture and re-export of items produced within an 'in bond' area. But of the remainder of the economic measures the planning for those services destined to favour social projects is the most important. The redistribution of land has been the thorniest social problem over the centuries, but, as has been seen earlier, the main impediment here is not the actual redistribution, but the provision of agricultural viability. Production has been increased by the use of improved seed, but only irrigation will completely change the real aspect of any particular cropping cycle. Introduction of gravity- and power-forced systems has been taking place since the late nineteenth century, but the area under irrigation is still comparatively small and much of the present equipment is fairly old and subject to breakdowns. Three means to improve this situation are seen. These are the increase of the areas watered, and here projects to irrigate over 200,000 hectares have been studied; the provision of government-guaranteed rural credits to purchase land, improved seed, and fertilizers; and the provision of expertise and credit to repair unserviceable irrigation and general farm equipment.

Current Movements in the Economy

The courageous decisions to change the course of the economy were taken late and, as we have seen, quite important amounts derived from post-war grants and loans were used to replace items of an outdated infrastructure which was based generally on a neo-colonialist posture. That a proportion of such monies was also used for purposes strange to economic and social rehabilitation is also evident, but this is ancient history and has little to do with our present problem. What can be drawn from the whole is that, although the Philippines is some way along the road to the establishment of a more evolved economy, she still shoulders the debts of much of a past era and these debts are not insignificant. By 1970, external obligations had reached some $ U.S. 1,700 million.

Lavish expenditure of funds usually reserved for capital investment in the country's economy does take place at the end of a Presidential term and as part of a studied campaign for re-election. This is a fact accepted internally and it dovetails in with the use of public time, transport, and current expenditure funds in vote-catching visits paid throughout the Philippines by the President and the senior members of his party in government. When, as in 1970, this accepted inflation had already taken place, when foreign exchange control was still fairly favourable, and when the proportion of external debts held as short-term exercises was not only high, but 45 per cent of the total fell due to mature during the year, the state of the economy, already somewhat in recession, gave grounds for serious misgivings. Not too long after, a further currency crisis, tied to the weakness of the United States dollar, brought with it more problems for the Philippine treasury.

The Philippines weathered the first crisis (her own), although considerable adjustment in loan distribution had to be negotiated and the IMF and World Bank authorities had to be convinced of the basic soundness of the country's economic and fiscal programmes.

As often happens in such circumstances, friends rally round to help in giving aid and reprogramming external obligations – and as also happens, after an examination of all the factors, the parity of the country's currency is reconsidered, found wanting, and a change in value is more or less imposed by outsiders. In the case of the Philippines in 1970, an application of a floating rate for the peso had to be accepted which resulted in its devaluation from a rate against the United States dollar of 3.90 to 6.40 pesos in a few months. As an exporting nation, much of her long-term contracts for the supply of raw and semi-finished items are expressed in foreign currencies – usually the United States dollar. Seasonal crops, such as coconut-palm products, pineapple, and other agricultural exports, are generally negotiated for periodically. As the staples of life are now in fairly good supply, imports here can be more easily controlled, although luxury items in all ranges have obviously shown a considerable advance in prices locally. Where, however, the bulk of the population is almost completely severed from the import market for much of its basic requirements,[7] such a devaluation is more salutary than disastrous. The requirement for hydro-carbon fuels, for industrial plant, machines, and for automotive and aircraft items and for invisible services (shipping and insurance) does throw an added burden on the economy, although the local assembly of cars, lorries, radios, refrigerators, air conditioners, and other heavy consumer goods assists to cut the cost at the point of purchase and to reduce the drain on foreign currency reserves. Despite this rather painful transition, the country's economy would seem to be sound and its long-range trade well balanced, always bearing in mind that the second Four-Year Plan specifically foresees an adverse balance of imports over exports for the next few years. This would establish and equip the export industries and the national infrastructure for a drive to complement home-grown foodstuff production in an all-out effort to provide for the country's growing population.

Now to the United States monetary crisis and the possible effects of the practical writing-down of the dollar and the enhancement of the value of gold and other currencies. There are a number of elements here and probably the most important are the identity of the country's trading partners, the character of long-term agreements, the extent of the importance to the Philippines of certain dollar-based invisibles, and the country's own domestic production of gold. Japan (whose massive revaluation of the yen provides a cross-current) has now replaced the United States as the Philippines' most important trading partner, with a current favourable Philippine balance of trade. The United States, which normally exports more to the Philippines than she imports from her, comes next. With the exception of local exports to Asian countries, balances elsewhere are adverse, including exchanges with the Netherlands and with Britain and West Germany, which total over 10 per cent of the country's gross entries, though trade with Australia and New Zealand is normally more or less balanced. These bare facts do not give a true picture. The majority of imports and exports are carried by foreign vessels, often Japanese, and, unless the written-in agreements for exportation terminate at a Philippine-based trading-point, transport charges will have increased as will have those for insurance. Most agreements, however, are normally concluded with the United States dollar as a base and the practical devaluation of this currency has resulted in a worldwide rewriting of all contracts. It may be some time before a true picture can be established here, but much of Philippine private investment has been made in the United States and American official sources did, in the past, contribute nearly $100 million annually in repayment for services provided at their military bases and establishments and for the counterpart of the pensions granted to Filipino citizens. On the other hand, gold production, which is officially subsidized and used to reinforce currency reserves, is increasing marginally (value $6 million at 1973 open market) and here there is a total gain for all practical purposes. It is scarcely doubted that there must be some considerable readjustment in Philippine trade agreements in the very near future, although there is no reason to believe that the transient weakness of the dollar will have greatly disturbed the real basis of the economy which produces so much of its own foodstuffs and which is rapidly increasing its primary exports, the majority of which are shipped to countries at present enjoying the benefits of relatively strong money.

The administration of the Philippines is based on universal suffrage against a background where politics are a permanent preoccupation and often a delight. The two major parties generally alternate in government and, even now, left-wing influences do not disturb overall stability. Fiscal and economic policies are quite skilfully planned and there is a suitable presence of expertise within the Philippines itself. The broad structure of budgetary control, tax collection, and the execution of economic development is well conceived and government agencies are often manned by efficient and painstaking officials. All this produces a climate which is satisfactory for the foreign investor, in a situation where sophisticated industrial projects require more capital than is available within the country and where local expertise for research and for planning and execution is difficult to find. Broadly speaking, therefore, future co-operation between successive Philippine governments and foreign entities, in both official and capitalistic sections, will in no way be impossible and it seems that, if the present administrative conditions and social climate can be extended in time, the current industrial programmes will be achieved and further active foreign participation obtained. This should ensure continuity in the future exploitation of natural reserves, pending the assumption of complete control by a new generation of Filipino industrialists and engineers.

As in all things, however, there are shadows. In the Philippines these mainly stem from corruption, lawlessness, and a neglect on the part of government agencies to counter such manifestations. Complacency also provides a threshold for the success of illegality and it is tragic to see how much influence this can bring to bear on the viability of a modern enterprise. In any consideration of participation in the Philippine economy, this continues to be an important factor for calculation.

[1] This could be greatly increased in a fairly short period by a nationwide encouragement of a viable apprenticeship scheme. As it is, this sector is at present fairly unevenly covered.

[2] An exception to this is the Lanao del Norte area, adjacent to the port of Iligan, which has been favoured by the hydro-electric potential of the Maria Christina complex. Elsewhere, general port areas in the more developed islands have evolved in an urban fashion, but are essentially tributaries of Manila.

[3] The new seed strains require the use of adequate supplies of fertilizer and, to give an optimum production, efficient irrigation to obtain more than a single crop a year.

[4] In addition to the Nonoc operation, Japanese interests have now finalized planning to bring the Rio Tuba (Palawan) deposits – one million metric tons of ore body at 2·2 per cent pure nickel content – to the export stage in 1976.

[5] Despite this, detailed prospection continues to reveal additional deposits of copper, nickel, and chromite in the non-ferrous group and iron-ore elsewhere.

[6] The maintenance of two systems with separate switching facilities is already an uneconomic complication. Presumably the future will see an eventual nationalization of the network, but this is not yet openly planned.

[7] Here, of course, there is always an important element of Philippine life which is dependent on imports. As we see in the next section, the bill for hydro-carbon oils in their crude form has increased. Transport and lighting (whether by electricity or kerosene) are among the services involved. Much of rural cooking is also done on kerosene.

Chapter 19

The Philippines in the World Today

POLITICALLY, the Philippines has continued a search to re-establish a national character which, according to popular legend, she lost with the colonization of the islands by the Spaniards in the sixteenth century. Logically, it is difficult to follow such thought. This predominantly Malay country, an earlier grouping of communities, has been in constant ethnic and cultural evolution throughout our era. A national and political consciousness was only born as the result of many years of Spanish occupation, although, before, there had undoubtedly been restricted local connections by affinity. Because of a fairly generalized way of life and the occupation of the islands by much the same type of settler, the lowlander tended to evolve in a way which was homogeneous and the later split between the confirmed Moslems and those people who had been converted to Christianity made a distinction similar to that between a Briton and a Spaniard of the seventeenth century. This cultural difference still exists, although it has been softened by latter-day practice.

Over the years, the predominance of the Iberian-influenced Christian has been confirmed, although significant changes have occurred since the beginning of the twentieth century. The Spanish language has almost disappeared as a medium and the Philippine revolution and United States occupation confirmed an early acceptance of liberalism, the latter adding a way of life and a readiness to assimilate a Western-based educational system, together with a dependence on North American symbols and outward trappings. The Filipino who represents his country commercially or officially is rarely far from the masses and many of the children at present living in remote *barrios* could well climb to the highest professional ranks within the country. This majority culture and its inherent strangeness within Asia are reflected in Philippine representation overseas.

What is then the impact of the Philippines on the life of, and on the history she now shares with, regional partners? For it is in this society that post-war governments have attempted to establish firm links and gain a sure foothold in a conscious process of decolonizing the national image.

In the East Indian area itself, the evolution of the last 1,500 years has resulted in few real political or cultural ties between the major elements, Indonesia, the Philippines, and Malaysia.[1] Despite geographical proximity, each component has been led on a different path by accidents of history and, although there is an almost ethereal, but sensed, affinity due to ethnic nearness, wide differences caused by the independent policies maintained by earlier outside influences again make the Filipino a stranger in these neighbouring lands. Today, the majority of the earlier settled peoples over the whole of the area are strikingly alike and the majority elements of the true indigenous populations are what they are generally considered to be – of a broad Malay heritage, although in the Philippines, hybridization is much more marked. However, in religion and political tradition, the three elements differ widely. For it was only in the Philippines that a conscious attempt was made by a European occupant to impose a religious belief over a long period and each of the three countries has not only inherited a degree of the way of life of its former colonists, but has also reacted quite differently to this political heritage. In current relations, the Philippine and Indonesian governments, despite the earlier fears caused by the Sukarno régime's expansionist policies, seem to be able to understand each other fairly well, but with Malaysia, problems have rarely been easy to solve since the establishment of the latter. Here, distrust remains, is mutual, and is essentially based on a sharp difference in the concept of political and administrative behaviour. On a wider scale, over the years, little real improvement can be discerned in the rehabilitation of an East Indian togetherness. The reason is not difficult to see: the vague affinity of blood ties and environment has never been strong enough to protect these peoples against the much stronger external influences which they have effectively absorbed; and none of these foreign currents has been wide enough in itself to engulf all of the three partners. Thus there is little East Indian solidarity outside ASEAN and the Philippines, in particular, looks further afield for ties. She looks both to the region and to the democratically aligned countries with whom she has an abundance of common ground, derived from an almost whole-hearted acceptance of the benefits of Western political and cultural systems.

In the wider region, essentially that of the non-Communist-aligned countries of South-East Asia and peripheral East Asia, the Philippines' position is a happier one than she enjoys in the narrower confines of the East Indies. The community's coherency was moulded both by an earlier polarization around the anti-Communist bloc and by the local presence of the United States as the giant antithesis of China. This situation has evolved considerably of late. First, a growing demand to become more independent of the former imperialistic powers has led to a lively search to learn more about each other and improve economic and political relations. Here over the last decade, formal and informal approaches have been made so as to broaden and supplement the meagre, predominantly military South-East Asia Treaty Organization's aims. Secondly, a highly important political development has changed much of the character of extra-regional pressure. A situation in which economic and social progress at home was being eroded by the maintenance of military forces and grants in aid to satellites has recently been viewed with alarm in the United States and to a certain degree in the Soviet Union, for, even in the latter country, populations have recently been enjoying a better standard of life and are becoming less and less isolated from the outside world. The post-Cultural Revolution manifestations of China have also tended to confirm a real lack of current expansionist policies, although, as has always been known, sensitivity is marked when any pressure is brought on or around physical or cultural frontiers. In such conditions, a more liberal exchange of views between the Communist-aligned countries and those of the regional group we are now considering has slowly grown up. Moreover, an increasing willingness on the part of the United States to come to terms and to withdraw troops has changed much of the character of political thought in these countries, where underdevelopment and population pressure are shared and where there is little time left to improve the situation in order to provide a surer, more deeply rooted, anti-Communist defence.

In this forum the Philippines is already an important component. Her strong economic links with Japan, an embryo super-power, tend to align her to this alternative world market where operations are now conducted in an atmosphere of mutual respect and negotiation rather than on the former basis of politico-military pressure exerted in the earlier part of the century. Relations here have also been tempered by the enormous reparations payments received and the awareness of recent Japanese administrations of the danger of ultra left-wing political organizations. Elsewhere, with the non-Communist parts of former Indo-China, with Thailand and with Formosa and South Korea, the Philippines not only shares a common peripheral physical position, but an improving regard for Japan, the former oppressor.[2] The forum, as we have seen, is now roughly formalized by ASEAN, but bilateral and multilateral exchanges are frequent. Here the Philippines is an appreciated partner. With firm non-Communist policies, which have a nationwide support at home, with a modern but run-in political and administrative structure, and a new willingness to live in an Asian society, she contributes an almost foreign influence which may well be the spearhead of change in this staunchly traditional area where roots run back to a former Pan-Sino community. The influence of the Filipino here is considerable; his culture is that of the islands, but his history and his ethnic make-up have formed him to understand those mainland currents which, in the past, have often passed him by. He speaks the accepted regional lingua franca, English, better than his partners, and he has been trained to think logically. Of all the community, his representatives are the most adaptable and are probably the most able to provide a natural source of liaison between the partners.

Although diplomatic relations now exist between the Philippines and the Soviet Union, an earlier reluctance to allow any formalized penetration by a Communist power led to a position where little cultural or commercial exchanges with the Sino-Soviet bloc existed. This situation still pertains today, despite indications that change is in the air. Elsewhere in the world, knowledge of the Philippines is strikingly disparate. In the United States, common history has brought with it a fund of information, which current contacts tend to maintain. Elsewhere, except perhaps in Spain, where memories are fast dying, the Philippines and the Filipino are scarcely known. Even in Australia, a country with considerable economic ties with the Malay world and a direct airline route to Manila, the image is fragmentary and is often blurred by the illogical reporting of a poor Press. In western Europe, where, all unbeknown to the local populations, there is a brisk exchange of commerce with the Archipelago, the situation is equally as badly appreciated. Outside an extremely restricted circle in any of these countries there is practically no opinion on either the actual place of the Philippines in the world or the eventual role which she might play in the same context.

In a personal assessment, I would like to take two poles of approach and against these attempt to produce something which is of use. The first is based on North American thought which I have encountered. The Philippines is a Christian country which, until United States tutelage, was corruptly governed under a system which scarcely allowed any economic development, and where this did happen, proceeds were drained out and re-investment rarely occurred. With United States occupation, a sound educational system was laid down and, soon afterwards, the roots of a democratic way of life were planted. Economic progress under capitalistic dynamism was almost immediate and the country soon found its place as a primary producer area where much of the funds in this sector remained, either in the form of wages or re-investment. Administrative independence was already obtained with the Commonwealth and an efficient simple national infrastructure had been built up by the 1940–45

War. War and Japanese occupation devastated the country, but, as promised, independence was granted. American aid and Japanese Reparations, the latter insisted upon by the United States after the Axis defeat, poured in and the Philippines was rehabilitated. Philippine loyalty to the American tutors was marked, was even touching. The country remained solid within the Allied cause throughout the 1940–45 War and has been firmly on the side of the anti-Communist bloc ever since; the armed forces fighting side by side with the Americans throughout the horrors of Bataan, continuing to operate bravely and successfully both in Korea and in their own country against the Communist terrorists. Certain modifications in economic planning have complemented a change in worldwide marketing profiles, but the United States still contributes institutionally and unofficially to the re-shaping of Philippine industry. Evolution in political loyalties continues, although some individual acts and statements of Philippine governments sometimes tend to cause sadness that such evolution is necessary. The political environment would seem to be stable, understandable, and conform to normal practice, although perhaps the mechanism of politics has turned out to be really too fascinating and some extravagances do occur.

The second pole is a remoter one, probably European, based, in many ways, on a more puritan outlook, and having nothing of the almost sentimental involvement of the first. It sees the Philippines as a distant nation in South-East Asia, somewhere between the Pacific and Indian Oceans, a former American colony populated by a people who live in conditions which seem to be an Asian caricature of Chicago in the 1930s. The current involvement of the United States is not necessarily understood and colonial or near-colonial status is often suggested. The cultural and religious base is also imperfectly appreciated (there is a fairly wide belief in Europe that Filipinos speak Spanish), as are the ethnic roots of the people. An almost complete ignorance of the make-up of this distant country has been aggravated by a Press which only reports violence and earthquakes.

Against these two differing, external opinions, I should like to offer a third view, based on the geographical, historical, economic, and political factors outlined above.

1. She is a hybridized Malay nation with an overwhelming Christian majority, whose historic background does not fit her at present to membership in a close East Indian association. In any case, real East Indian coherency is not for now.

2. She is strikingly mature as a nation. Her educational and administrative systems already have firm roots in history, and are well managed, despite occasional lapses in detail.

3. She has considerable resources, both human and material, and she could well become a reserve of skilled labour for the region. She is already an important producer of coconut and sugar-cane products, non-ferrous mineral ores, and timber. She is generally self-supporting for staples and produces much of the dietary additives necessary for her existing population. She is poised for self-sufficiency, although she is still dogged by functional inefficiency, part of an accepted system which has failed to eradicate nepotism and petty corruption.

4. She has a physical position in Asia which presents an enormous legal barrier to the free movement of aircraft and shipping, and here her sovereignty is immense, although there are practical reasons at present to underplay its importance.

5. Although still in many ways anchored to United States political (until recently) and economic traditions, she is slowly decolonizing herself. In this context, her future in the South-East Asian region seems to be both economically and politically acceptable, and the character of her representation in regional politics is interesting in the domain of expertise and liaison. Despite the decolonization process, however, the government still depends on the internal support of a restricted number of influential families, and unless this support is forthcoming in a particular context, development plans fail to get off the drawing board.

6. She is, nevertheless, an underdeveloped country relying, in the majority, on a quite primitive agricultural sector and an export potential which is still one based on primary and semi-finished products. In her future struggle for economic and political sovereignty, her viability will rely on her ability to feed, maintain, and improve the lot of a fast-expanding population and to pay the luxury of greater contribution towards external and internal security. Some concrete steps have already been taken to transform the economy, but if the population is to number 80 million people by the first decade of next century, the future for such a country in a world where the gulf between rich and poor is always widening will be tragically unsatisfactory.

Viability, therefore, if everything else runs truly to course, depends on the number of Filipinos to feed and maintain in the future, on the evolution of the primary-products market, and eventually the build-up of a processing infrastructure and a marketing organization to obtain a greater share of industrially produced wealth. Are these three separate factors complementary or can the second supply the answer without some positive action on the limitation of births, essential if the future Filipinos are to be considered as anything but permanently underprivileged? Within eight years, unless some satisfactory steps are taken, time will already be running short. Despite goodwill, stable political conditions, and a pushing-ahead of economic rephasing, the race between an increased population and an increased national product may well be gained by disaster. In such circumstances, by the beginning of next century, the Philippines will have to rely on something not yet found or accepted to maintain an unchecked increase. This is not an unknown problem in the world today, but for the Philippines, strong institutionalized pressures continue to be maintained so as to make it currently impracticable to do much to disseminate any knowledge which would ultimately change this present course. A change here, however, would assist the present population in its initial economic struggle as well as that of the future, which could already have been overwhelmed *a priori* by miseries caused by unfulfilled targets.

Her future political evolution is difficult to foresee. United States tutelage and earlier Philippine political acumen produced a well-based constitution, armed with tried democratic safeguards. Its liberalism was marked and it engendered a political life which relied on a strong central government which, once elected, was guided by traditionally conservative policies, a touch of individuality, if the President of the day so wished it, and the tug-of-war influences of social and economic pressure-groups. A reliance on this long-range type of operation and the past incapacity of administrations to stamp out lawlessness and irregularity were two important reasons why constitutional reform was programmed during President Marcos's second term. The promulgation of the new, more summary, constitution demonstrated that for the first time since the Commonwealth (outside the period of Japanese conquest), government action had left the rails of a mandate given by the Filipino people. Although it can well be argued that the present state of exception, which might eventually be replaced by the rule by an elected assembly, headed by a Prime Minister and cabinet, is expedient and produces an efficient administration, it is also nevertheless true that the upheaval has been traumatic. The shock of this severance with the past, rather than any belief that there might be a threat to the long-term liberty of the individual, is probably the overriding impression. Political evolution, therefore, although taking place under not wholly unsatisfactory conditions, is no longer on a calculable course. There is, however, no sign at present that anything but progress may be expected, even though a progress outside the framework of normal parliamentary practice. There are few countries in the world today where older democratic procedures have proved expedient if rapid and permanent change is desired.

It would be wrong for a book on the Philippines to be concluded with too many sad reflections. Although the future might well hold continuing material disadvantage in store, it is not in the Philippine character to muse too long on things which might, in the event, never happen. Despite differences caused by wealth, dialect, social environment, and even ethnic fragmentation, there is a pattern in these islands which shows the Filipino as a sensitive human being, generally warm-blooded, generous, pleasure-loving, and attractively brown in some timbre or another. This is a generalization, but it is significant that the popularly accepted national character image echoes all of these and adds a few words on laziness, profligacy, and a tendency to disregard the importance of law and order. These brightly coloured facets make up much of Philippine life and to capture some of them for just a little time is tempting. An almost spontaneous friendliness, sometimes pushed to the stage of indiscretion, is almost universal and is both inherent and inherited. In this context, a Philippine home can almost always receive a guest, although the majority of the population has, to Western eyes, practically nothing to live on. We have already seen that personal cleanliness means much. Here is at least one of the reasons why it is not difficult for someone of poor family to climb the ladder fast, for, with his inbred desire to be clean comes a fine eye for attractive, even flamboyant, clothes and together with the greater family, where someone at least is reasonably well off, and the sense of equality which is everywhere, comes the sure knowledge that all is just a matter of opportunity.

The *fiestas*, with the religious processions, politically prompted entertainments, and a hospitality stemming from quite spontaneous roots, match the love of music, the noise of fireworks, the excitement of the cockfight, the dances, and the enthusiasm of the crowd at almost any public manifestation. Even natural disasters can be accompanied, after initial punch-drunk lethargy, by enthusiastic efforts to make and mend, often helped by laughter and song. Mass and Benediction are not a duty in the Western sense. They form part of a welcome relief to the humdrum things of the week and, for this and other reasons, are revered. Children, over-numerous perhaps, are to our mind infuriatingly noisy and curious, but this is only because the foreigner fails to understand that he too is a welcome change from the humdrum way of life. If there is any real cause for correction by adults, it is accepted without argument. Resentment can vanish as quickly as it appears, but here there is a dangerous area for, unmitigated by some act of conciliation or even a gesture, it can build up and explode. This is also the case with unrequited love, political frustration, and personal envy, all manifestations of the same character of things.

The majority, the rural and semi-rural Christian population, with its only too shabby working clothes, puts on its Sunday best once a week; the male, complete with his broad-brimmed straw hat and a fighting cock under the arm. In the hills and forests live the less evolved pagan communities with their Stone Age customs, their seemingly inadequate clothing, and their separate languages. They are, however, Filipinos like the rest and many have the vote and follow politics quite closely. In the south, the Moslems supply the last element of the population, their women, often heavily made up, walking proudly, unveiled, along the dusty roads: the men working in the rice, root, or maizefields, or perhaps, as in some villages in the Sulu Archipelago or on Ilana Bay, contemplating loot, murder, smuggling, or some other typically East Indian practice.

Thus life goes on in the Philippines. The often suave, but not too remote from the grass roots, official or businessman of the city is at heart the boy playing in the *barrio* or starting off his working existence in the fields. His uncles and cousins are still there and he may be doing something to help them in their rural struggle or to assist them in giving at least one of their children a complete education. The nationwide machine is awaiting these children and the economy will later do its best to absorb them and give them a job commensurate with their value. Whether it will be able to do so or not depends on the progress which the Philippines is able to make against those factors carried over from a previous era and which are still actively maintained inside and outside the country today: illegality and corruption may well continue to sap the national wealth and violence assists them in harming the national image; but these pale when faced with economic servitude and overpopulation, both of which are capable of bringing ruin to this island nation.

[1] It is curious to record here that the game of golf, closely adhering to the spirit in which it was conceived so far away, provides an important *trait d'union* between East Indian dignitaries.

[2] Thailand technically also waged war on the Allies. This episode, however, in no way changes the unity of the present partners, as she was occupied in a *de facto* sense.

Appendix

Concise Data Tables

Major Indigenous Languages Spoken – Mother Tongue Statistics

(*Source:* Philippine census)

Language	*Percentage of Total Population*	
Cebuana	24.1%	(Visayas and Mindanao)
Tagalog	21.0%	(Luzon and Mindanao)
Iloco	11.7%	(North Luzon and Mindanao)
Panay-Hilagayan	10.4%	(Visayas)
Bikol	7.8%	(South Luzon)
Samar-Leyte	5.5%	(North Visayas)
Pampango	3.2%	(Central Luzon)
Pangasinan	2.5%	(Central Luzon)
Magindanao	1.5%	(Mindanao and Sulu)
Tausog	1.1%	(Mindanao and Sulu)
Aklanon	1.1%	(North Visayas)
	89.9%	

Major Religions Practised

(*Source:* Philippine census)

Christian Sects (major professions)	92.9% (83.8% RC)
Moslem	4.9%

Note: the percentage of the whole population claiming to practise these two religions has increased at the expense of the small Buddhist and pagan communities owing to both missionary activities and their higher birth-rates.

Mining Production

(*Source: Mining Annual Review*, 1972)

Gold (oz.)	639,000
Silver (oz.)	1,910,000
Copper (metric tons)	208,300
Zinc (metric tons)	4,200
Nickel (metric tons)	225
Mercury (flasks)	4,800
Iron ore (metric tons)	2,066,800
Chrome ore (metric tons)	422,100
Manganese (metric tons)	5,100

Philippine National Balance Sheet 1971

(Figures in US dollars)

Imports	$1,830 million
Exports (without invisibles)	$1,160 million
Imports (*major heads*)	
Machinery	$255.1 million
Mineral oils, etc.	$141.2 million
Transport equipment	$122.2 million
Exports (*major heads*)	
Forest products	$261 million
Coconut products	$254 million
Sugar cane products	$220 million
Minerals	$217 million
Fruits	$41 million
Abaca	$15 million
Tobacco	$15 million

During the first six months of 1972 invisible surpluses produced $117 million. GNP growth for 1973 and 1974 should be 6 per cent and 7 per cent respectively, and the balance of trade should return to an even result by 1974.

Short Bibliography

On the area

Charles Robequain: *Malaya, Indonesia, Borneo, and the Philippines* (translated by E. D. Laborde), London – New York – Toronto, 1954.

On the country and its history

Alzona, Encarnacion: 'The Origins of the Commonwealth of the Philippines', *Philippine Commonwealth Handbook*, Manila, 1936.

Araneta, Francisco, SJ, 'Some Problems of Philippine Education', *Science Review*, Manila, March 1961.

Benitez, Conrado: *A History of the Philippines*, Boston, 1954.

Berreman, Gerald D.: *The Philippines: A Survey of Current Social, Economic, and Political Conditions*, Cornell Southeast Asia Program, Data Paper No. 19, Ithaca, 1966.

Beyer, H. Otley: *Population of the Philippine Islands in 1916*, Manila, 1917.

—: *Early History of Foreign Relations with Foreign Countries, Especially China*, Manila, 1948.

— *et al.*: *Philippine Saga: A Pictorial History of the Archipelago since Time Began*, Manila, 1957.

Blair, E. H., and Robertson, J. A.: *The Philippine Islands, 1493–1898*, Cleveland, Ohio, 55 vols., 1903–09.

Coates, Austin: *Rizal: Philippine Nationalist and Martyr*, Kuala Lumpur, 1968.

Costa, Horacio de la: 'History and Philippine Culture', *Science Review*, Manila, May 1961.

—: *The Jesuits in the Philippines, 1581–1768*, Cambridge, Mass., 1961.

—: *The Trial of Rizal*, Manila, 1961.

—: *Readings in Philippine History*, Manila, 1965.

Farwell, George S.: *Mask of Asia. The Philippines Today*, New York, 1967.

Forbes, W. Cameron: *The Philippine Islands*, 2nd edition (one volume), Cambridge, Mass., 1945.

Fox, Robert B.: *Prehistoric Source Materials for the Study of Philippine History*, Manila, n.d. [1968?].

Grunder, Garel A., and Livezey, W. E.: *The Philippines and the United States*, Norman, Okla., 1951.

Hall, D. G.: *A History of South-East Asia*, London, 1964; New York, 1968.
Hayden, Joseph Ralston, *The Philippines: A Study in National Development*, New York, 1942.
Hill, Percy A.: *Romance and Adventure in Old Manila*, Manila, 1964.
Huke, Robert E.: *Shadows on the Land*, Manila, 1963.
Le Gentil de la Galasière, *A Voyage to the Indian Seas* (translated by W.A.B.), Manila edition, 1964.
Mitchell, Mairen: *Francis Andreas de Urdaneta, OSA*, Manila, 1964.
Nelson, Raymond: *The Philippines* (New Nations and Peoples series), London and New York, 1968.
Palma-Bonifacio, V.: *The Trial of Andres Bonifacio*, Manila, 1963.
Power, John H., Sicat, Gerardo P., and Mo Huan-Sing: *The Philippines and Taiwan: Industrialization and Trade Policies*. Published for the development centre of the Organization for Economic Co-operation and Development. London – New York – Kuala Lumpur, 1971.
Ravenholt, Albert: *The Philippines: A Young Republic on the Move*, Princeton, 1962.
Romani, John H.: *The Philippine Presidency*, Manila, 1956.
Saleeby, Najeeb M.: *The History of Sulu*, Manila, 1908. Reprinted Filipiniana Book Guild, Manila, 1963.
Schurz, William Lytle: *The Manila Galleon*, New York, 1939.
Smith, John: *Philippine Social Life*, London, 1965.
Smith, Robert Aura: *Philippine Freedom 1946–1958*, New York, 1958.
Wickborg, Edgar: *The Chinese in Philippine Life 1850–1898*, New Haven and London, 1965.
Yabes, Leopoldo Y.: 'The Literature of the Filipino Peoples', UNESCO Symposium on Culture, Manila, February 1961.
Zaide, Gregorio F.: *Philippine Political and Cultural History*, Manila, 1953.
—: *Philippine History*, Manila, 1962.

Official works

The Philippine Economic Atlas, Program Implementation Agency, Manila, n.d.
Census of the Philippines: Population and Housing Summary, Manila, 1963; Agriculture, Summary, Manila, 1965.
The Philippines. A series of 24 publications issued by the Philippine Committee on ECAFE affairs, Department of Commerce and Industry, Manila, 1963.
The Philippines. A single pamphlet issued by the Department of Commerce and Industry, Manila, 1966.
Four-Year Economic Program for the Philippines. Fiscal Years 1967–1970, 1971–1974, Manila, Office of the President, 1966, 1970.

Maps

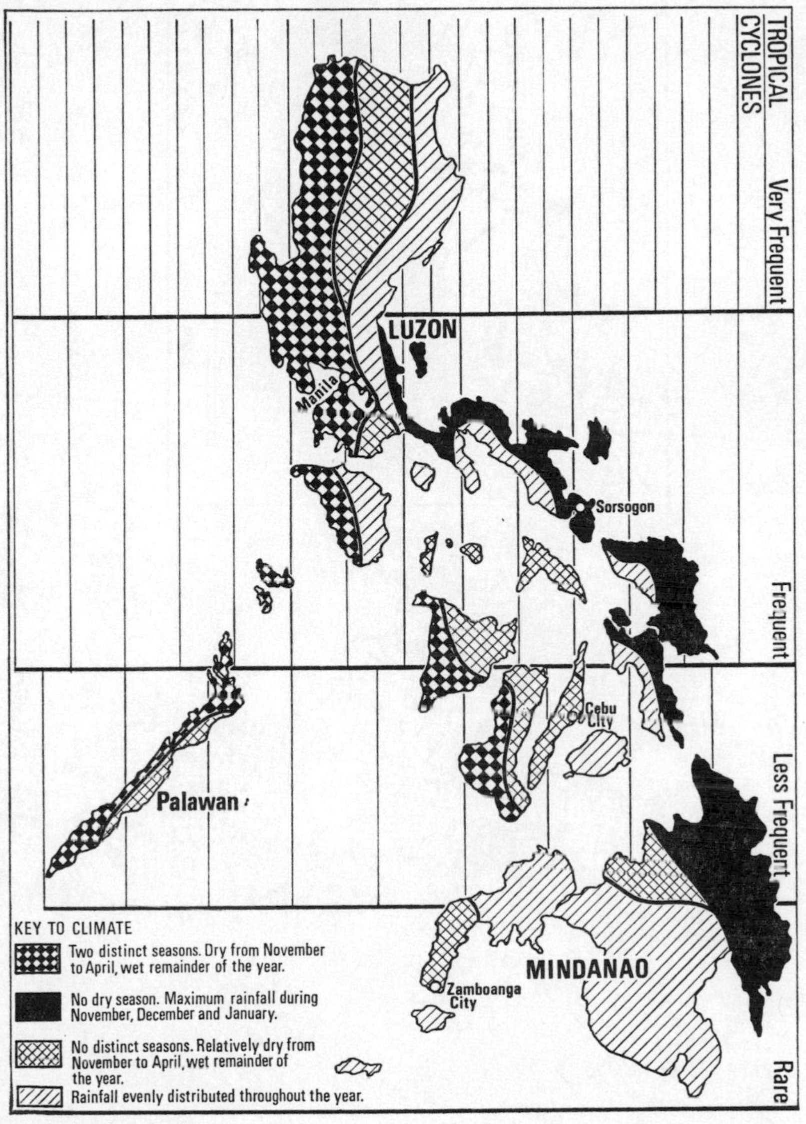

1 Climate in the Philippines

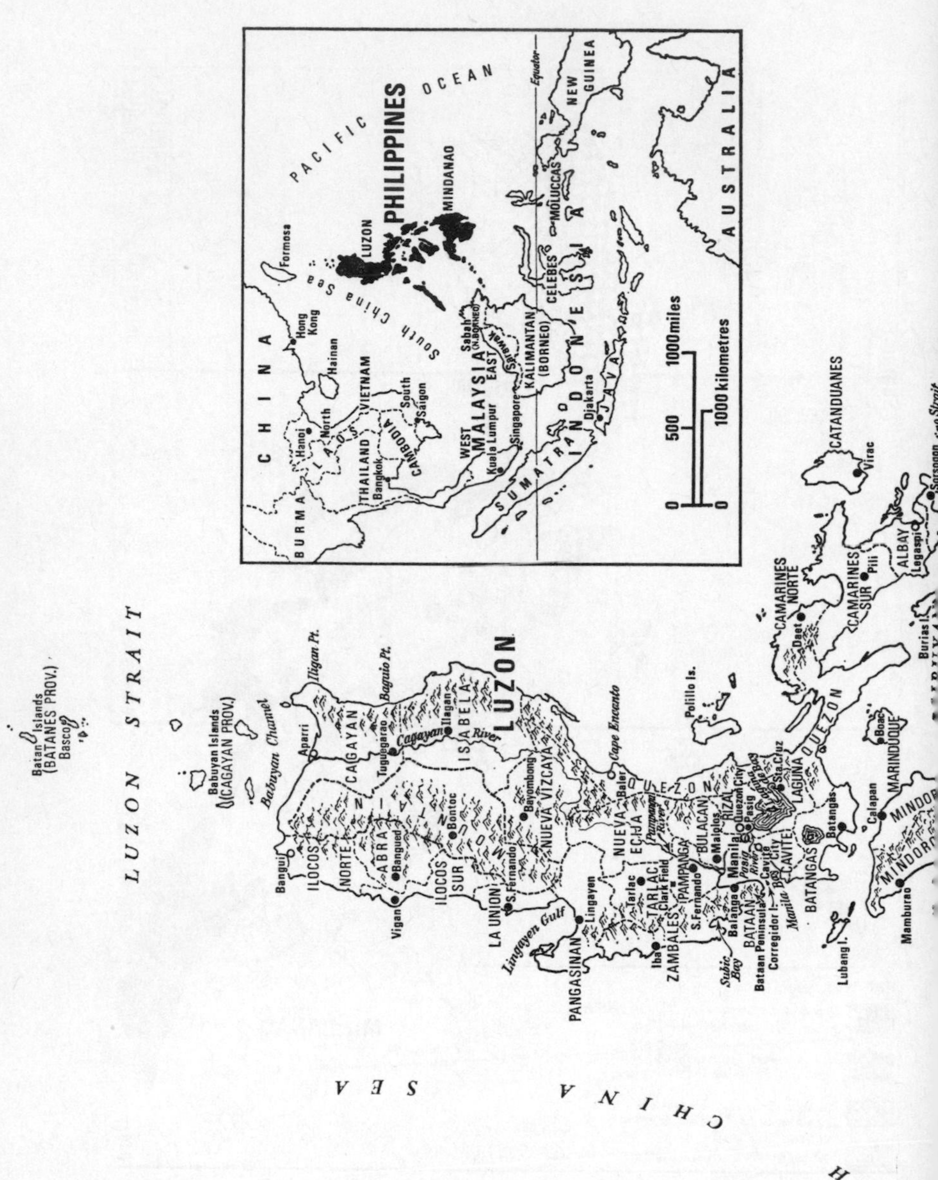

2 The Philippines – general map

N
W
E
S
Calamian Group
Busuanga I.
Culion I.
Linapacan I.
STRAIT
Cuyo Is.
Dumaran I.
Palawan
Puerto Princesa
Bugsuk I.
Balabac I.
SULU SEA
Cagayan Sulu I.
Tablas I.
Sibuyan I.
SEA
Masbate
Masbate
Samar
Catbalogan
Biliran I.
Tacloban
Ormoc
Leyte
Kalibo
Roxas
AKLAN
CAPIZ
Panay
ANTIQUE
ILOILO
Iloilo City
S.Jose de Buenavista
Guimaras I.
Bacolod
OCC.
NEGROS
Negros
NEGROS OR.
Dumaguete
Siquijor I.
Cebu
Cebu City
Camotes Is.
Bohol
Tagbilaran
SOUTHERN LEYTE
Maasin
Surigao Strait
Dinagat I.
Siargao I.
Surigao
SURIGAO DEL NORTE
MINDANAO SEA
Mambajao
Camiguin I.
Butuan
SURIGAO DEL SUR
MISAMIS OR.
AGUSAN
Agusan River
Dipolog
Oroquieta
Cagayan de Oro
BUKIDNON
Malaybalay
ZAMBOANGA DEL NORTE
MISAMIS OCC.
Iligan
Marawi
LANAO DEL NORTE
Pagadian
ZAMBOANGA DEL SUR
LANAO DEL SUR
MINDANAO
Illana Bay
DAVAO
Davao City
Bongo I.
Cotabato City
Rio Grande de Mindanao
DAVAO GULF
MORO GULF
Lebak
COTABATO
Zamboanga City
Basilan Strait
Basilan I.
Pilas Group
Pangutaran Group
Jolo
Samales Group
Tapul Group
Tawitawi I.
Tawitawi Group
Sibutu I.
Sulu Archipelago
Sarangani Is.
CELEBES SEA
0
50
100
150
200 miles
0
100
200
300 kilometres
Provincial Boundary
Provincial Capital

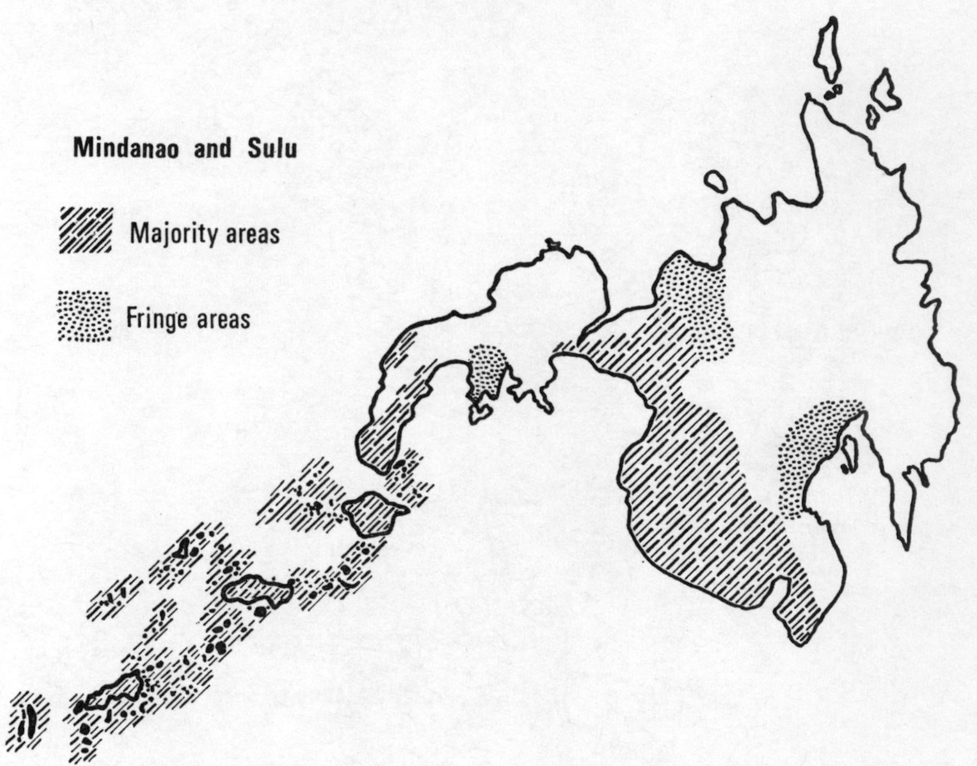

3 Traditional Moslem areas

Index

Index

Printed in Great Britain
by W & J Mackay Limited, Chatham